BRITAIN and IRELAND

Country Inns and Back Roads

Country house hotels,
bed and breakfast, traditional inns,
farmhouses, guest houses,
and castles

By Norman T. Simpson
The Berkshire Traveller

A Harper Colophon Book

1817

HARPER & ROW, PUBLISHERS, New York
Cambridge, Philadelphia, San Francisco,
London, Mexico City, São Paulo, Singapore, Sydney

TRAVEL BOOKS BY NORMAN T. SIMPSON

Country Inns and Back Roads, North America
Country Inns and Back Roads, Britain and Ireland
Country Inns and Back Roads, Continental Europe
Bed and Breakfast, American Style

COVER PAINTING: Bickleigh Cottage, Devon, by Alan King, Malvern, U.K.
DRAWINGS: Janice Lindstrom

First HARPER COLOPHON edition published 1985. An edition of this book was originally published in 1984 by the Berkshire Traveller Press.

Library of Congress Cataloging in Publication Data

Simpson, Norman T.
Country inns and back roads.

(Harper colophon books)
Includes index.
1. Hotels, taverns, etc.—Great Britain—Directories.
2. Hotels, taverns, etc.—Ireland—Directories.
I. Title.
TX910.G7S57 1985 647'.944101 84—48624
ISBN 0-06-091268-5 (pbk.)

85 86 87 88 89 10 9 8 7 6 5 4 3 2

CONTENTS

PREFACE

I love prefaces, introductions, or whatever they're called. They give an author a chance to say all the things he couldn't put in the book. He can explain the "mystique" of the book, acknowledge a few friends and teachers in his past, and generally spread an agreeable glow over everything connected with the work.

This preface is no exception.

My intense preoccupation with things British probably began when I was nine years old, reading Charles and Mary Lamb's *Tales from Shakespeare,* and it was given a glowing boost in high school by my teacher, Abraham Lass, who introduced us all to the entangling webs of the Thomas Hardy novels. Diggory Venn and Eustacia Vye, where are you now?

During my freshman year at Bucknell University, a splendid college in Lewisburg, Pennsylvania, I was cast as Feste the jester in Shakespeare's *Twelfth Night.* As the years moved swiftly onward, I was to take several other roles in the same play, including Orsino and Sir Toby Belch. While still attending an occasional class at Bucknell, I was further spurred by courses in Tennyson and Browning, taught by Professor C. Willard Smith; Shakespeare, by Professor Coleman; and British history, by Professor Johnson. (I'm sure *he'd* be very much surprised to learn the result!)

During World War II, I was stationed in India where I acquired an intense interest in the "Empire." I also saw Lawrence Olivier in the film, *Henry V,* at the Lighthouse Cinema in Calcutta. How that speech at Agincourt thrilled me!

That was one of my first British films. I didn't miss a single one of Dirk Bogarde's "Doctor" series, nor any of those early Hitchcocks, like *Lady on The Train and The Lady Vanishes.* Leslie Howard was my idol, a position he still shares with C. Aubrey Smith and David Niven. I spared no pains to see all of the Alec Guiness films, not to mention the six times I saw *Genevieve.*

In more recent years I've enjoyed some of the television imports like "Upstairs, Downstairs"; "The Duchess of Duke Street"; "Poldark" and all the other Masterpiece Theatre offerings hosted by that most urbane of Englishmen, Alistair Cooke.

My first trip to Britain was in 1973, a portion of which was described in *Country Inns and Back Roads, North America.* I knew eventually I would have to travel all over Britain and Ireland and write a book about my experiences.

In 1976, I included several British and Irish inns, country house hotels, and B&Bs in *Country Inns and Back Roads, Europe,* and a few years later, this book was born. Today, *Country Inns and Back Roads, Continental Europe* includes many countries on the Continent, but not Britain and Ireland. On the other hand, *Britain and Ireland,* which is in its third revision, does not contain any travel experiences on the Continent.

The two books are revised alternately every other year. This revision is effective for 1984 and 1985, and I have made a provision for that in estimating the rates for a year in advance. I am sure the reader realizes that these are not firm quotations but merely estimates.

Everyone enjoys traveling in Britain: retired people, students, newlyweds, the first-time traveler, and the sophisticated, experienced traveler. This book has something for everyone, especially for the reader who may *never get* to Britain. Charlie Lovett of Lovett's Inn, Franconia, New Hampshire, refers to this volume as a "wish book." I guess for some readers that tells the story best.

As far as cost is concerned, I tend to look at the accommodations I have selected as a many-layered cake, a slice of which provides expensive frosting on the top and then continues through various gradations to include castle hotels, country house hotels, traditional inns, guest houses, and B&Bs. I try to provide a travel menu that allows the traveler to splurge on one night and perhaps be accommodated more modestly on the following night. While I have yet to find the perfect inn (hotel), the reader will notice very few, if any, negative comments.

This book is written for the North American reader and after nearly twenty years of writing about inns, I think I understand my audience. I find it very interesting to compare my accounts of visits to some of these places with what my good friends, the British travel writers, have to say about the same places.

The reader will find no ratings, stars, or rosettes displayed beside any entry. The length of my descriptions have nothing to do with the excellence of the accommodations. If I have used more space in writing about one place than I have for another, it simply means that as a writer, I found an anecdote or story to share.

In Britain and Ireland I set out to find the same qualities that I look for among inns in North America: warm, friendly, personal lodgings that are the expression of the owner and his or her family. For the most part, these are proprietor-managed places and provide the opportunity for the traveler to get "the feel of the country."

As in North America, I looked for inns and country house hotels that I felt would continue to operate for many years to come. I searched for a feeling of stability.

If the reader finds as much about *people* as he does about half-timbered houses, hearty roast beef, and English antiques, it is because I believe the heart and soul of these accommodations are the proprietor, his family, staff, and the guests themselves. The setting, food, lodgings, service, furnishings, diversions, and surroundings, of course are of prime importance, but the main factor that makes this journey unique and enjoyable is personal involvement.

Rising Sun Hotel (See pg. 167)

COUNTRY INNS IN BRITAIN AND IRELAND

For the past eighteen years I have defined the word "inn" in North America as a certain type of lodging that conveys something of the innkeeper's personality, along with friendly hospitality and service in unique surroundings.

However, I've discovered that in Britain the term, "inn" has a more specific meaning. It's a type of pub (public house) that has a license clearly defining the hours when it must be open or closed. When overnight accommodations are available in a pub, they are frequently called inns. These are sometimes the old traditional inns, frequently with colorful and imaginative names. Most of the time they are located in the center of the villages. The food and accommodations range from simple to sophisticated.

The popularity of traveling in Britain in recent years has seen the emergence of the "country house hotel." For the most part, these are sizable houses built a hundred or more years ago by affluent Britons for pleasure and residence away from the city. Today they have been converted into very good, smallish hotels, usually set in several acres of grounds and woodlands and located away from the towns and villages. They are not, by strict interpretation, inns. Proprietorship usually runs the gamut from retired naval and military personnel to younger couples who, like some North American innkeepers, are establishing new careers. If a British country house hotel were located in North America, it would be known as a country inn. If North American country inns were to be transferred to Britain, they would be called country house hotels.

The third type of establishment is the B&B, which is short for "bed and breakfast." The old American slang expression, "You pays your money and you takes your choice," applies here. Some B&Bs are splendid, others leave much to be desired. I have included as many as possible, and while I have seen all of them personally, I have not necessarily remained overnight.

One final category is the guest house. These, like the B&Bs, are frequently in farms and private homes. Breakfast and dinner are usually served in the family dining room, and besides sharing the living room, there is usually that wonderful institution only to be found in Britain, the residents' lounge, where there's usually a small "telly," a fireplace (or an electric fire), and many books and magazines. The rates at guest houses are higher than at B&Bs, but lower than inns or country house hotels.

HOW THE BOOK IS PLANNED

I've divided this book into the principal touristic sections of Britain, plus London and Ireland. A large map of England shows these sections, and there are separate maps for Scotland and Ireland.

Each of these sections has its own keyed map showing the approximate location of every accommodation. Of further assistance is the Addendum-Index, which lists the hotels alphabetically as well as showing rates and last times for dinner orders. There's also a map in this section showing the location of every county.

The italicized paragraphs following each narrative account of my visits contain essential information about the amenities offered and nearby recreational and cultural attractions. Reasonably explicit driving directions are also included.

To understand the italicized factual information, the following explanation may prove helpful:

NAME OF HOTEL, Village, (Nearby larger town), County, Country, Postal code.

TELEPHONE NUMBER: This is in two parts: The first number in parenthesis is the STD code. When outside of the immediate area of any of the accommodations, step into the nearest friendly red phone booth and dial all of the STD number plus all of the numbers that follow. In some cases, where an operator may be necessary, I have included the name of the individual exchange.

Many U.K. points can be dialed direct from overseas. The country code for England, Scotland, Wales, and Ireland is 011-44 plus the STD code and the individual number.

CREDIT CARDS: except as noted, all places accept some major credit cards such as American Express, Barclaycard, Master Charge or Visa. British traveler's checks are excellent.

The rest of the italicized paragraphs is self-explanatory.

RATES

Rates for a room with bath for two people for one night with breakfast are included in the Addendum-Index of this book. They are not to be considered firm quotations, but should be used as guidelines only. The traveler who is willing to travel British-style (booking a room with a shared bath) will appreciate the lower rates.

MAKING RESERVATIONS

A travel agent can frequently be the traveler's best friend. These people are professionals and know how to make the necessary contacts for reservations. Since a very high percentage of the hotels and inns pay travel agents' commissions, this should not be an additional expense for the traveler. However, in some cases, the smaller accommodations do not pay commissions, and the travel agent is entitled to charge the client a fee equal to the usual commission. It's also reasonable for the travel agent to charge the client for the cost of telephone calls or telex messages.

Because the Thomas Cook Travel Agency has offices in all parts of Britain, they can confirm reservations most readily.

The best way to assure a firm reservation is to contact the inn or hotel by telephone and then send a deposit which is held against the first night's stay.

HOW TO TELEPHONE GREAT BRITAIN TO MAKE A RESERVATION

If you are calling from North America, you may directly dial the numbers that are in this book. The first thing to do is to dial 011 if you want a station-to-station call, or 01 for calls requiring operator assistance (collect, person, etc.). Next, dial 44, the country code. Now refer to the telephone number given for each accommodation. One very important point: if calling from North America, omit the first zero; otherwise, dial the number as given. If direct international dialing is not available in your area, you will still get the dial rate on a simple station call, just dial 0 and give the details of your call.

If telephoning from point-to-point *within* Great Britain, read the instructions carefully that are posted in each telephone booth and be sure to dial the 0, which is omitted when dialing from North America to Great Britain.

The most economical way to telephone Great Britain is to call between 6:00 P.M. and 7:00 A.M., local North American time (British time is 5 hours later than Eastern Standard Time). This is for a call that does not require operator assistance. It costs about 25% more to dial direct between 1:00 P.M. and 6:00 P.M., and about 50% more to dial between 7:00 A.M. and 1:00 P.M. Operator-assisted calls are considerably more expensive. Your telephone company can fill you in on further details. Dial toll-free 1-800-874-4000.

LUGGAGE

For years I've been taking two- or three-week extended trips to the U.K. and the Continent, using only carry-on luggage consisting of a garment bag and a soft travel bag. This eliminates any waiting for luggage or any other type of delay. The garment bag holds one jacket, which is necessary for the evening meal, and one pair of suitable dress trousers. I also include at least one sweater, an additional pair of trousers, and a raincoat, which serves many purposes. I usually carry three drip-dry shirts and three drip-dry shorts, and four pairs of wool socks. Of course, this means that I am doing a hand laundry every night, which, under the circumstances, will dry in just a few hours. The ladies will have a different list, but keeping your luggage to a minimum will simplify your travels all the way around.

CANCELLATIONS

In Britain, acceptance of a hotel booking by telephone or in writing, is generally regarded as a legally binding contract. If it's necessary to cancel, advise the hotel immediately. If they are unable to re-let the room, the hotel may be entitled to claim compensation—usually two-thirds of the agreed price, and any deposit would be included as part of this payment.

AIR FARES TO BRITAIN

Even in these days when escalating air fares keep pace with the rising cost of jet fuel, I find that it's possible to shop around and get bargains. For example, Pan Am, as well as all the other airlines, have standby tickets which require an obvious flexibility of schedule. When this doesn't suit my convenience, I order my ticket in advance under one of several plans which effect a savings.

ARRIVING IN BRITAIN

Though large and somewhat complicated, Heathrow Airport, just outside London, is most efficiently designed. Part of the hassle is reduced by luggage trolleys and moving walkways. Immigration and customs are easily negotiated, and the traveler emerges into the International Arrivals Section, where currency can be exchanged and information about lodgings can be obtained. This is also where there are literally hundreds of people waiting for arriving friends and guests. Many of them have small signs with the name of the arriving person printed on them—that's how chauffeurs and other people meeting strangers get together.

At Heathrow there's a choice of two types of transportation into the center of London. The first is airport coaches going to Victoria Station and two other London railroad stations. You can then take a cab to your hotel.

The second way is to use the Underground, which runs from Heathrow right to the heart of London. Follow the signs in the airport and use the moving walkways; there are no traffic tie-ups. Travelers arriving at Gatwick Airport can take the train or bus directly to Victoria Station.

RENTAL CARS

After much trial and error I found the most satisfactory car rental arrangements in both Britain and Europe, from the standpoints of both convenience and cost, could be made through Auto-Europe, whose offices in North America are at P.O. Box 500, Yorktown Heights, New York 10598. The toll-free number for the U.S. is 800-223-5555. (New York State: 800-942-1309.) Canada: 800-268-8810. Arrangements can also be made to pick up cars in principal cities and airports in Britain and drop them off in other countries.

I always advise travelers not to plan on driving their rented cars in the city of London. Take the Underground or the airport coach to center London and then a cab to your hotel. Pick up a rental car when leaving the city. The Auto-Europe cars can be picked up and/or dropped off in London, Heathrow, Gatwick, and Prestwick airports, and many other points.

Many experienced travelers visit London at the conclusion of their trip, engaging a rental car on arrival at the airport and spending the first night at one of several countryside accommodations listed in this book. At the end of their travels, the car can be dropped off at one of various locations, including Edinburgh, Glasgow, York, Oxford, Cambridge, Exeter, or even Heathrow or Gatwick. The trick is to take the train back to London and avoid the traffic.

DRIVING TIPS

In Britain, automobiles are driven on the left-hand side of the road. This should not alarm anyone, since it's very easy to make the adjustment. I'd suggest an automatic, rather than a stick shift, automobile. A U.K. operator's license is not necessary.

Enter the roundabouts (traffic circles) on the left and circle clockwise. The traffic already in the circle has the right of way.

Ancient church, Bosham

DINING IN ENGLAND, SCOTLAND, WALES, AND IRELAND

Basically menus in Britain and Ireland fall into three categories. First, there's pub food which is usually salads, sausages, cold cuts, meat pies, and patés. Pub food is most generally served at midday.

Some lunch and nearly all dinner menus include hearty British food such as roast beef and Yorkshire pudding, various cuts of lamb, veal, ham, and poultry which might include pheasant, partridge, and other game birds.

At dinner, British dishes frequently share the spotlight with French cuisine, both traditional and *nouvelle*. I found a great many French chefs working in British kitchens.

There are local food specialties in various parts of Britain. Most of the time they are easily recognizable on the menu and may even be called to the traveler's attention through the "Taste of England," "Taste of Scotland," and "Taste of Wales" programs, which can be found in many restaurants.

The latest times dinner may be ordered vary greatly from one place to another, and these times are listed in the Addendum-Index in the back of the book.

DEPARTING LONDON

As noted earlier, the Underground is a quick, always sure, direct method of getting from Heathrow to Center city. I have found that the reverse is also true. It is possible to catch the airport buses leaving from Victoria Station and two other railroad stations in London and going directly to the Heathrow departure counters for all airlines. For overseas flights, I find that it is best to arrive at least 90 minutes ahead of time. You can always enjoy yourself watching the fascinating crowds at Heathrow after being ticketed and going through passport control. Major overseas airlines all have special reservation numbers for checking vital departure information. The PanAm reservation number in London is 01-409-0688.

FLOATING THROUGH EUROPE

A unique way to spend part of a holiday in Britain is to book passage on one of the luxury barges that ply the hundreds of miles of canals and rivers in the U.K. For full information, contact Floating Through Europe, 501 Madison Avenue, New York, New York 10022. Tel: (212) 832-6700. I first mentioned this organization in the original *Country Inns and Back Roads, Europe* and have received many letters of commendation.

ACKNOWLEDGMENTS

This book is really a team effort. Behind the scenes were literally dozens of individuals and organizations who gave generously of their time and advice in order to bring their experiences to this published fruition.

To start with, the British Tourist Authority in both New York and London was immensely cooperative in helping me plan my trips. Equally helpful was the Irish Tourist Board in New York and in Dublin.

PanAmerican Airways has always been very helpful with information and travel assistance. There are different toll-free 800 numbers in various sections of North America for information and reservations.

This book was designed and the drawings created by my longtime associate, Jan Lindstrom.

Virginia Rowe, the editor, is responsible for the accuracy of all the facts and keeps a watchful eye on my literary style.

As has been the case for almost twenty years, the Studley Press, Dalton, Massachusetts, with its usual high standards of efficiency and competence, set the type, prepared the negatives and plates, ran the presses, and provided us with bound books.

I am also grateful to the hundreds of readers of my earlier books who have been kind enough to share some of their favorite places in Britain and Ireland. This book will be revised again in 1986 and further suggestions are most welcome..

Maps in this book are reproduced with the kind permission of the British Tourist Authority. The poem: "Helford Creek" is reproduced with permission of the publishers of *This England,* magazine.

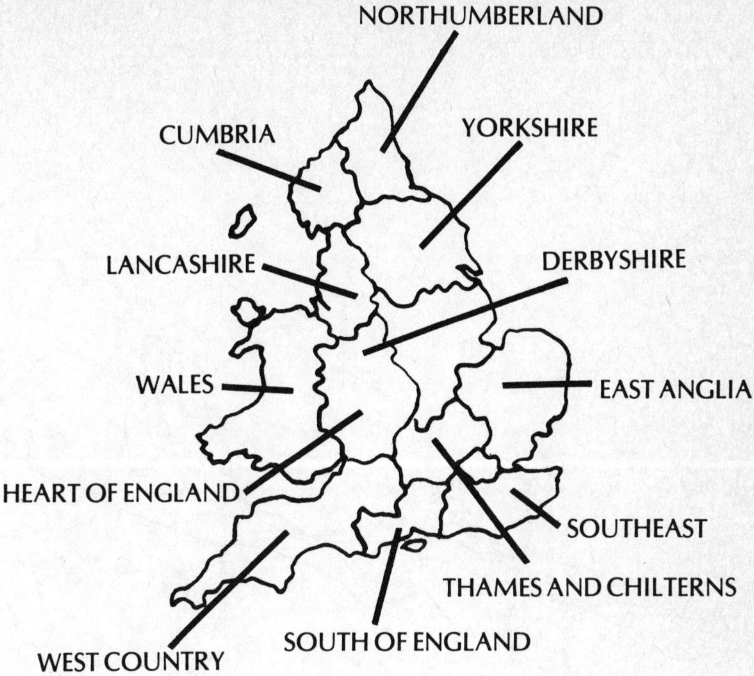

ENGLAND

Contents

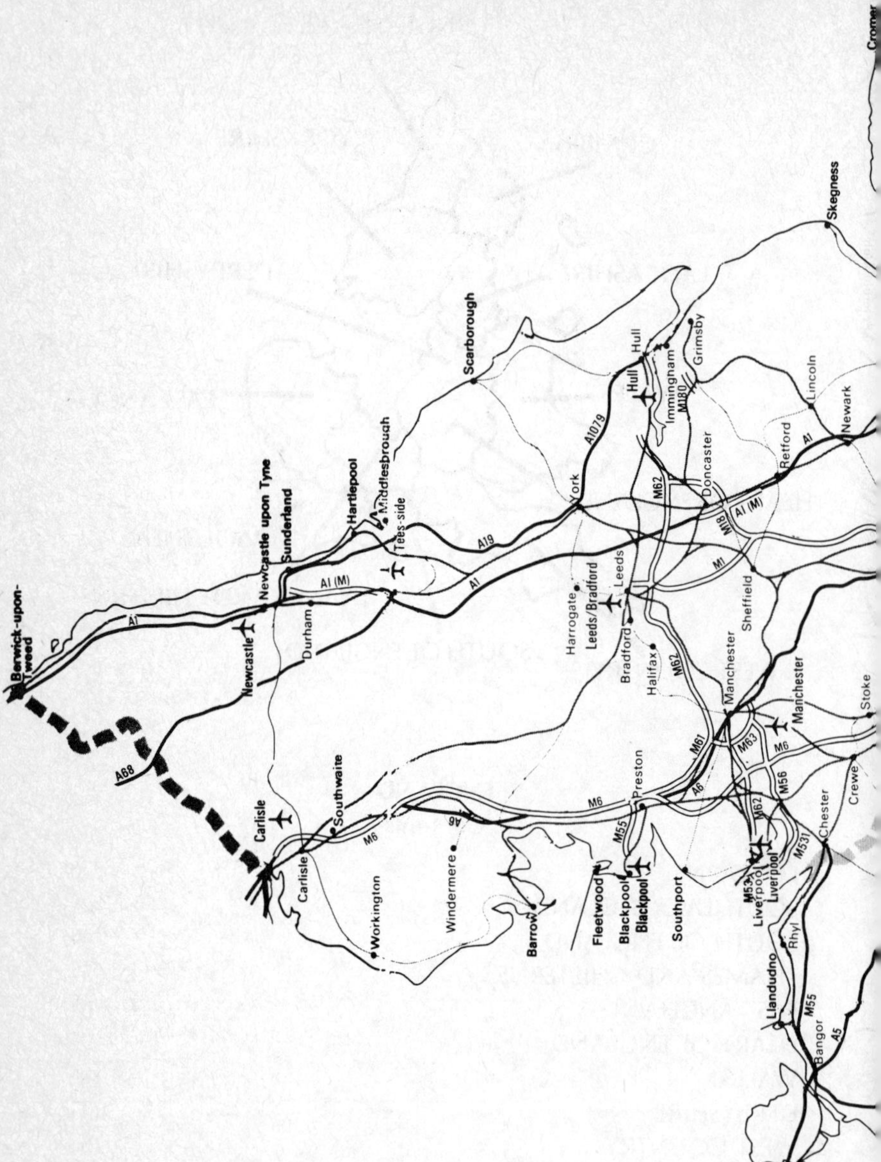
Berwick-upon-Tweed
A1
Newcastle upon Tyne
Sunderland
Hartlepool
Middlesbrough
Tees-side
Scarborough
A1 (M)
Durham
Newcastle
A68
Carlisle
Carlisle
Southwaite
M6
Workington
Windermere
A6
Barrow
Fleetwood
Blackpool
Blackpool
M55
Preston
Southport
M53
Liverpool
Liverpool
M62
M531
Chester
Rhyl
Llandudno
M55
Bangor
A5
Holyhead
Crewe
M56
M6
M63
M61
A6
Manchester
Manchester
Stoke
Halifax
Bradford
M62
Harrogate
Leeds/Bradford
Leeds
Sheffield
M1
M18
A1 (M)
A1
A19
York
M62
Doncaster
A1079
Hull
Hull
Immingham
M180
Grimsby
Retford
A1
Newark
Lincoln
Skegness
Cromer

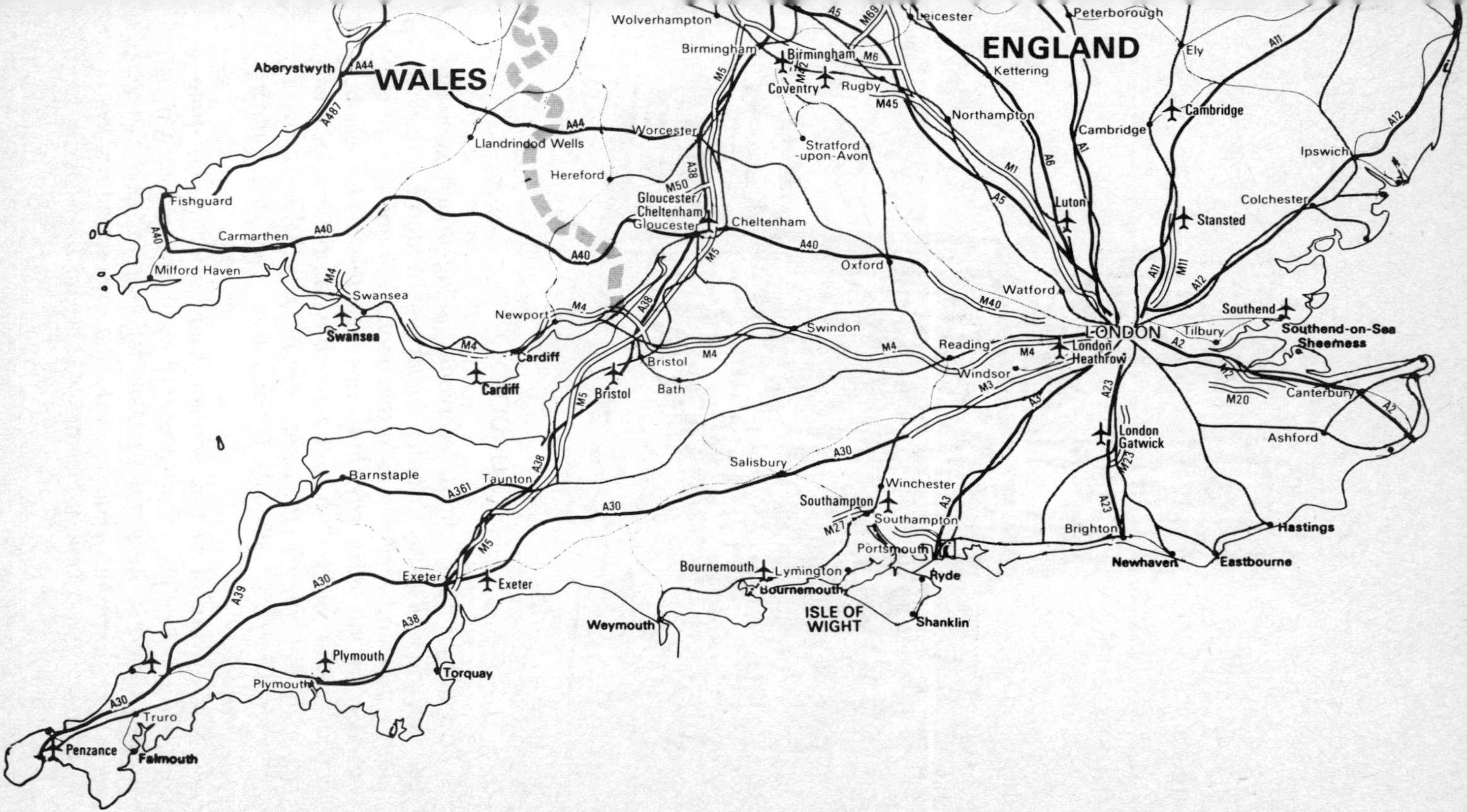

ENGLAND
WALES
LONDON
Aberystwyth
Fishguard
Carmarthen
Milford Haven
Swansea
Swansea
Llandrindod Wells
Hereford
Worcester
Wolverhampton
Birmingham
Birmingham
Coventry
Rugby
Leicester
Peterborough
Kettering
Ely
Northampton
Cambridge
Cambridge
Stratford
-upon-Avon
Gloucester/
Cheltenham
Gloucester
Cheltenham
Newport
Cardiff
Cardiff
Bristol
Bristol
Bath
Swindon
Oxford
Luton
Stansted
Watford
Reading
Windsor
London
Heathrow
London
Gatwick
Ipswich
Colchester
Southend
Southend-on-Sea
Sheerness
Tilbury
Canterbury
Ashford
Hastings
Eastbourne
Newhaven
Brighton
Winchester
Southampton
Southampton
Portsmouth
Ryde
Shanklin
ISLE OF
WIGHT
Lymington
Bournemouth
Bournemouth
Weymouth
Salisbury
Taunton
Barnstaple
Exeter
Exeter
Torquay
Plymouth
Plymouth
Truro
Falmouth
Penzance
A44
A487
A40
M4
A38
M50
M5
M6
M42
M45
M69
A5
M1
A6
A1
A11
M11
A12
M40
M3
A3
A23
M23
A2
M2
M20
A30
A361
A39
M27

LONDON

Sooner or later, almost everyone visiting Britain goes to London, and well-a-day that they do because London is alive with interest, fun, and excitement. In this book I will not attempt an overview of this great city, but hope that the reader will be encouraged to visit London, walk as much as possible, and feel free to mingle, not only with the Londoners, but also the thousands of other visitors. I have walked the London streets very late at night in complete safety.

Now a word of caution and some advice for the first-time visitor to London! Do not attempt to drive an automobile within Greater London. The ground transportation from Heathrow or Gatwick is speedy and frequent. You will not need a car in the city of London. If you land at Heathrow, and your baggage can be handled conveniently, it is possible to take the Piccadilly Line to center London, where a cab can then be taken directly to your hotel.

Getting around in London is easy. The London Underground is fast and efficient; goes everywhere and is good for excursions that are some distance away. The double-decker buses, as well as the green buses, provide an opportunity to see London above-ground. The hotel concierge can supply a very essential map which gives all of the bus lines by number, and it's quite common to see tourists standing in front of a chart on a post, reading the numbers of the buses that are going to stop here.

There are dozens of books about sightseeing in London; one of the best is London, Your Sightseeing Guide, *published by the British Travel Authority.*

London Hotels

Because almost everybody traveling to Britain will be planning to stop in London for a few days, I have included a group of moderate-sized London hotels in various price categories. (See price list in Addendum-Index.)

Many of these hotels have representatives in the United States, but they can also be contacted directly for reservations. A telephone call at the low-rate time is well worth the effort. Once a reservation is made it should be followed up as soon as possible by an air-mail letter with a deposit.

THE BASIL STREET HOTEL
Knightsbridge, London SW3

The Basil, as it is known in London, is the "Americans' home away from home." It is located right behind Harrods Department Store near where Brompton Road, Knightsbridge, and Sloane Street all come together. It's just a few steps away from the Knightsbridge Station on the Piccadilly Line on the Underground.

All London hotels have an indispensable man known as the Hall Porter. I'll use The Basil Hall Porter as a model for others. Guests soon discover that his desk is the nerve center to the smooth running of their holiday or business trip. Hall Porters provide information on everything from sightseeing and transport, to religious services, hotel reservations at the next destination, restaurants, theatres, mail, newspapers, messages, laundry and valet services, parcels, luggage, and taxis. He's on duty from 9 a.m.

to 9 p.m., at which time his duties are taken over by the Night Porter.

Guest rooms at the Basil vary in size and price. A majority have private bathrooms.

Besides several different dining rooms, The Basil also has the Parrot Club, which is a delightful meeting place for women, used mostly by daytime visitors to London, but also available to hotel guests.

The Basil lounge is a good place to meet friends in London, and also provides an opportunity to chat with other travelers. The afternoon teas are first-rate.

I've stayed at the Basil several times and I have American friends who prefer it above all other London hotels.

BASIL STREET HOTEL, Knightsbridge, London, SW3 1AH. Tel: (01) 581-3311; U.S. reservations: 800-223-9868; telegrams: Spotless London SW3; telex: 28379. A 103-room (mostly private baths) hotel located near Sloane Square, Hyde Park and Harrods Department Store. Breakfast, lunch, tea, dinner, and snacks served every day of the year. Setphen Korany, Managing Director. (See Addendum for rates.)

Directions: From Heathrow Airport take the Piccadilly Line Underground (it's the only one available) to Knightsbridge Station, which is just a few steps away from the hotel. From London air terminals, take airline coach to central London, and then a taxi cab.

BROWN'S HOTEL
Dover Street, London W1A

In the city of institutions, Brown's Hotel in the center of fashionable Mayfair, is a true London institution. I realized this when I was presented with a 32-page color brochure which chronicles the hotel's history, ownership, expansion, and distinguished visitors.

Brown's was discovered by North Americans a number of years ago and became a very *chic* place to stay. Along with a couple of London's other smaller hotels, Dukes and the Stafford, Brown's is a very elegant hotel and favored by a great many experienced travelers.

BROWN'S HOTEL, Dover Street, London W1A 4SW. Tel: (01) 493-6020; telex: 28686. A 135-room well-known, smaller hotel conveniently located close to London nightlife, as well as Buckingham Palace and Green Park. Bruce P. Banister, General Manager. (See Addendum for rates.)

DUKES HOTEL
35 St. James's Place, London SW1A

Dukes, like the Stafford and Brown's Hotel, is located close to Piccadilly and the London theater district, although all three of them are very quiet. Dukes was originally composed of "chambers" for the younger sons of the nobility; it has been a hotel since 1908. I've included it in *CIBR, Britain* since the first edition.

Dukes is probably the closest thing to a private London club—the essence of restrained elegance with a friendly and accommodating atmosphere. It's located on one of the few remaining streets in London enjoying romantic gas lighting.

Baskets of fruit are provided for each arriving guest, and the *London Times* is left at each door every morning. Although the dining room, which has been considerably enlarged, is open for breakfast, most of the guests prefer to enjoy breakfast in their rooms.

All of the rooms are named after historic dukes and decorated in a ducal style. They are on the medium-to-small size.

I have a feeling that Beau Brummel, the arbiter of London fashion who lived at 39 St. James's Place, would thoroughly approve of Dukes today.

DUKES HOTEL, 35 St. James's Place, London, England SW1A 1MY. Tel: (01) 491-4840; U.S. reservations: 1-800-223-5581; telex 28283. A 54-room luxury hotel in the heart of London's West End, convenient to Piccadilly, the Strand, and the theater district. Adjacent to Green Park, Buckingham Palace. Open every day. Breakfast, lunch, tea, and dinner served to non-residents. (See Addendum for rates.)

STAFFORD HOTEL
St. James's Place, London SW1A

The Stafford Hotel is just about two blocks away from Dukes Hotel on St. James's Place, one of London's well-kept secrets. St. James's Place has its own history. Oscar Wilde lived here, and also Sir Francis Chichester. Some of the famous London clubs, such as Bootles, Whites, and Brooks were located here, and one of the principal walks was 'Green Walk' between the mall and Park Wall where Charles II met Nell Gwyn.

The Stafford housed various London clubs, then added buildings on each side, and then became the Stafford Hotel. During World War II, it was a club for Canadian and American overseas officers. I stayed there a couple of times and found the rooms very comfortable and the staff very amiable.

THE STAFFORD HOTEL, St. James's Place, London SW1A, 1NJ, Tel: (01) 493-0111; telex 28602. A 70-room hotel located in the Mayfair district of London within walking distance of theatres, Oxford Street, and Buckingham Palace. Breakfast, lunch, tea, dinner served daily to non-residents. Terry Holmes, Managing Director. (See Addendum for rates.)

Directions: First-time visitors should take a bus to the air terminal and a cab to the hotel.

BRYANSTON COURT HOTEL
56 Great Cumberland Place, London W1

This is a very pleasant hotel located just a few blocks from Marble Arch. It is convenient for walking to Oxford Street and Piccadilly.

During my visit, an entirely new dining room and kitchen were being installed which, I understand, has now been completed.

Great Cumberland Place is a quiet, dignified street and the hotel has a demeanor to match.

BRYANSTON COURT HOTEL, 56 Great Cumberland Place, London, England W1. Tel: (01) 262 3141. Telex: 21120 Ref 2637. A 60-room hotel on a quiet street a few blocks from Marble Arch. Open every day. Breakfast, lunch, tea, and dinner served to non-residents. E. Theodore, Resident Proprietor. (See Addendum for rates.)

DURRANTS HOTEL
George Street, London W1H

Durrants Hotel is a former Georgian coaching inn owned and run by the same family for over a half a century. It is in London's fashionable West End opposite the Wallace Collection. It's within a short walk of Oxford Street, Piccadilly, and Marble Arch. It has a very pleasant lobby and entranceway, and a comfortable lounge area with deep leather chairs.

Durrants is a quiet conservative hotel generally preferred by travelers for whom London is a frequent stop.

DURRANTS HOTEL, George Street, London W1H 6BJ, England. Tel: (01) 935 8131. A pleasant hotel just off Manchester Square and a few blocks from Oxford Street and Marble Arch. Open every day in the year. Breakfast, lunch, tea, and dinner served to non-residents. J.P. Leveque, Director. (See Addendum for rates.)

THE GORING HOTEL
Beeston Place, Grosvenor Gardens, London SW1W

The Goring is located within walking distance of the Thames Embankment, as well as the Royal Parks, Westminster Abbey and the Houses of Parliament, Victoria Station, the West London Air Terminals, and the Pan Am Terminal.

Departures and arrivals from Gatwick Airport are transported directly to or from nearby Victoria Station by train.

The Goring manages to be sedate and informal at the same

time. One of its virtues is the fact that there is a beautiful lawn and garden in the rear which also provides views of the posteriors of a group of small London townhouses.

THE GORING HOTEL, Beeston Place, Grosvenor Gardens, London SW1W OJW. Tel: (01) 834-8211; telex 919166. A 100-room family-owned hotel near Victoria Station, London, and Pan Am Air Terminals. Breakfast, lunch, tea, dinner served daily to non-residents. William Cowpe, Manager. (See Addendum for rates.)

NUMBER SIXTEEN
16 Sumner Place, London

Number Sixteen is actually the name of a small, tidy hotel in a lovely residental area reasonably close to, but not a part of, central London.

It is located at 16 Sumner Place in the South Kensington area, which is also the name of the stop on the underground.

Because of the system of house numbering in London, once having found Sumner Place it may be necessary for you to go around the block and come up the other way in order to locate Number Sixteen.

It is actually three townhouses that were built in 1848 and have been preserved for their architectural charm. There is no hotel sign, but the street number is very plain. Inside, the reception area is most attractive and friendly. I saw many of the 24 bedrooms, which were furnished in a comfortable and appropriate manner.

There is a pleasant sitting room and also a private bar, which is open in the evening. A continental breakfast is served to every guest; however, a full English breakfast is also available.

The hotel won the most recent "London in Bloom" competition for its garden that stretches across the entire three-townhouse area in the rear.

Number Sixteen isn't for the traveler who ordinarily stays at one of the more palatial hotels near the Marble Arch or Park Lane; however, you will not be the first London visitor to discover it. If form holds true, you will want to do what everyone does who visits it—tell the whole world about your new London hotel.

NUMBER SIXTEEN HOTEL, 16 Sumner Place, London, England SW7 3EG. Tel: 01-589 5232. Telex: 266638. A 24-bedroom (private baths) townhouse in a quiet section of London. Continental breakfast included in the room rate. Open year-round. A few moments from Harrods, Knightsbridge, Hyde Park Corner, and Piccadilly by cab, foot, bus, or underground. Michael Watson and Tim Daniel, Hoteliers.

Directions: After arriving at Heathrow Airport, take the underground to South Kensington Station and ask directions to 16 Sumner Place; it is just around the corner. Otherwise take the regular airport bus to central London and then take the short cab ride to the hotel.

HARRODS

I was browsing in the meat shop at Harrods, one of London's great department stores.

What a glorious fantasia of sights and enticing aromas greeted me! It was Elysian at the very least.

The first thing I saw hanging from the domed ceiling, mind you, were hundreds of hams, sausages, pumpernickels, salami, and dozens of their relatives in the "wurst" family. A great many of them were imported from different countries in Europe, and there were numerous items which were totally new to me.

Below them was a large center section of cases with such delights as pork pies, steak and kidney pies, ham pies, and chicken pies. There were 27 varieties of salads, including oriental, Spanish, Russian. The displays themslves were beautiful. There were tins of caviar and small fish, and dozens of varieties of paté. There were jellied eels, absolutely sumptuous-looking bacon, and beautiful quiches. I walked around the center at least three times planning picnics and cold buffets.

However, to further add to my delight, all around the outside of this square were counters with gorgeous displays of fowl, including turkey and pheasant. There were cuts of pork, lamb, veal, beef—just about everything. Particularly intriguing was the display of fish including kippers, shellfish, halibut, sole, Scotch salmon, and many others. There was also a large fish sculpture in ice.

All of these great treats were beautifully displayed in a setting of intricately tiled pillars and ceiling. There were many colors of tiles forming a fascinating succession of patterns.

The next stop was the cheese department which was equally as exciting. There were all kinds of cheeses done in all forms—in crocks, jars, cans, hanging loose, sliced, in cases for slicing, and hanging from the ceiling. There were cheeses from all over the world—Beaumont, Brie, Port Salut, Jarlsburg, provolone, to name a few. There were cases of cheese of all colors—yellow, green, white, and speckled cheeses. I saw wheels of cheeses and cheese patés.

The aroma and sight are still in my mind.

SOUTHEAST ENGLAND
Counties of Sussex, Kent, and Surrey

All roads in southeast England originate from (or lead to) London, consequently, almost every weekend, the motorways and main roads from London's Marble Arch are abuzz with small English cars being driven on the left-hand side of the road, at slightly-less-than-breakneck speed, through the pleasant countryside to the three southeast counties and the towns and villages of Chichester, Brighton, Eastbourne, Hastings, Rye, Folkstone, Dover, and Canterbury.

Surrey is the county closest to London, and has beautiful hills, woods, and heathland, including the highest point in the south of England: Lythe Hill. There are many "great houses" in Surrey, and it has been the scene of some of the stirring events of England's past, including Runneymede where King John signed the Magna Carta in 1215 on the banks of the River Thames.

The county of Sussex, divided into East and West Sussex, extends from the southern borders of Surrey south to the coast, and eastward to Kent. Sussex has delightful combinations of peaceful forest, undulating downland, and attractive seaside towns and villages.

The South Downs (high rolling hills) sweep across Sussex from the border of Hampshire to Eastbourne, and there are several of the famous hill figures carved on the sides of the hills. Some of these are rather ancient, but a surprising number have been created since 1900. The Glyndebourne Opera is also in Sussex, as is the city of Chichester and its harbor.

The Kentish coast bends around southeast England for 126 miles and is replete with many resort towns. This is the land of Anne Boleyn, Henry VIII's second wife, who was beheaded (and whose ghost still walks); Winston Churchill, whose home, Chartwell, is now maintained by the National Trust; Charles Darwin; and General Wolfe, who figured prominently in the history of the New World. It is a place of many cathedrals, abbeys, churches, castles, and ruins. One of the principal attractions is the old city of Canterbury with its famous cathedrals.

Oddly enough, this section of England is not the prime objective for North American visitors who are far more apt to go from London north to Stratford-on-Avon, the Lake Country, and on to Edinburgh. The AA Touring Guide To Britain *outlines twelve tours in this region.*

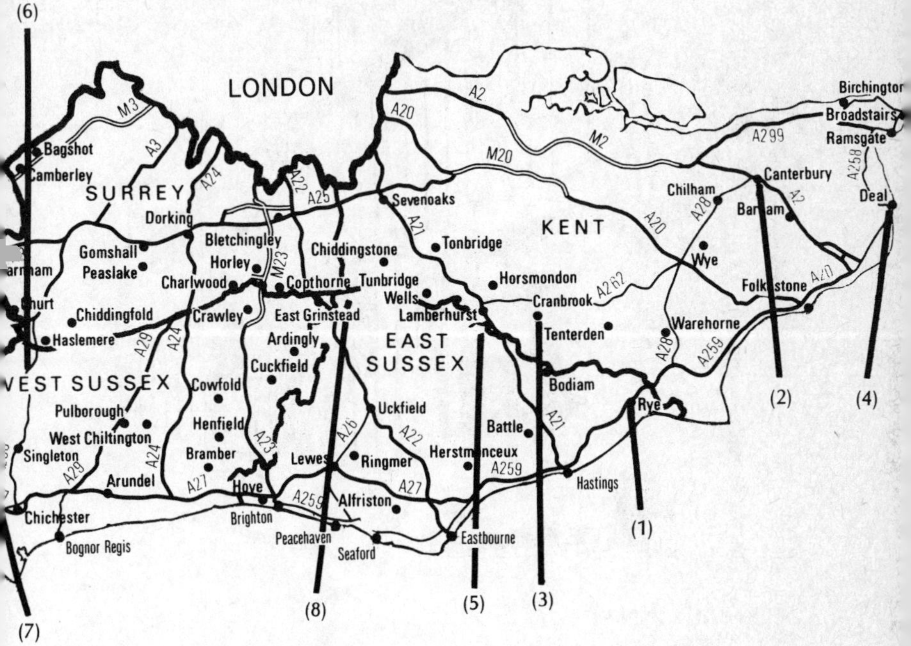

SOUTHEAST ENGLAND

(1) MERMAID INN, Rye, Sussex, 30
(2) ABBOTT'S BARTON HOTEL, Canterbury, Kent, 32
(3) KENNEL HOLT, Cranbrook, Kent, 34
(4) ROYAL HOTEL, Deal, Kent, 35
(5) THE PRIORY, Rushlake Green, East Sussex, 37
(6) SPREAD EAGLE HOTEL, Midhurst, Sussex, 39
(7) WHITE HORSE INN, Chilgrove, Sussex, 40
(8) GRAVETYE MANOR, East Grinstead, Sussex, 41

MERMAID INN
Rye, Sussex

"Good night, Norman, I will see you at breakfast. Will 8:30 be suitable?" That was Michael Gregory speaking, owner and innkeeper of the Mermaid Inn in Rye. We had spent a most congenial evening in the dining room with a dinner of good English roast beef and Yorkshire pudding, and then in the lounge over second cups of coffee.

Naturally most of the talk centered around the Mermaid. "How old is it, Michael?" I asked. "Do you really know?"

"Well, we think it was rebuilt in 1420 after the French had burned the town in 1377 on one of their frequent raids. Local legend says that the inn was visited by Queen Elizabeth I when she visited Rye in 1573.

"The inn has seen and made its own episodes in history," he pointed out. "During the Reformation many priests were sheltered here during their flight to France."

He took me upstairs to point out the initials "JHS" in one of their bedrooms. "This was the symbol of the escaping clerics," he said. Then he showed me the secret staircase which was probably used many times as members of the clergy slipped away from their oppressors. In the huge Back Lounge of the inn I saw the "Priest's Hole." "Just take a look up the chimney," he said. "That's another hiding place. A bit warmish, but quite safe.

"The history of the inn has always reflected the history of the town. Perhaps the most exciting period was during the times when smugglers' gangs were the bully boys of Rye. One group called the Hawkhurst Gang didn't do our reputation any good at all. They sat about in the windows of the inn cursing and carousing with their loaded pistols on the tables, and no magistrate would interfere with them.

"In February, 1735, a smuggler named Thomas More who was out on bail went to the Mermaid and dragged the bailiff from his room and into the street by his heels taking the bail bondsman's warrants with him. The bailiff was taken to a ship in the harbor but eventually rescued by the captain of another ship. I could go on at great length about famous people who visited here," Michael said, "and, of course, the ghosts."

Jan Lindstrom's drawing of the inn shows the Elizabethan half-timbers and entrance arch. The entrance hall reflects the motif of the entire building. The walls are faced with oak paneling and the timbered ceiling is supported by a kingpost. In a way, four centuries just fall away.

Michael and I said good night and I walked up the staircase past "Dr. Syn's Lounge," which is another whole piece of Mermaid tradition.

I fell asleep quickly, but in the middle of the night I awakened hearing whispers in the hall and a clicking sound like the cocking of an ancient pistol. Footsteps went down the passageway and stairs and then it was quiet. When I asked Michael about it the next morning, he just smiled.

MERMAID INN, Rye, Sussex, England. Tel: (0797) 22 3065; Telex 957141. A 30-room traditional inn located in one of England's most historic ports 65 mi. from London. Open all year. Breakfast, lunch, dinner served to non-residents. Reservations may also be made for Abbot's Barton in Canterbury and the Royal Hotel in Deal. M. Gregory, Resident Owner.

Directions: From London, take A21 through Tunbridge Wells, and then A268 from Flinwell directly to Rye. There are dozens of alternate routes.

Rye at Dawn

Michael Gregory told me that Rye was fascinating at sunrise, and an early morning walk over hill and dale and into the town, with all its fascinating little shops, proved him to be altogether correct. The old houses and the flowers lining the cobbled streets; the church at the top of the hill with its ancient churchyard graves; Battings Tower, built in 1250, and redolent of English history; and that place on the hill where stood (until a bombing in 1940) the garden house of Henry James, who had lived there from 1898 to 1916, were all part of a magical sunrise walk through Rye.

ABBOT'S BARTON HOTEL
Canterbury, Kent

It was in the prologue to the *Canterbury Tales* that Geoffrey Chaucer wrote, "And specially, from every shires ende of England, to Caunterbury they wende."

Today, I myself was a pilgrim to Canterbury, driving on the famous Dover Road which leads from the South Coast of England to Canterbury and London. Here, I would not only view the famous Canterbury Cathedral, but also visit Abbot's Barton Hotel.

I easily found the hotel which is a Victorian building on the Dover Road just a short distance from the cathedral and the center of the city. It sits back from the road with broad lawns and attractive gardens.

Legend suggests that the hotel now stands on the site of the Canterbury Abbey barley farm or granary. In old English, "Bere Tun" means storage of crops, hence the name "barton."

The building is of a rather imposing red sandstone construction and the older portion on the front is quite interesting. Additional rooms and facilities have been added in the rear in the same architectural design. Most of the fifty rooms have their own bathrooms.

The general decor of the bar and restaurant depicts historic Canterbury, and the days of pilgrimage and of Chaucer. While I was not able to remain for dinner or overnight, I did enjoy an excellent bar lunch.

Abbot's Barton proved to be an excellent center for visiting the historic city of Canterbury and its famous cathedral, and also for a very pleasant holiday in Kent. It is just a few miles to Dover and the famous chalk cliffs, as well as the north Downs and the seaside towns of Sandwich, Deal, and Folkstone. I was quite surprised by the number of golf courses in Kent. The University of Kent at Canterbury has a very good theater company, and there were also various types of recitals and concerts.

The bulletin board at Abbot's Barton is jam-packed with suggestions about places to go and things to visit including Chartwell, Winston Churchill's home.

It is possible to make convenient reservations at the Royal Hotel in Deal and the Mermaid Inn in Rye, as well as other small hotels on the South Coast.

ABBOT'S BARTON HOTEL, New Dover Road, Canterbury, Kent, England. Tel: (0227) 60341; Telex 957141. A 50-room in-town hotel set in three acres of lawn located about ¾ mi. from the Canterbury Cathedral. Breakfast, lunch, and dinner served to non-residents. Open every day of the year. Located near many historic and cultural treasures in Kent. Associated with the Mermaid Inn, Rye, and The Royal Hotel, Deal.

Directions: From London take the A-2 (M-2) eastward to Canterbury.

CANTERBURY

Canterbury dates back to Roman times and was used by the Romans as the seat of government for the tribes of Kent. In 597 A.D.

St. Augustin traveled from Rome and converted the King of Kent, and restored some of the town's earlier Christianity. The present cathedral dates from 1070 and was the scene of the brutal murder of Archbishop Thomas Becket for his denial of the king's authority over the Church. It remains to this day one of the great and inspiring attractions in the United Kingdom.

In addition to the abbey and cathedral, it is possible to view the city wall bastions: the West Gate; Grey Friars, the first Franciscan settlement in England; the Weavers, a house of Flemish weavers in use in the 16th century; and the poor priests' hospital, now used as the regimental museum.

Canterbury is a compact, inspiring city. Perhaps nowhere else is it possible to see so much history within a few hundred yards. It is a real center of English religion and learning.

Although not a native of Kent, Geoffrey Chaucer (1340(?)-1400) has proven to be the best press agent for Canterbury. The celebrated Canterbury Tales *is made up of the stories of a group of pilgrims, representing all types of English life, as they journeyed through the April sunshine and showers from the Tabard Inn in Southwark (near London) to Canterbury and back. Chaucer apparently finished twenty-one of these humorous, earthy tales which reveal his love of nature and his fellow man.*

It is said of Chaucer that he found English a dialect, and left it a language.

KENNEL HOLT HOTEL
Cranbrook, Kent

Kennel Holt was one of the first places I visited in England. It was an Elizabethan, beamed, manor house, and today it is a country house hotel set in five acres of landscaped grounds with a natural pond, rosebeds, croquet lawn, and cobnut walks. It still sits at the end of a secluded lane, 300 yards from the main road, overlooking a wooded valley in the heart of the rolling orchard country of Kent.

These days it is amiably presided over by Patrick Cliff, a former RAF fighter and helicopter pilot, and his wife, Ruth, who, among other things, is totally in charge of the kitchen. She is a Cordon Bleu-trained cook .

There are seven bedrooms all with color TV and private bathrooms.

There are over fifty historic houses, gardens, and castles within easy driving distance of Kennel Holt. I'm afraid I can't list them all, but I will mention Chartwell, Sir Winston Churchill's

family home. The Cliffs have a very comprehensive book and maps of all of the fascinating places nearby.

Wing Commander Cliff points out that Kennel Holt would make an excellent first or last stop for guests using Gatwick Airport. I should imagine that the peace, quiet, and the comfort of the log fires in the residents' lounge would be most reassuring to all guests.

Kennel Holt is also just an hour away from London by train (Charing Cross Station).

If you'd like to have the pleasure of staying at a country house hotel and don't want to drive down into the country, you can be collected at Staplehurst Station and enjoy a few days in the Kent countryside.

KENNEL HOLT HOTEL, Cranbrook, Kent, England TN17 2PT. Tel: (0580) Cranbrook 712032. A 7-bedroom country house hotel (all private baths) 50 mi. from London. Rates include dinner, bed and breakfast, and early morning tea. Central location for touring Kent. No credit cards. Mr. and Mrs. Patrick Cliff, Resident-Owners.

Directions: Cranbrook is 1 mi. southeast of the A262-A229 cross-roads, which is 10 mi. south of Maidstone. The hotel is on the A262 between Cranbrook and Goudhurst.

THE ROYAL HOTEL
Deal, Kent

Deal is a modest-sized town on England's southeast coast, barely sixty minutes by ferry from the European continent. I arrived on a very sunny morning in late April and was immediately delighted by one of the main streets, which has the English

Channel on one side and the wonderful old business buildings of various sizes and shapes on the other. Compared to Brighton, Rye, and Dover, Deal is smaller, more conservative and quiet.

The Royal belongs in Deal. It's an unobtrusive structure whose front entrance is on the long street next to the water, and because it is the only building on the water side, the back of the hotel looks directly out over the Channel.

Visited by the great and near-great for over three hundred years, the most notable guests may have been Lord Nelson and Lady Hamilton. There are two adjoining sea-view rooms with their names on the doors. Another of the impressive rooms facing France is called the Wellington, named after the famous duke who was the victor over Napoleon at the Battle of Waterloo. There are several Wellington prints on the walls of the dining rooms and parlors in the hotel.

Besides these large and impressive rooms, there are smaller accommodations that are clean and quite comfortable, about half of which have their own baths. (When traveling in Britain, it is well to bring a bathrobe for journeys to "hall" bathrooms.)

The newly appointed manager of The Royal was Mr. Hollis, who had recently joined the hotel after twenty-five years in the hotel business in Kenya, Africa. He had grown up in Deal, and was very much enjoying being back in his home town.

I asked him what it was that the English tourist found most attractive in Deal and in typically British fashion, he replied, "Peace and quiet. The Briton, of course, prizes this above all else. Guests enjoy the walks along the sea wall, visits to Walmer Castle, which now houses the Wellington Museum and has superb gardens, and the other castle in Deal which was built during the reign of Henry VIII. It's just a short drive to Dover, Canterbury, Sandwich, and the North Downs. There is fishing from the pier and also boat fishing.

"We have a very fine golf course in Deal. Some of the preliminary rounds for the British Open are being played on our links. Many of our guests come here for a golfing holiday."

The Royal is like visiting the home of a favorite aunt, because there are many delightful surprises. It is really very comfortable; natural. The British and French have known about it for years. I think it would be particularly enjoyable in June, September, and October.

THE ROYAL HOTEL, Beach Street, Deal, Kent, England. Tel: (03045) 5555; Telex 957141. A 30-room seaside hotel (15 private baths/ showers), 8 mi. from Dover. Open every day. Breakfast, lunch, dinner served to non-residents. The Royal is located on the beach overlooking the English Channel. Many golf courses nearby. Limited facilities for children. P. Hollis, Manager.

Directions: There are several roads from London to the Kentish coast. Consult the map for one of your choice.

THE PRIORY COUNTRY HOUSE HOTEL
Rushlake Green, Heathfield, East Sussex

One sensation I feel at least half a dozen times while traveling in the U.K. is the "awe of antiquity." I have experienced it in ancient castles, hoary forests, hidden country churches, staunch bridges, and weathered towers on high hills. Now, in the full moonlit East Sussex night, I was experiencing it at The Priory at Rushlake Green.

Peter Dunn, whose family was deeded the property at the time of Henry VIII, and who today terms himself "an English farmer," pointed out that it was originally developed by the Dominicans in 1412. "They came up from Hastings to start a new splinter group," was the way he termed it.

The squarish main building of weathered local stone, brick, and half-timbers exudes a somewhat monastic feeling of austerity which is belied by the comfortable furnishings and decor of the interior. The wonderful kind of eery feeling of antiquity was considerably heightened by the remnants of the walls of ancient buildings, now disappeared.

As I walked through the gardens and adjacent lawns, I peeked through the window into the sitting room where a fire was creating

a warm, generous atmosphere, encouraging guests to delve deeper into conversation. I turned onto the country road determined to enjoy a constitutional, following a sumptuous English dinner consisting of a rack of lamb and vegetables from the garden, served in covered individual saucepans. The waitress's skirts matched the pattern of the tablecloth, and there were fresh flowers on the candlelit tables. An interesting curiosity was a table for two set within the confines of a presently unused fireplace, part of which had also been an old bread-baking oven.

Now, the quiet of my lavender-scented evening was broken by the whirr of a duck who flew up from a nearby miniature pond, beating the air and setting up such a quacking that it quite startled me. I continued on, realizing that under this gorgeous full moon and the stars in the south-of-England sky this was about as quiet a moment as I have ever experienced. I could literally hear nothing.

The rather thrilling chill of the night air returned me to the parlor and the fireplace where I joined an American couple and their English friends who were carrying on a rather elegant conversation about English history. I found that they were staying at The Priory for four of five days and enjoying day trips into Sussex and Kent. They spoke very glowingly of walking on the nearby South Downs, a stretch of high hills along the southern coast.

One of these guests summed up The Priory rather neatly, "They even have a plate of fruit and a tin of biscuits at bedside," he said, "and a hot water bottle with a quilted cover to help warm up the sheets. I think this is one of the most *civilized* places I have ever visited."

THE PRIORY COUNTRY HOUSE HOTEL, Rushlake Green, Heathfield, East Sussex, England TN219RG. Tel: (0435) 830553. A 12-room secluded country house 5 mi. from Heathfield and 55 mi. from London. Open January 18 to December 24. Lunch, tea, and dinner served to non-residents. Not suitable for children under 9. Conveniently located for several scenic, cultural and recreational attractions including South Downs, English Channel, Chartwell, Leeds Castle. Fishing, croquet, rough and game shooting, clay pigeon shooting, walking on grounds. Tennis, golf, horseback riding, nearby. Mrs. Jane M. Dunn, Resident Owner.

Directions: From London take A21 to last exit for Tunbridge Wells. From Tunbridge Wells, take A267 to Heathfield, then B2096 (Battle Road) through Punnets Town about ¾ mi.; turn right at Three Cups Pub. Next fork left marked Dallington. Priory Hotel sign at next crossroads. Continue down drive ¾ mi. long.

THE SPREAD EAGLE HOTEL
Midhurst, Sussex

The Spread Eagle dates back to 1430, and the "newer section" was built in 1650. It is knee-deep in tradition and "olde worlde" atmosphere.

In early Elizabethan days, it was the center of much feasting and merriment for the Queen and her lords after hunting in the surrounding forests. I found it intriguing to imagine that some of the old cobblestones in the courtyard were trod upon by Cromwell's men. As recently as 1906, the king's horses were stabled here.

There are some very interesting aspects to the rambling, half-timbered building including the fact that the third-floor lodging rooms, accessible by tiny staircases, are up underneath the eaves, and one must have a care lest one knock one's head on the steeply slanted ceiling.

The dining room has a smoke-blackened brick fireplace, and the huge beams and posts are hung with an array of highly burnished copper utensils.

Dinner is by candlelight. The menu and food are adequate. Afterward, guests enjoy the bar lounge with still another fireplace and deep, comfortable furniture, leaded windows, and much old cabinetry. I was attracted by the caricatures signed "Sneak." They punctured the ego of important figures in British life during the last quarter of the nineteenth century.

Midhurst is one of the oldest and most attractive towns in England, and even four hundred years ago was of considerable importance. The Tudor and Georgian buildings are separated by narrow streets and lanes, affording opportunities for a pleasant stroll.

THE SPREAD EAGLE HOTEL, Midhurst, Sussex, England GU29 9NH. Tel. (073 081) Midhurst 2211. A 27-room village hotel (most rooms have baths and/or showers). Breakfast, lunch, tea, and dinner served every day in the year. The South Down hills, the city of Chichester with its famous theater, the Roman Palace, and many museums nearby, as well as many distinguished great houses, castles, and parks. Sandy and Anne Goodman, Proprietors.

Directions: From London take the A3 to Guildford and then A286 south to Midhurst.

For room rates and times for last dinner orders see Addendum-Index.

WHITE HORSE INN
Chilgrove, Sussex

I happened to stumble willy-nilly into the White Horse Inn while making a wandering backroad trip between Midhurst and Chichester. The whitewashed building with its red chimney sits back from the highway in the meadows where there were some sheep and new lambs placidly grazing. The front entrance had many tubs of daffodils and other spring flowers heralding a welcome. I couldn't resist a visit.

I was immediately attracted to the decorations and furnishings inside the pub and dining room. It was most comfortable and inviting. Although it was running very close to the start of a busy Saturday lunchtime, proprietor Barry Phillips explained that he was in the rather lengthy process of buying the place from the brewery proprietors (a great many pubs in England are actually brewery-owned), and it would soon be what he termed a "free house."

The White Horse is a traditional English country pub. If it had rooms I would typify it as an inn or a residential pub. It can boast of a marvelous countryside setting, an interior that would be quite at home in an English movie, and a very extensive menu of some considerable reputation in the south of Sussex.

"We serve lobster, grouse, pheasant, partridge, woodcock, mallard, teal, widgeon, hare, salmon, venison, calves liver, and Aylesbury duck," asserted Barry. "Our menu is à la carte. We offer lunch and dinner. And many people who are staying in Midhurst, Chichester, and other surrounding towns eventually find their way to us. They are surprised that in our rather small place we have such a wide variety of choices."

The most recent news from Barry Phillips is that not only is he the sole owner of the White Horse Inn, for which he has our congratulations, but he also had the honor of a visit for luncheon from H.R.H. Prince Philip. I'm delighted to know that things are humming at the White Horse Inn.

WHITE HORSE INN, Chilgrove, (Nr. Chichester) Sussex, England PO 189HX. Tel: (024-359) East Marden 219. A traditional country pub (no lodgings) 7 mi. north of Chichester near Goodwood House, Chichester Festival Theater and the South Downs. Lunch and dinner served Tuesday through Saturday except bank holidays. B.C. Phillips, Owner.

Directions: Proceed north from Chichester on A286 toward Midhurst. Through Lavant take B2141 signposted "Petersfield" and proceed 5 mi. to village of Chilgrove.

The Wooded Lanes of Sussex

Surrey and West Sussex have some extremely attractive back-roads that wander through forests, border meadows, and follow the course of the many brooks and rivers. It is easy to get lost on them, but not "perilously so." It is beautiful in springtime, especially during the daffodil season, and I found myself stopping to look at gnarled old trees with ivy growing up the trunks, and lingering by the meadows with centuries-old stone and thicket walls. In the spring the rock gardens appear with all the lovely spring colors.

In this part of England what are called speed bumps in North America are known as "sleeping Bobbies."

GRAVETYE MANOR
(Near East Grinstead) West Sussex

The memories of my first visit to Gravetye (as it is known) were immediately revived as I followed the winding drive through the park-like grounds and saw the weathered stone and oaken door of the front entrance. The Sussex countryside was bathed in the light of an autumn sun, heightening the muted tints of beige, brown, and russet. The flowers of autumn in the famed Gravetye gardens, encouraged by the warmth, turned their faces toward the sun.

Gravetye is an Elizabethan manor house built about ten years after the defeat of the Spanish Armada. According to the records, Roger Infield built it for his bride, Katherine Compton. Their initials, "R" and "K," are carved over the entrance to the formal gardens. To add to the romantic note, the likenesses of Roger and Katherine are carved in oak over the fireplace in the master bedroom.

The manor's most notable owner, William Robinson, had a worldwide reputation as one of the greatest gardeners of all time. He bought Gravetye and the one thousand acres on which it stands in 1884, and lived there until he died, well into his nineties, in 1935. It was here that he realized many of his ideas for the creation of the English natural "garden style" which is now admired and copied all over the world. His book, *The English Flower Garden,* is still in demand. His simple good taste is much in evidence both inside and outside of the manor house. He paneled the interior with wood from the estate and enriched the rooms with chimney pieces and fireplace furnishings kept entirely in the Elizabethan mode.

Today, the proprietors are Susan and Peter Herbert who have devoted time, effort, and considerable investment in carrying on

Mr. Robinson's ideals, while at the same time preserving much of the tradition and antiquity. A new baby daughter will be of help in the future.

The menu for lunch and dinner is basically French, but a note points out that if the guest's preference is for *simply* cooked food, this can be accommodated. Even now while writing this paragraph, my mouth begins to water at the memory of a crêpe filled with scampi, sole, shrimps, and scallops and served in a cream and brandy sauce which has been glazed. The "sweet" menu is a Mozart sonata.

There are basically two types of guest rooms. One group is done in the grand manner with canopied beds and walls that are intricately paneled. The master bedroom is a classic—the furniture is "manorial" to say the least.

The other type of room is a bit smaller and has a more modest demeanor. However, they, too, enjoy many of the same views of the gardens and countryside.

"Garden" is a key word at Gravetye. In a country where gardening is a national sport, the gardens here which cover many acres are some of the most impressive I've ever seen. For example, the kitchen garden has over a full acre of leeks, parsley, endive, chicory, spinach, dill, thyme, mint, hyssop, broccoli, french beans, radishes, lettuce, and several different types of berries and fruits. It is all tended by a gardener named Trevor, whom Peter says is really "a magician." Naturally, these all appear on the table.

Thanks to Roger Infield, William Robinson, and Susan and Peter Herbert, Gravetye Manor has been preserved, and is entering into its most useful and exciting period, because it is available for all of us to enjoy.

GRAVETYE MANOR (Nr. East Grinstead), West Sussex, England RH19 4LJ. Tel: (0342) Sharpthorne 810567. A luxuriously appointed 14-room country manor hotel, 30 mi. from London. Open all year. Lunch, dinner served to non-residents. No credit cards. Suitable for children over 7 years old. Beautiful gardens on grounds as well as trout fishing, croquet, and clock golf. Golf and horseback riding nearby. This area has many famous houses and gardens for touring. Peter Herbert, Managing Director.

Directions: From London, leave A23 at Exit 10 for Crawley, turn east on A264 towards East Greenstead. At roundabout by "Duke's Head," turn right onto B2028 through Turner's Hill. 1 mi. south of village, fork left for West Hoathly; after 150 yds. turn left up Vowels Lane. Hotel on right after 1 mi. (Hotel drive 1 mi. long.)

SOUTH OF ENGLAND
Counties of Hampshire and Dorset

These counties, which are only about two-and-a-half hours' drive southwest of London, include the woods and heaths of the New Forest, the megaliths of Stonehenge, the great cathedrals of Winchester and Salisbury, Thomas Hardy and Jane Austen country, and among other great houses, Broadlands, the treasure-filled residence of the late Lord Louis Mountbatten.

Broadlands is located in Hampshire and contains an impressive collection of art, as well as numerous mementos of Mountbatten's naval and Asian campaigns. The River Test, one of Britain's trout streams, runs through the grounds of Broadlands, which is south of the town of Romsey and near Southampton.

The AA Touring Guide To Britain *outlines three enchanting tours in Dorset and three more in Hampshire.*

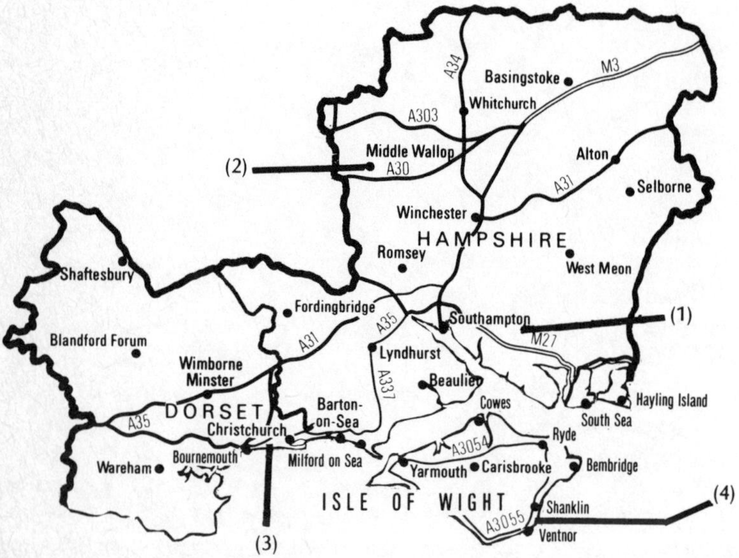

SOUTH OF ENGLAND

THE OLD HOUSE HOTEL AND RESTAURANT
Wickham, Hampshire

"This is a duck's nest coal-burning hearth." Annie Skipwith was showing me the lodging rooms at the Old House in Wickham. We were in a most attractive second-floor bedroom where the stately windows overlooked the other Georgian townhouses on the hollow square in the center of the town.

Everything about this inn was delightful. The young inn-keepers, Richard and Annie, were full of *joie de vivre.* They are a most handsome couple. Richard is a debonair Englishman and Annie is a delightful French girl.

Each of the ten lodging rooms is totally different. The furniture was refinished by Richard. The upstairs hall has some engaging prints originally done by a man named Gould, and curtains have been found whose patterns match the prints. There are several small things that make it seem very much like a private house. For example, there is a little cabinet in one corner of the hallway downstairs which is filled with carved pieces and china.

In the back of the house, which was part of an old barn, the bedrooms have exposed beams, beautiful flowered wallpaper in tones of blue and green, and curtains to match. There was one double bedroom with dozens of books. In fact, there are books in every bedroom on the nightstands.

There are porcelain door knobs on the paneled doorways and all of the floors in this house of many levels are shining clean and well-varnished.

On the first floor, a series of small lounges all show Richard's and Annie's interest in prints. One room has some excellent sailing prints and also a collection of different size keg taps mounted.

The restaurant is part of the old converted barn and has exposed beams with a big window that overlooks the garden in the rear. This is an excellent breakfast room.

The menu is made up of French provincial dishes. For lunch that day I had a dish with green peppers, tomatoes, onions, garlic cooked in spices and herbs and then topped with a whisked egg white which, when put in the oven, turns into a four-inch meringue. It was just right. Other main courses were pot-roasted chicken and escalloped veal and sirloin served with tomatoes and garlic sauce and topped with olives.

In discussing the inn clientele, Richard said that for the most part people stayed for one night, although many businessmen stay here while traveling during the week. "They like our little garden in the rear and our countryside is appealing." Please note that the hotel bedrooms are not available on Saturdays and Sundays.

OLD HOUSE HOTEL, The Square, Wickham, Hampshire, PO175JG England. Tel: (0329) 833049. A 10-room in-town hotel 9 mi. west of Portsmouth. Closed Sat. and Sun., 2 wks. in July and Aug., 2 wks. at Christmas, and 1 wk. at Easter. Lunch and dinner served to non-

residents. Restaurant closed all day Sunday, and also for lunch on Monday and Saturday. Pleasant rose garden on grounds. Sailing and golf nearby. Mr. & Mrs. Richard Skipwith, Proprietors.

Directions: From London take M3 southwest to Exit 5 and follow A32 to Wickham, 45 min. from Motorway exit.

FIFEHEAD MANOR HOTEL AND RESTAURANT
Middle Wallop, Hampshire

I felt a very strong kinship with this section of England, because Middle Wallop is just a few miles from the village of Stockbridge; however, it is not in Berkshire (pronounced "Barkshire" in Britain), but in Hampshire, which is frequently referred to on local signposts as "Hants." Another coincidence is the fact that Salisbury, Connecticut is about the same distance away from Stockbridge, Massachusetts, as is Salisbury, Hampshire, from Stockbridge, England.

I liked the feel of Fifehead Manor almost as soon as I arrived, because it seemed to be a family place. Being a Sunday, there were several families from the local area who had driven over for a Sunday dinner. Some well-dressed children were playing outdoors in the October sunshine, and several others had pulled some games and puzzles from the shelves in the living room and were stretched out on the carpet enjoying themselves.

I soon discovered that proprietress Margaret Leigh Taylor is capable of carrying on an animated conversation not only in English, but also in French, German, and Dutch, and this rather modest manor had a decidedly international air with several visitors from the Continent.

She was able to spare me a few moments from her supervisory duties in the kitchen to point out that during the bizarre history of this old manor house, which dates from the eleventh century, it has been a nunnery and, later, the home of the Earl of Godwin whose wife at that time was Lady Godiva, the famous horsewoman of Coventry.

There have been so many additions to the oldest part of the house it is a sort of architectural "Pictures at an Exhibition." For example, the center section has typically medieval stone mullion windows, and the Victorian newer portion has gingerbread ornamentation. There were two fireplaces in the room where the children were playing, one Jacobean and the other Elizabethan.

Middle Wallop (wonderful name, isn't it?) is just a few miles from one of the most famous trout streams in all the world, the River Test. In fact, one of the specialties on the menu is fresh trout from the Test which is prepared in several different ways. The menu also lists Dover sole, roast lamb, veal, and beef in various forms.

The rather large guest rooms in the main house have been augmented recently by the addition of attractive, modernized bedrooms in an old barn.

Because it is such a relatively short distance from Heathrow Airport, Fifehead Manor would make a most sensible place to stay for the first night or two after arriving in the U.K. It is very quiet and relaxed and only a short distance from Salisbury, Stonehenge, and Winchester.

"Our guests from North America often stay here to recover from their jet-lag and then go west to Devon and Cornwall, or north to the Cotswolds," commented Mrs. Leigh Taylor.

I can think of many enthusiastic fisherman who would love to start a holiday wetting a line in the River Test!

FIFEHEAD MANOR, Middle Wallop, Stockbridge, Hampshire, England S020 8EG. Tel: (0264) Andover 781565. A 12-room rural inn (all with private baths), 10 mi. west of Salisbury, convenient to the famous trout-fishing Test River, and Stonehenge. Open every day except two weeks at Christmas. Breakfast, lunch, tea, and dinner served to non-residents. Restaurant closed Sunday evening. Mrs. M. Leigh Taylor, Resident Owner.

Directions: Fifehead Manor is located on A343 at Middle Wallop. There are several different routes. It is best to locate Middle Wallop and work backwards to where you are (West of Salisbury).

A LAZY SUNDAY AFTERNOON

Stockbridge, England, and Stockbridge, Massachusetts, have one common denominator. They are villages with a long main street, although the Hampshire village's street is much longer than the one in New England. A dissimilarity is the fact that the English Stockbridge has fewer trees.

This is a very important fishing area, and there are two streams that literally run through the town. These were frequented, on a sunny Sunday afternoon, by resident ducks. There were a few guest houses, a number of B & Bs, and one rather large hotel. Several small restaurants served teas and light lunches.

From Stockbridge, I took the country road which runs next to the Test River through the village of Houghton which, I understand, is one of the great fishing centers. I turned left over the river on a humpbacked bridge into another world. It was, to say the least, the most idyllic of all English scenes, worthy of a Constable.

A series of these small bridges spanned the river as it wound its way through the woodland copse. Overhead the leaves were turning yellow and brown against the wonderful blue English sky. A flock of crows added their own particular chorus to the chirping of other small birds.

The water on one side of my bridge was so placid and clear that the vegetation on the bottom looked like cabbages and cauliflowers. I could easily see the trout. However, on the other side of the bridge, the surface changed as the water rushed out into a broad channel where the sun danced and sparkled. The eddies spun around and around before proceeding on their short journey to the sea. A few ducks fished for their Sunday dinner. Along the banks there were blackberries, plump and ready for the picking.

I drove on and came to a small village which had a fascinating triangular village green; a group of people were sitting in the sun at the Crown Inn enjoying a bar lunch. Some of the village lads were leaning up against their cars. A sign announced that it was

"Hampshire Weekend," and there were some small stalls nearby where people returning from church stopped off and purchased various crafts and other country things on sale. A very British girl prevailed upon me to "have a go" at one of them.

I saw a poster announcing that a "country and western dance" would be held with music by the Rustlers. Admission would be one pound and twenty-five pence including supper, but an additional note said "no leather jackets."

CHEWTON GLEN HOTEL
New Milton, Hampshire

It felt good to be back once again at Chewton Glen enjoying a very pleasant evening with proprietor Martin Skan and greeting some of the members of his staff whom I remembered from my first visit about four years ago.

I had driven from Rushlake Green in East Sussex across the South Downs with a brief stop at Wickham to visit Richard and Annie Skipwith at the Old House Hotel. Then, I drove through the New Forest and arrived at Chewton Glen in time to enjoy a dip in the pool before tea.

Chewton Glen is a deluxe country house hotel set in thirty acres of parkland right on the fringe of the New Forest, just a few miles from the South Coast. Their elaborate full-color brochure shows extensive views of the house, the several drawing rooms, the beautiful bedrooms, and the cuisine, and depicts the varied activities that are available to guests, either on the grounds or nearby.

At dinner, Martin described the many changes that had been made at the hotel recently, and outlined his plans for a new indoor swimming pool, a sauna, and a par-three golf course. "We are a true destination resort," he said. "We have everything to make a suitable holiday for a weekend to a month. Besides the tennis courts, putting greens, and swimming pools here on the grounds, we have excellent horse-riding, fishing, and twelve golf courses within a radius of twenty miles, some of which are championship calibre."

Dinner is really an Event at Chewton Glen with a table d'hote and à la carte menu in French (fortunately for me there are English explanations). One of the totally British attributes is the handsome silver trolley which is wheeled deftly from table to table proudly displaying a magnificent standing rib roast of beef. This is cut with great flair to the preference of each guest.

After dinner we wandered out into one of the drawing rooms for coffee and the talk turned to the rather impressive history of Chewton Glen which Martin has wisely included in a very small booklet.

The house has a famous literary link through Captain Frederick Marryat who lived here for periods in the 1840s when he gathered material for his novel, *The Children of The New Forest.* Marryat had a reputation as a sailor and was at St. Helena when Napoleon died, making a drawing of him on his deathbed. He was also active in hunting for smugglers who were operating in this area 150 to 200 years ago. Several aquatints after drawings made by Marryat are displayed in the main hotel lounge.

I was up early enjoying morning coffee on the terrace of my room and listening to the lowing of the cattle in a nearby field. The morning sun was rising behind the fir trees, and the mist over the rolling meadows was drifting away. The rain had stopped and there was good fall nip in the air which boded well for all of the guests at Chewton Glen.

CHEWTON GLEN HOTEL, New Milton, Hampshire, England BH25 6OS. Tel: (04252) Highcliffe 5341. U.S. reservations: 800-223-5581. A 53-room luxury resort-hotel 10 mi. from Bournemouth. Open all year. Breakfast, lunch, and dinner served to non-residents. Tennis, putting, outdoor heated swimming pool, croquet on grounds; golf, riding, and fishing nearby. Within a short distance of the New Forest and South Coast. Martin Skan, Proprietor.

Directions: Chewton Glen is situated on the A337 between New Milton and Highcliffe. From London take the M3 and A33 to

Southampton and turn left on M27. Leave M27 at A337 marked Lyndhurst and then follow A35 to a sign marked New Milton on the left side of the road. IGNORE THIS SIGN. Proceed toward Bournemouth and turn left on the road marked Walkford and Highcliffe (opposite The Cat and Fiddle Public House). From this turning, drive 1.3 mi. through Walkford as far as a forked junction. Ignore all signs to New Milton; turn left on A337 to Lymington. Chewton Glen is ¼ mi. on the left.

THE NEW FOREST

The New Forest stretches over heath and woodland in a 145-mile-square area west of Southampton. It is one of England's most attractive and popular natural areas. There are free-roaming animals of all kinds, including pigs, cattle, and ponies, and motorists are required to drive with great caution.

Being British, naturally, the forest has great walking areas and public footpaths, as well as some narrow gravel roads for automobiles. The flowers, trees and bushes, beautiful in themselves, are inhabited by hundreds of species of birds.

It's been called the "New Forest" ever since William of Normandy chose this part of Hampshire for his royal hunting grounds, as it was convenient to his palace and castle at Winchester. However, the area has prehistoric burial mounds and earthworks showing earlier occupation.

King William II later imposed such outrageous laws on the New Forest that it is said his death during a hunting expedition might have been an assassination. Both King John of Magna Carta fame, and Charles I have a close association with this wooded area.

Many of the ancient laws of the forest still exist, but I don't believe that poachers are beheaded any longer.

LUCCOMBE CHINE HOUSE
Shanklin, Isle of Wight

Ah, the Isle of Wight! I have always heard much about it—the connection with Queen Victoria, its strategic position as an off-shore naval base, and its present popularity for holiday excursions.

The day was marvelous; I had driven across Sussex and Hampshire and at Portsmouth, I found the foot ferry to Ryde. I left my luggage at the ferry entrance and drove about two blocks away to the multi-storied car park.

I had decided to try the ferry that did not take autos (there are others that do). After a very pleasant voyage, along with many dozens of other holiday-seekers, I arrived at Ryde, where a train was waiting on the pier. My journey continued along the famous Sunshine Coast through several little towns, finally ending at Shanklin, where my hostess, Stella Silver, awaited my arrival with a car.

Stella proved to be as enthusiastic as she was informative and I got a running history of the island, as well as interesting information about the flora and fauna as we drove through the village of Shanklin. The road went out into the country with occasional glimpses of the sea.

She turned down into a sheltered and secluded valley (chine) and entered a long private drive with lovely ferns, trees, lawns, and a profusion of hydrangeas. I had arrived.

The house itself has an interesting history and is definitely Victorian in feeling, although there are Tudor half-timbers and casements on the upper stories. The Silvers have done some marvelous things to make it very attractive and homelike rather than grand. It looks like what it is—a comfortable, upper middle-class home.

The bedrooms are sensibly decorated with period pieces, but there is an emphasis on comfort with wool blankets and even clock radios.

The first thing I did after getting settled was to take a walk on the grounds, with a visit to the Watch Tower overlooking the coast. The tower was built in the days when smugglers abounded.

I was tempted to continue on the footpaths that lead in all directions, many with magnificent views of the sea.

All of this vigorous outdoor activity, on top of the ferry trip, made for a very healthy appetite, and after a consultation with Mr. Silver I placed an order for pork cutlets. Everything is cooked to order and the sauce for the cutlets was simply marvelous.

I awakened in the morning to the wonderful sound of one of the fourteen cascades that musically assist a small brook as it twists, tunnels, and tumbles through the chine down to the sea below.

My stay on the Isle of Wight also included a visit to the Godshill Church. This is a country where ancient churches are to be found everywhere, but this one is quite exceptional. If you visit, be sure to ask about the famous legend.

And, oh, yes, I must not forget Osbourne House, where Queen Victoria lived and died, which is open for visitors.

By all means take the time (at least two nights) to visit Luccombe Chine House on the Isle of Wight. There are dozens of things to amuse a visitor, including riding, swimming, tennis, saunas, and so forth, but there's also the wonderful sense of tranquility in just looking out over the sea.

LUCCOMBE CHINE HOUSE, Shanklin, Isle of Wight, England PO37 6RH. Tel: (098 386) Shanklin 2037. A 6-bedroom (private baths) country house hotel located in a quiet corner of the Isle of Wight, overlooking the sea. Breakfast and dinner served daily. Open all year. Conveniently located to enjoy all of the myriad diversions and recreations of the Isle of Wight. Great walking country. Paul and Stella Silver, Hoteliers.

Directions: If you are not planning to stay for more than two nights, don't bring a car to Luccombe Chine House. There are several different ways to get to Shanklin, including the train from Waterloo Station in London to Portsmouth; then the ferry to the Isle of Wight, and then another little train to the end of the line. For full information about car ferries, foot ferries, etc., call Mr. and Mrs. Silver for schedules.

THAMES AND THE CHILTERNS
Counties of Oxfordshire, Buckinghamshire, Bedfordshire, and Berkshire

The Thames Valley and the Chilterns extend from the London city limits to the western borders of Berkshire and include Oxford, the edge of the Cotswolds, and Bedford to the north.

The Thames meanders through towns and villages and eventually through London. It ripples down from its source in the Cotswold Hills, gathering momentum and becoming a full-fledged navigable river. It passes through peaceful countryside, historic towns, lush meadows, lovely old inns, and waterside gardens; negotiates locks, rushing weirs, and leafy backwaters; slices between the wooded hills of Goring Gap; and slides lazily by Windsor taking in memorable views of the town and castle.

The Chiltern Hills, many of which are crowned with ancient beech groves, are located roughly to the northwest of London, and the narrow country roads leading out of High Wycombe, Chalfont, and Wendover, provide a very pleasant alternative route to Oxford.

The Thames and Chilterns are rich in history, architecture, and tradition. There are hundreds of years of family history to explore, and every one of its many great houses has its own unique story—of great men and wicked men, men who won battles, built empires, and gambled away fortunes.

TheAA Touring Guide To Britain *outlines four intriguing tours in this area and two more in the neighboring Cotswolds.*

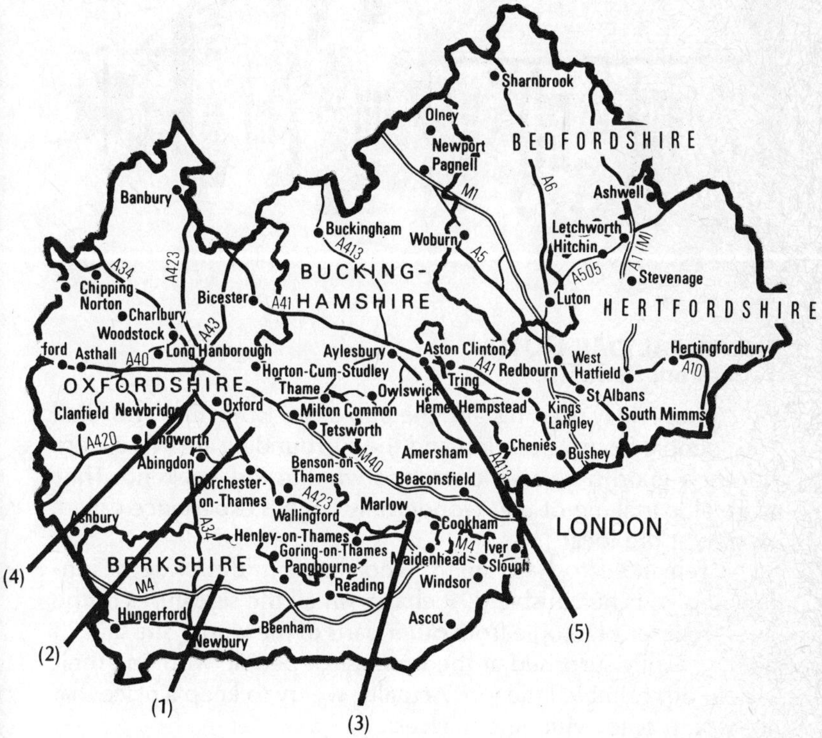

THAMES AND CHILTERNS

(1) ROYAL OAK HOTEL, Deal, Kent, 56
(2) STUDLEY PRIORY, Horton-cum-Studley, Oxford, 57
(3) COMPLEAT ANGLER, Marlow-on-Thames, Buckinghamshire, 60
(4) WESTON MANOR, Weston-on-the-Green, Oxfordshire, 61
(5) THE BELL INN, Clinton, Buckinghamshire, 63

THE ROYAL OAK HOTEL
Yattendon, Berkshire

It was Friday evening, and the pub of the Royal Oak was filled with people from Yattendon and the surrounding area who were having a good time and looking forward to the weekend. They were all partaking of that wonderfully English experience called, "a pint at the local."

I remarked to Kate Smith, who shares in the pride of innkeeping with her husband, Richard, on all the signatures in the guest register of people from other parts of the world. She said, "I am constantly surprised at the number of people who find their way to our humble little inn. Actually, we try to keep a place that we would enjoy visiting ourselves.

"The Royal Oak started life as an inn during the 16th century and, despite the extensions and improvements carried out over the years, one feels that the founding landlord would still readily recognize the inn. There is no doubt that the strong oak beams and fascinating chimneys, together with the unusual brickwork, are unchanged in nearly five hundred years.

"With five bedrooms and five bathrooms, the hotel is small enough for a completely personal service, yet it's big enough to provide the facilities demanded by the discriminating guest. A good English breakfast is served in the restaurant, and a continental breakfast may be served in the guests' rooms."

Only fifty miles west of London, the Royal Oak is in the center of the tiny village of Yattendon. Kate speaks of it as "the prettiest and quietest village in England." It is mentioned in the Doomesday Record, dating to Norman times.

One of its earlier inhabitants, Sir John Norreys, was accused of having an adulterous affair with Anne Boleyn, one of Henry VIII's wives. He was executed at the Tower of London after refusing to compromise the Queen.

The village includes a classic square surrounded by wisteria and vine-covered cottages and a blacksmith's shop, buildings that are virtually unchanged since Oliver Cromwell billeted his troops here before the second battle of Newbury. I understand that the cricket ground is one of the best in the area, and the village team will certainly welcome anyone who would like to play.

Winding lanes lead through the woods and farmlands to the Chilterns, the upper regions of the Thames, historic Oxford, and other beauty spots.

In addition to its multiple functions as a local pub and an internationally famous hotel, the Royal Oak is also a restaurant acclaimed by many of the food writers in Britain. I can certainly attest to the excellent roast duck I enjoyed at my evening meal. The dining room was very busy and Kate moved deftly among the tables, much concerned with her guests' comfort.

Because the village is only forty-five minutes from Heathrow Airport, many overseas guests arrange to spend either their first or last nights in Britain at the Royal Oak. Either way, it would be a most enjoyable experience.

THE ROYAL OAK HOTEL, Yattendon, Newbury, Berkshire, England RG16 OUF. Tel: (0635) 201 325. A 5-room village inn approximately 45 minutes from London Heathrow Airport. Breakfast, lunch and dinner served to non-residents. Open every day. Short distance from Thames and Chilterns recreational, scenic, and cultural attractions. Kate and Richard Smith, Innkeepers.

Directions: Going west on M4 (from London or Heathrow) use Exit 12 and follow signs toward Pangbourne (A340). Take first turn left (200 yds.), signposted Yattendon. Go straight on to cross-roads at Bradfield and follow signposts to Yattendon, 4 mi. [Don't miss Exit 12, because the next exit is miles to the west. I know.].

STUDLEY PRIORY HOTEL
Horton-cum-Studley, Oxfordshire

"Well, I trust you had a refreshing sleep!" A smiling Jeremy Parke greeted me in the dining room of the Studley Priory Hotel where the sun was streaming in through the stone mullioned windows. All around me the overnight guests were eating their breakfasts with what was obvious enthusiasm.

"I did, indeed," I responded. "However, I had a dream in the middle of the night that someone was galloping along the London Road, and that people were lighting bonfires and celebrating some portentous event!"

Jeremy smiled and said, "Oh, I think I can explain that. You fell asleep remembering our conversation about Studley Priory, and I told you that the main part of the house was finished just one year before the defeat of the Spanish Armada. I'm sure it stirred your imagination."

Dinner the previous evening had been a gastronomic adventure; Jeremy explained that his *chef de cuisine* has introduced a radical new style of French cuisine. "It is Cuisine Legere. It includes a subtle new combination of tastes and imaginative uses of new ingredients." Starters were a quail consommé flavored with truffle and a velvety scallop soup with a dash of white wine. Main courses included baron of baby rabbit served with a delicate sherry vinegar sauce, calf's sweetbreads braised on a bed of vegetables, and an interesting group of three fillets of beef, pork, and lamb. The dining room is named for John Croke, who built this Elizabethan-style house and whose family owned it for over 300 years.

In 1966, Studley Priory was chosen as the home of Sir Thomas More for the film, *A Man For All Seasons.* The hotel was used for exterior shots of the house and grounds.

A short walk through the grounds after breakfast gave me an interesting perspective on the lovely, mellowed Cotswold building which stands in its own parkland with many magnolia, redwood, and oak trees. It was late April and as usual the daffodils were in glorious profusion. They would be replaced throughout the summer by other colorful flowers. Nuthatches and goldfinches darted back and forth, busy at their springtime tasks.

There were pleasant views in all directions including Blenheim Palace, the Cotswolds, and the Chiltern Hills. The grounds, while neat and tidy, had a good, natural feeling and didn't seem overgroomed.

Walking out to the driveway to wish me a pleasant journey, Jeremy smiled and said, "You'd be surprised how many other guests have had that same dream!"

STUDLEY PRIORY HOTEL, Horton-cum-Studley, Oxford, England 0X9 1AZ. Tel: Stanton St. John 203 and 254. A 19-room country house hotel in a handsome Elizabethan house 7 mi. from Oxford. Breakfast, lunch, tea, and dinner served every day of the year. Just a

few miles from the Thames River, the Chiltern Hills, and the Cotswolds. All of the cultural attractions of Oxford are within a very short distance. Tennis and clay pigeon shooting on grounds. Squash, riding, and golf available nearby. Jeremy Parke, General Manager.

Directions: Take the London-High Wycombe Road through Headington to A40 roundabout. Take the second left off the roundabout, signposted "Horton-cum-Studley 4 mi." Follow signs to Horton-cum-Studley. Hotel is situated at the top of the hill in the village. Turn right at an entrance to a drive.

THE GREY SPIRES OF OXFORD

Long before I had walked along the High or stood at the Carfax, the main crossroad of Oxford, or had seen for myself the Magdalen College deer park, or admired Wren's Sheldonian Theater, or browsed in Blackwell's Bookstore, I had dreamed of being in Oxford.

I expected to find a quiet town basking in the afternoon sun with groups of undergraduates casually strolling to appointments with their tutors, or trotting toward the cricket field, or dreaming on the river bank.

Instead, I found a vibrant, active city where town and gown alike enjoy the fruits of learning and pleasure. The quadrangles of the thirty-four colleges, each providing a superb example of almost every architectural period, are woven into the fabric of the commercial and residential life of the town.

Oxford has left its mark on some of the world's intellectual and literary giants. A list of scholars and graduates is a veritable "Who's Who" of English letters. Balliol College claims John Wycliffe, Adam Smith, Robert Southey, Matthew Arnold and Algernon Swinburne. Thomas Moore, Robert Burton, John Ruskin, and W.H. Auden were members of Christchurch.

Magdalen Hall looked down upon a youthful John Keats.

Perhaps of more contemporary interest is the fact that J.R.R. Tolkien was a Fellow and a Professor of English Language and Literature at Merton from 1945 to 1959.

Cardinal Wolsey, Roger Bacon, Geoffrey Chaucer, Shakespeare, Alexander Pope, Jane Austen, Wordsworth (a Cambridge man who wrote two sonnets about Oxford), Thomas Hardy, Henry James, and Dylan Thomas visited Oxford and came under its sway.

For an interesting satirical contrast between Oxford and Cambridge, first read Sir Max Beerbohm's novel, Zuleika Dobson, *and then read* Zuleika Goes to Cambridge. *The latter is attributed to "S. Roberts" which may be a Beerbohm pseudonym.*

COMPLEAT ANGLER HOTEL
Marlow-on-Thames, Buckinghamshire

The Thames River (which is a story in itself), in its eastward journey across England through London to the English Channel, presents one of its most attractive aspects as it skirts the Chiltern Hills in a series of delightful loops between Abingdon and Windsor. The town of Marlow stands on such a loop and the Compleat Angler is on the south bank of the river facing the town.

Three hundred and fifty years ago, when Izaak Walton wrote his immortal work on fishing, he was a guest at the inn. Today, I would term it an elegant luxury hotel. The forty-two bedrooms all have private baths, and the French à la carte menu is quite extensive.

The drawing rooms and dining rooms overlook the river, which at this point is made even more dramatic by the presence of some falls. Guests may enjoy a walk on the nigh-perfect turf of the extensive gardens which border the river.

My guide through the hotel was a young assistant manager wearing striped pants and a cutaway coat. He was the very height of courtesy and good humor. Over a cup of tea in one of the lounges, he explained that this part of the Thames was particularly popular for sculling and that many of the boating clubs had brisk workouts on the river. As if on cue while we were chatting, several such shells reversed directions in the river, almost within touching distance.

The Compleat Angler is one of the most publicized and hence, popular hotels in Britain. Its location near Windsor Castle and Runnymede, and its proximity to London, make it a very popular place for lunch or dinner. It is only a short distance from Heathrow Airport, and thus it could be a place to spend the first or last night of a visit to Britain. I think I would prefer the latter.

COMPLEAT ANGLER, Marlow Bridge, Marlow, Bucks, England SL7 1RG. Tel: (06 284) 4444. A 42-room luxury hotel on the banks of the Thames River approximately 30 mi. west of London. Conveniently located for recreational and cultural attractions in the Thames and Chiltern area. A short drive from Heathrow Airport. Open every day. Lunch and dinner served to non-residents. Not particularly suitable for children. Tennis and fishing on grounds. Golf, swimming pools, riding stables nearby.

Directions: From the M4 and Heathrow, take Maidenhead Exit and follow A423 to Marlow.

WESTON MANOR
Weston-on-the-Green, Oxfordshire

Visiting Weston Manor is like having a slice of eight-layer cake decorated with a delicious frosting. The layers of the cake are the periods of its history, commencing with the eleventh century, and including the fourteenth, sixteenth, and nineteenth centuries.

After the Norman invasion, the Manor passed by marriage into the hands of a great friend of William the Conqueror and remained in this family until the early thirteenth century, when it was given as a marriage supplement to another family. Having second thoughts, the first family tried unsuccessfully to regain possession of the Manor, but eventually, it passed to the Abbots of Osney Abbey.

When Henry VIII dissolved the church property, he gave the Manor to a friend of his, and during the reign of Queen Elizabeth, the disputed ownership from earlier years eventually led to a private war for which both participants were heavily fined by the Queen.

In 1631, the Manor passed to supporters of Charles II. During the English Civil War, Rupert of the Rhine came to England in 1642 to support the Cavalier cause against Oliver Cromwell. Rupert's cavalry was defeated, and the prince sought refuge at the Manor on

the very same night that the victorious General Fairfax, commander of Cromwell's army, also stayed in the Manor. It is reported that the General actually slept in the room where Rupert was hidden in a secret closet. Rupert escaped in the morning, disguised as a dairy maid.

Still another layer of the cake is the story of a young nun from a nearby convent who fell in love with one of the monks. Unfortunately, one fateful night, she was discovered in her lover's cell; tried and found guilty of breaking her chastity vow, she was burned at the stake on the Manor grounds. Since that time, the ghost of the young nun, known as Mad Maude, has returned for a number of visits.

Today, the frosting on the cake is the fact that Mr. and Mrs. Dudley Osborn, the present owners of the Manor, are keeping a very happy and accommodating country house hotel where the emphasis is on personal service and good food. I asked Mr. Osborn whether or not the stories of the Manor's past have any chilling effect on the guests. "Not a bit of it," he said jovially, "our guests love those stories and some of them even claim to have seen Mad Maude."

Mention should also be made of the highly sculptured topiary garden at Weston Manor which has been cultivated over the centuries. The famous box hedges have been trimmed and formed into large arches, birds, animals, and other fascinating figures.

WESTON MANOR HOTEL, Weston-on-the-Green, Oxfordshire, England. Tel: (086950) 621; U.S. reservations: 800-528-1234. A 23-

room country house hotel; 14 rooms with private bath or shower, located 9 mi. from Oxford. Breakfast, lunch, and dinner served every day in the year. Blenheim Palace, Oxford University, Stratford-on-Avon, the Cotswolds Hills, and the Thames Valley, all nearby. Squash, swimming pool, croquet, walking, either on the grounds or nearby. Mr. and Mrs. Dudley Osborn, Proprietors.

Directions: From London take the motorway M40 to Oxford. On the northern outskirts of Oxford, take the A43 (Northhampton Road) north to Weston-on-the-Green.

THE BELL INN
Aston Clinton, Buckinghamshire

"Let me tell you the unusual story about that clock." Innkeeper Michael Harris and I were on a leisurely tour of the Bell Inn, and at the moment were standing in the main hallway.

"In 1797, William Pitt, who was responsible for the income tax, imposed a tax of five shillings a year on clocks. It applied equally to pocket watches, increasing to ten shillings a year for a gold watch. As a result, people refused to buy clocks and watches and many disposed of those that they owned. Thousands of craftsmen became unemployed. For the convenience of their patrons, and to attract those who no longer carried a watch or owned a clock, British innkeepers installed large clocks in their inns. The tax was repealed within a year, but the inn clocks remained popular, and many are in their original positions to this day. They are known as Act of Parliament clocks."

We stepped into the bar where there was a cheery coal fire against the light chill of a somewhat rainy April afternoon. Michael Harris continued his narrative: "I grew up here at The Bell, and it was quite natural that I should acquire some of the knowledge and enthusiasm that my parents had for history. My father, Girard, was a solicitor by profession and a gourmet and restaurateur by inclination and adoption. He and my mother, Daphne Harris, who has been responsible for most of the decorations and furnishings of the inn, were great collectors and some of the Hogarth prints and the painting of the Punch Club are part of their many acquisitions. They started the collection of brass bells over the fireplace."

We strolled across the street to the old brewery where there are fourteen additional lodging rooms in the converted stables and malt houses which form an attractive group around the cobbled courtyard. "We tried to preserve the simplicity and charm of the old buildings as far as possible," he said. "Each apartment has been especially designed by my mother, who has chosen all of the curtains and wallpapers individually.

"I think we take a justifiable pride in our food. The head chef, Mr. Jack Dick, is a Bavarian and he has created a menu which has some traditional English dishes. However, fine French cooking predominates. Meals are à la carte except on Saturday evening when we offer a six-course menu at a fixed price."

The Bell was once a part of the estate of the Duke of Buckingham and was known as an inn as far back as 1650. It was a modest country inn when Mr. Harris, senior, took it over. Today it is one of the most prestigious inns in Britain and member of the Relais de Campagne.

THE BELL INN, Aston Clinton, Buckinghamshire, England HP 225 HP. Tel: (0296) 630252. A 21-room luxuriously appointed village inn about 40 mi. from London. Breakfast, lunch, and dinner served every day in the year. Located at the foot of the Chiltern Hills. Conveniently situated for walking and sightseeing. Blenheim Palace, Waddesdon, Woburn and other stately homes nearby. Golf, riding, tennis available. Michael Harris, Managing Director.

Directions: Take M1 out of London and use Exit 8 through Hemel Hempstead and on to A41 through Berkhamsted. Take Tring Bypass toward Aylesbury. The Bell Inn is 4 mi. from Tring.

Guests making reservations at the Bell are provided with a notice that the hotel appreciates the fact that sometimes patrons are unavoidably prevented from taking up their bookings. The notice continues: "If this occurs, we do ask that you advise us as early as possible, as in many cases, it may be possible for us to offer the accommodations to someone else. If, however, we receive less than twenty-four hours' notice of cancellation, we must with regret, impose a cancellation charge of half the rate. In the event of a non-arrival without *prior notice, there is a cancellation charge at full rate. All bookings are accepted on this condition." Unfortunately, many travelers on both sides of the Atlantic are quite careless about their booking obligations, and many are highly offended when they are charged for lodgings which are not used, but not canceled. I believe the Bell at Aston Clinton has stated the case most clearly.*

For room rates and times for last dinner orders see Addendum-Index.

EAST ANGLIA
Counties of Sussex, Suffolk, Norfolk, and Cambridgeshire

East Anglia starts at the Thames estuary and runs north to King's Lynn and the Wash. It bulges into the North Sea to the east, and its coastline is opposite Europe. To the west it borders the Thames, the Chilterns, and the Heart of England.

Essex is the county closest to London. Its great attractions are the seaside towns and villages and the historic town of Colchester.

In the thirteenth century, Flemish weavers settled in Suffolk and established a cloth trade that was to make the county one of the great centers of medieval England. Some of the towns in mid-county like Long Melford and Lavenham still have great churches, houses, and colorful cottages. Suffolk is Constable country and the great English painter saw great beauty in the quiet pastoral scenes near Dedham. Newmarket is a famous racing center.

Norfolk has the famous inland waterways known as the Norfolk Broads. These reed-fringed lagoons are thought to be the remains of Saxon peat diggings which are now flooded and connected by a complex network of six rivers. Norwich is its ancient capital, and there are castles and many great houses in this section. Norfolk is also well-known for its seaside resorts.

Cambridgeshire, besides being the site of the famous univeristy also has the cathedral town of Ely where the King's School was founded by Alfred the Great. Other towns include Kimbolton where Mary, Queen of Scots was imprisoned for a time; Soham, one of the last areas of natural habitat for fenland wildlife; and St. Ives.

Many individuals from East Anglia have left their mark on England, if not the entire world. The great landscape painter John Constable was inspired by the tranquil countryside. Sir Issac Newton was seated in the garden of his manor in nearby Lincolnshire when he formulated the law of gravity as he watched an apple fall from a tree. Oliver Cromwell, the Protector of England, attended the grammar school which is now the Cromwell Museum in Huntingdon.

The AA Touring Guide To Britain *outlines five backroad drives in East Anglia.*

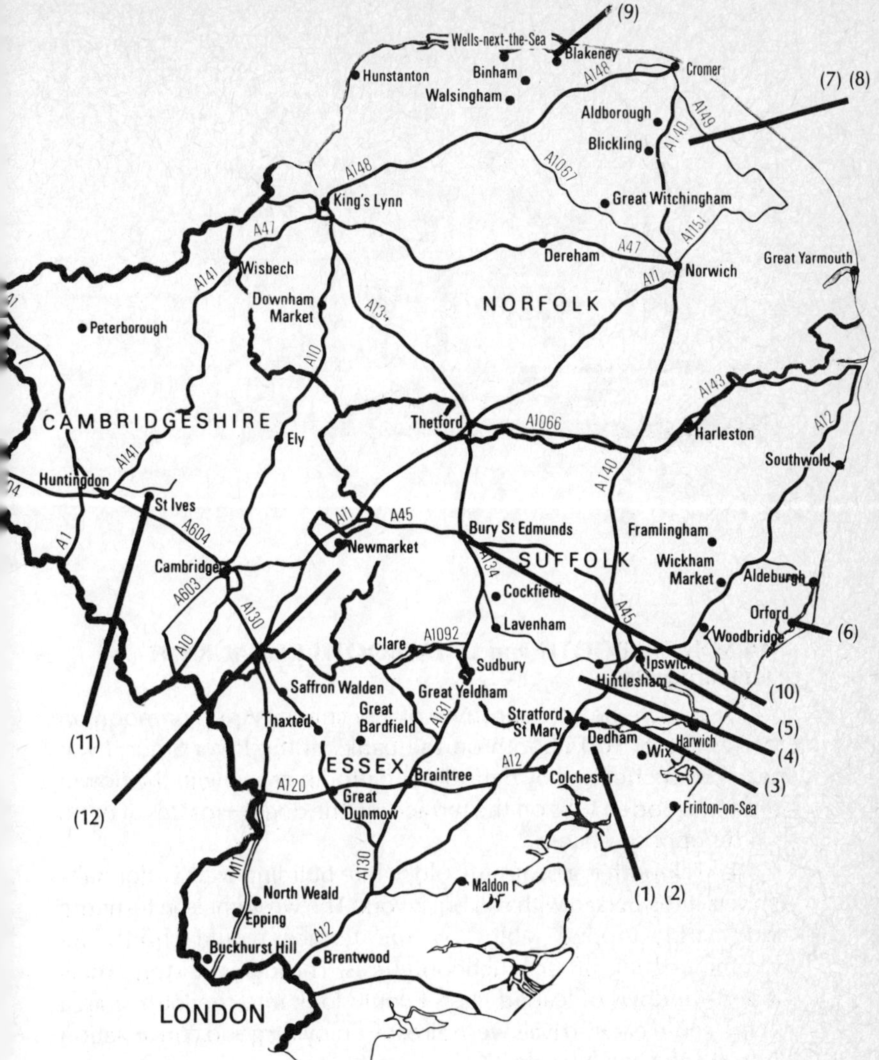
(9)
Wells-next-the-Sea
Blakeney
Cromer
Hunstanton
Binham
Walsingham
(7) (8)
Aldborough
Blickling
A148
A149
A140
A1067
King's Lynn
Great Witchingham
A47
A1151
Wisbech
A141
Dereham
Norwich
Great Yarmouth
A11
Downham Market
Peterborough
A134
NORFOLK
A10
A143
CAMBRIDGESHIRE
Thetford
A1066
Harleston
A12
Ely
Southwold
Huntingdon
St Ives
A140
A45
Bury St Edmunds
Framlingham
A604
Newmarket
SUFFOLK
Wickham Market
Aldeburgh
A1
Cambridge
Cockfield
A603
Orford
Lavenham
Woodbridge
(6)
A130
Clare
A1092
Sudbury
Ipswich
Hintlesham
(10)
Saffron Walden
Great Yeldham
Great Bardfield
Thaxted
A131
Stratford St Mary
Dedham
(5)
(11)
Harwich
Wix
(4)
ESSEX
Braintree
A12
Colchester
(3)
A120
Great Dunmow
Frinton-on-Sea
(12)
M11
A130
Maldon
(1) (2)
North Weald
Epping
A12
Buckhurst Hill
Brentwood
LONDON

EAST ANGLIA

MAISON TALBOOTH and LE TALBOOTH RESTAURANT
Dedham, Essex

Seated in the pale sunshine of a promising April forenoon on the terrace of Le Talbooth on the banks of the River Stour, I was nearly overwhelmed by daffodils—daffodils growing in the flower beds, in wooden tubs on the terrace, on the dock—masses of them on the opposite banks.

Le Talbooth is a beautiful, old, white building with Tudor half-timbers interspersed with red brickwork. The wrought iron furniture and marble-topped tables on the terrace would shortly be accommodating other luncheon guests. Through the stone mullioned windows of leaded glass, I could look into the lounge area where some early arrivals were already enjoying good conversation in front of a small bright fire.

Gerry Milsom joined me for a few moments before lunch. "We still have time to run over to Dedham Village," he said. "There's something over there that I think you might find rather extraordinary."

As we walked across the lawn, he told me that the house was built early in the 16th century. "The name, 'Talbooth,' probably derives from the fact that tolls were collected at the bridge. It may have been used to collect tolls also from the barges that work their way from Harwich."

I remarked on how beautifully the building had been restored.

"By the 1930s," he said, "the house was in a sad state of disrepair. Abandoned lime kilns occupied the site of the River Room, and the oak timber frame of the house, so characteristic of East Anglian domestic architecture, was concealed by the original lime plaster, crumbling and long past making good.

"We arrived on the scene in 1952 with everything in a near-shambles. It took a lot of time and a lot of work, but we finally opened. During the first week, the takings were 27½ pence!"

I might add, parenthetically, that now Le Talbooth is a rousing success and a member of the prestigious Pride of Britain Partnership.

As we sped over the country road towards the village of Dedham, Gerry explained that there are two establishments; one is the restaurant Le Talbooth, and the other is a country house hotel with the appropriate name of Maison Talbooth.

In the village I saw the old grammar school attended by the painter John Constable. Gerry pointed out a brick building with a sun dial on the front. "This building, Sherman Hall," he said, "has direct connections with the General Sherman who gained some notoriety during the American War Between the States."

Maison Talbooth is an elegant country house hotel with fine views of the Constable countryside. As Gerry says, "We work on the assumption that everybody who comes here really has a first-class home, and they don't want to experience anything less than they are accustomed to."

There was no reception desk; instead, we were met in the reception hall by a very attractive hostess who obligingly showed me through the individual rooms and suites, all with sumptuous furnishings. The bedrooms were beautiful, but words fail me on the subject of the bathrooms. Each of the ten was entirely different, and two of them had round sunken bathtubs large enough for two people. Very contemporary.

During the half-mile return trip to the restaurant, Gerry commented that the Vale of Dedham is known throughout the world because of the many Constable paintings. "There is a painting, hanging in the National Gallery of Scotland, of Le Talbooth itself in a view across the vale. We're fortunate enough to have a copy."

I still have fond memories of lunch, which included a delicious slice of pork brought to the table on a silver carving tray. The kitchen is staffed with enthusiastic men and women well-versed in the art of French cuisine, who also turn out such regional specialties as Yarmouth herring with cream cheese, Colchester oysters, and Suffolk stew.

Gerry proved to be a walking fountain of information about the virtues and attractions of East Anglia, and his last word before my departure was, "I hope all of your readers will visit East Anglia. It's the uncrowded, natural England for which so many people are searching."

MAISON TALBOOTH and LE TALBOOTH RESTAURANT, Stratford Rd., Dedham, Colchester, Essex, England CO76HN. Tel: (0206) Colchester 322 367. U.S. reservations: 800-323-3602. A 10-room luxury hotel and restaurant located about 8 mi. from ancient city of Colchester. Lunch and dinner served every day. Closed Dec. 25 to Dec. 30. In the heart of Constable country, it is very convenient to many of the Essex and Suffolk cultural, scenic, and recreational attractions. Tennis, swimming, riding, golf, fishing, available nearby. Member: Pride of Britain. Gerald Milsom, Proprietor.

Directions: Follow A12 from London. Above Colchester, watch for exit at Stratford St. Mary and Dedham. Follow road down hill. Take right turn toward Dedham. Maison Talbooth is ½ mi. on right.

DEDHAM VALE HOTEL
Dedham (near Colchester), Essex

Gerry Milsom had prepared me to expect some changes at the Dedham Vale Hotel, although as I sat in the conservatorylike atmosphere of the Terrace Restaurant, I was certain that even in my most imaginative musings, I never dreamed of anything quite like this.

Actually, the entire redesigning of Dedham Vale came out of Gerry's vivid imagination. He is also the owner of Le Talbooth Restaurant and Maison Talbooth Hotel, nearby. Dedham Vale was for many years the home of his father and mother, who operated this beautiful building as a hotel. "It was here that I got my first taste of the restaurant and accommodations business," he commented.

Basically, the entranceway was exactly as I had remembered it, through a very sedate front doorway into a quiet parlor. However, as Gerry led me through the doorway to the Terrace Restaurant, it opened on an entirely different world.

It was as if I had walked into a magical garden with glass walls and ceilings. There were large bushes and small trees adorned with gaily colored lights and a profusion of brightly hued flowers.

"We had an Edwardian-style glass conservatory in mind," Gerry said. "The glass panels provide an intimate view of the garden outside and we wanted a total *al fresco* feeling."

To add further to the fun and enjoyment, Gerry pointed out

that the poultry and some of the main meat dishes served at the restaurant, such as chicken, duckling and lamb, are barbecued on the largest rotisserie that I have ever seen. Other main courses, such as sirloin steak, fillet of pork, and halibut steak, are cooked on the grill. A heavily laden sweet trolley rounds out the evening meal.

However, the wonderful British features are still in glorious profusion, including the really outstanding garden, which is the habitat of wrens, wagtails, thrushes, and finches. The rustic bench is still snuggled up to the tremendous tree with a girth equal to some I've seen in northern California, and the miniature waterfall creates a counterpoint to the songs of the birds.

Ten of the original twelve bedrooms have now been converted into six handsome suites all with their own bathrooms, television, radio, and telephone service.

"Between Le Talbooth and Dedham Vale Hotel we feel that our guests can now have a choice of two different types of atmosphere," Gerry remarked. "Things are a bit more informal here at Dedham Vale and the barbecued main courses provide an interesting contrast to the French menu at Le Talbooth."

If, by some chance, your British journey begins in East Anglia, may I suggest that you take the train from the Liverpool Street Station in London, ride to Colchester, and pick up your car at that point. AutoEurope cars can be dropped off at many different places in the British Isles.

DEDHAM VALE HOTEL, Dedham (near Colchester), Essex, England CO7 6HW. Tel: (0206) Colchester 322273. A 6-bedroom (all private baths) hotel in the Constable country, just a few miles from Colchester. Open every day. Continental breakfast included with room tariff. Dinner served nightly. Luncheon to houseguests. Conveniently located to enjoy the meandering Stour River, Dedham Village, and other cultural, recreational, and scenic attractions in Suffolk and Essex. Gerald Milsom, Proprietor.

Directions: From London on the A12, continue 6 mi. beyond Colchester and turn off at large sign on left marked, "Stratford St. Mary." After ½ mi., bear right over bridge crossing the A12. The hotel is 100 yds. away at bottom of hill on right.

DEDHAM HALL
Dedham, Essex

"This entire area—the Vale of Dedham—is a walker's and painter's paradise." Bill Slingo and I were taking a stroll about the

grounds at Dedham Hall as he explained some of the many interesting aspects of this splendid guest house.

"Actually," he continued, "the Vale of Dedham is a wide valley through which flows the River Stour, the boundary between the counties of Essex and Suffolk. John Constable discovered its wonderful, paintable qualities and it was made famous by his landscapes. Fortunately, the Ministry of the Environment has declared it an area of outstanding beauty and national importance, so it's changed very little since he painted it."

As we made the turn around Dedham Hall, he indicated a timber-framed, white-plastered house with one side almost completely of glass. "Because so many of our guests are interested in painting, we made this old 14th-century building available for painting courses that are held throughout most of the year. Visiting tutors are experienced in oils, water colors, and pastels. I do a bit of picture framing here if it's desired."

There are ten very comfortable bedrooms at Dedham Hall, and besides the full English breakfast, which includes homemade bread or croissants, Elizabeth Slingo provides a hearty dinner. Most of the eggs and meat come from the Hall grounds, and she's very proud of the home-grown vegetables. Dinner is served at 7:30 p.m., but reservations are necessary no later than 9:30 a.m., because everything is cooked to order.

"Our guests gather in the drawing room every night," Bill commented, "and it is sometimes one of the best times of the day."

Our turn around the grounds brought us back to the front

entrance, and I could see the often-painted tower of Dedham Church rising above the trees. The village of Dedham and the surrounding countryside remain one of the most beautiful and unspoiled areas in England. Small wonder that John Constable was so inspired.

DEDHAM HALL, Dedham, Colchester, Essex, England CO7 6AD. (A Wolsey Lodge.) Tel: (0206) Colchester 323027. A 10-bedroom (4 rooms with private baths) guest house in the heart of Constable country. Rates include breakfast. Dinner served to houseguests and friends with 12-hr. advance notice. Closed Jan. and Feb. Inquire about painting courses held frequently with visiting tutors. Most conveniently located to enjoy Dedham Vale and wonderful walks in the country. Mr. and Mrs. William Slingo, Proprietors.

Directions: Take Dedham exit from A12; follow through village and look for guest house sign on the left.

THE OLD VICARAGE
Higham (near Colchester), Suffolk

We American Anglophiles who watch "Masterpiece Theatre" regularly are certainly familiar with English countryside and with English country houses. That's why, when I stopped off at the Old Vicarage, I felt as if I had been there before. It's really a private house, because there is no sign indicating that there are accommodations available. The Parkers are country people who have "a few guests now and again." I think the great appeal is that it is indeed a private family; however, Meg Parker has a way of taking people up and making them feel as if they are very much part of everything that is going on.

I phoned from about a mile away in the center of the village and had no difficulty following her directions to reach the pink house. There were other personal guests visiting at the time, and for a few minutes we all gathered in the comfortable drawing room and talked travel, discovering that we had all visited several of the same places.

They went off to play tennis on the courts just outside the door, and Meg and I stayed long enough to have a late-morning cup of coffee and to get acquainted.

"That's the River Brett just behind us," she pointed out. "It joins Constable's favorite river, the Stour, just a little bit farther on. You know we are right on the Essex and Suffolk borders."

While we were talking we were joined briefly by a couple of friendly dogs, who rendered their approval of me and then went outside to enjoy the June sunshine. Meanwhile, we could hear the sounds of the tennis game going on, and another guest came in to take a plunge in the swimming pool.

The house itself is, like other East Anglian structures, Elizabethan in design. There are six bedrooms, three of them with private baths and the other three share two bathrooms. A full breakfast is included and Meg mentioned that there are times when she invites her guests to use her kitchen to prepare a light evening meal for themselves.

We continued our chat, strolling around the grounds and the most impressive garden. She pointed out that the sweet little church that adjoins the Vicarage dates back to the 14th century. "It is a typical small wool church," she explained, "so-called because the people who lived up here were all in the wool business. The church is still in use today, and on Sunday the church bells are rung by the village carpenter."

I think you'll have a lot of fun finding the Old Vicarage, but you'll have even more fun as a guest.

THE OLD VICARAGE, Higham (nr. Colchester), Suffolk, England. Tel: (0206-37-248) Higham 248. A 6-bedroom (some shared baths) private home in the Constable country of Suffolk. Full breakfast is included in the room rate. Included in Wolsey Lodges plan. Open all year. Tennis court and swimming pool on grounds. Conveniently located for excursions to the Suffolk coasts, as well as enjoying the footpaths and back roads. Meg Parker, Proprietress.

Directions: Take the Stratford St. Mary exit from the A12 (halfway between Ipswich and Colchester), and follow the road toward Dedham and Langham to Stratford St. Mary. In Stratford St. Mary, there is a turning marked Higham; follow this 1 mi. and look on the right for a pinkish house with a black barn and 3 pink deer beside a sign marked "Church."

BELSTEAD BROOK HOTEL
Belstead Road, Ipswich, Suffolk

I think it's fair to say that, with the exception of the "GIs" who served there during World War II, East Anglia remains relatively undiscovered by the North American traveler. During my visit to the four counties in this section, I made several happy discoveries and among them was the Colchester-Ipswich area which can be enjoyed during a stay at the Belstead Brook Hotel.

Peacocks and Muscovy ducks strutting among the newly-greening willow trees on the bank of the brook immediately caught my eye as I entered the hotel grounds. The many rosebushes already had buds; in a few weeks the garden would come completely to bloom—and just two miles away was the bustling center of Ipswich.

Belstead Brook is a family-owned hotel; the present manager is a young, handsome Englishman named Iain Hatfield. His father, George Hatfield, founded the establishment a number of years ago, and is one of the most respected hoteliers in Britain. There's a pleasant air of comfortable sophistication about the hotel. The lounges, restaurant, and other public rooms have been decorated in harmonious colors and furniture. There were 24 guest rooms at the time of my visit, all with contemporary furnishings, color TVs, radios, and intercom systems.

Several new suites have been built recently which are entirely in keeping with the general atmosphere. Each has its own sitting room and bedroom with a king-sized bed, clock radio, a trouser presser, and there is also a whirlpool bath. These are known as the Garden Suites.

The dining room is particularly attractive with handsome candlesticks and bright red candles on each table. A bevy of very comely young ladies wearing long gowns serve the diners.

I enjoyed a steak and kidney pie accompanied by broccoli and parsnips. I'm particularly fond of buttered parsnips, and the English variety has a flavor that I've never found anywhere else. The dinner menu was à la carte and had an unusual number of selections, including fresh seafood from the nearby North Sea.

Iain Hatfield joined me for coffee and proved to be well versed in the history of both the hotel and this section of East Anglia.

"Ipswich is at the head of the estuary of the River Orwell," he said. "It's on the site of an Anglo-Saxon settlement, and was already a flourishing trading community of seafaring people when King John granted its first charter in 1200. In the Middle Ages, Suffolk was one of the richest counties of England due entirely to its cloth trade.

"The hotel was originally a Saxon manor house. Our front door would have been the main door, and it was an important house because wings were added centuries ago on each end of the center building. During Jacobean times, when James VI of Scotland became James I of England, another wing was added. We have left exposed some the herringbone-patterned brick walls which were obviously on the outside of the building, as well as some Tudor half-timbering, so that this earlier construction can be easily observed."

These half-timbered houses are one of the interesting features of this area, and there are many to be found in the small villages nearby.

"A favorite activity of our guests is to get maps of all of the footpaths nearby." He stopped when he saw I was smiling. "Oh, I see you've already learned how keen we Britons are on walking. We even have a little packet of eight different walks in southeast Suffolk with a map and a description of each."

Of no small importance to the international traveler is the fact that it is only a short drive to Felixstowe and Harwich where there are ferries to Germany, Holland, and Scandinavia.

BELSTEAD BROOK HOTEL, Belstead Rd., Ipswich, Suffolk, England IP2 9HB. Tel: (0473) 684241. A 30-room country house hotel located in the pleasant outskirts of Ipswich. Breakfast, lunch, tea, and dinner served daily year-round. Ipswich is conveniently located for many attractive day trips in East Anglia, including Colchester, Yarmouth, Bury St. Edmonds, Lavenham, Harwich, and Felixstowe. Swimming, sailing, golf, riding, squash, tennis available nearby. Iain Hatfield, Manager

Directions: Take the A12 from London to the first significant roundabout in Ipswich and inquire at the nearest petrol station as to the location of Belstead Road, which is relatively close. Follow Belstead Road approx. 2 mi. through the residential area, keeping a sharp lookout for the hotel sign on right.

KING'S HEAD INN
Orford (near Woodbridge), Suffolk

Once a fortified port on the coast of Suffolk, Orford is a delightful fishing village bordering the North Sea. It has a high church tower that for centuries has served as a landmark for mariners. The town also boasts an equally high castle keep built by Henry II. The tower of this castle has a stunning view of the sea, harbor, and surrounding marshlands.

I saw all of this and more during my visit to Orford on a bank-holiday Saturday. I was originally interested in Orford because a New Hampshire village has the same name.

I dislike using the word "typical" in referring to inns or hotels anywhere, because the one thing that all inns can certainly boast of is a remarkable individuality. However, the Englishman is able to feel at home in a pub wherever it may be located because of certain common denominators. For example, at the King's Head, patrons were picking up plates of food at the bar from hostess Phyl Shaw and her son, Alistair, and taking them out into the wonderful sunshine to sit against the wall of the inn or underneath the trees in a little adjoining park. I knew that just as the patrons of the King's Head were enjoying this holiday scene, it was also being reenacted in all parts of England.

Incidentally, the cold buffet on the day of my visit was fresh crab, roast beef, and salmon. The King's Head also has a rather impressive evening menu that includes lamb, sweetbreads, and various local fish.

I had a brief opportunity to speak to Phyl Shaw, even though it was 2 p.m., at the height of the bar lunch rush. I stayed long enough to take a quick tour of the bedrooms which, as with the Silent Inn in West Yorkshire, were small but serviceable. Five double bedrooms share two bathrooms. There were basins with hot and cold water in each of the rooms.

In the rear of the inn is a craft shop with a very good selection of baskets and several other locally made crafts. Next to that, in what was formerly a stable, is one of the most popular spots in the village—the ice cream shop.

Orford is a great sailing center and much of the village reflects this nautical interest.

KING'S HEAD INN, Orford (nr. Woodbridge), Suffolk, England 1P12 2LW. Tel: (03945) Orford 271. A 5-bedroom (sharing 2 baths) traditional inn located in one of Suffolk's most natural villages. Breakfast, lunch, and dinner every day. Closed January. Closed from 3 p.m. to 5 p.m. every day, but arrangements can be made

to check in in advance. Orford is a sailing center. The entire area has a great deal of historical interest. Conveniently located for all of the recreational, cultural and natural attractions in this part of East Anglia. Phyl Shaw, Innkeeper; Alistair Shaw, Chef.

Directions: Take A12 north from Ipswich. After passing Woodbridge, look for signs to Orford and follow them to the village. Inn is on the left.

For room rates and times for last dinner orders see Addendum-Index.

FELMINGHAM HALL
North Walsham, Norfolk

An Elizabethan manor house! With few additions and permutations, it has been standing on this spot for four hundred years. Its architecture and design is quite different from the Georgian and Victorian which are so predominant in Britain. Built of red brick with plaster trim, the two main sections are separated by a smaller center section. At a distance, it looks like a small, willowy child standing between two sturdy adults.

The entrance is through a formidable front door into a large reception area and living room with a tremendous sunken fireplace, which would play an important role, I discovered that evening, in the hospitality of Felmingham Hall.

My bedroom was reached by well-worn stone steps leading to the second floor, and through its deep windows, it looked out in two directions over the fields and parkland. I could see the vegetable gardens on one side and many grazing sheep on the other. The date carved in the stone mantelpiece said 1569.

The Elizabethens apparently had large rooms, but they didn't have the central heating or the generous bathtubs or conveniences provided for today's guests. However, the remnants of their lives were around me, including many old trees and ancient brick walls adding to the atmosphere of this beautiful house.

After a few moments of rest and a quiet walk, during which I raised several pheasants and woodcocks in the fields, we were all summoned to an attractive dining room to enjoy the evening meal. Along with several other guests, I was served by a very pleasant young woman with whom I had a lively conversation about the nearby Norfolk Broads. Following a choice of starters, I enjoyed some Norfolk turkey, fresh vegetables, and a trifle for dessert.

After dinner we all gathered in the front reception area where the log fire had been stirred up to new heights, and we settled down around it. The evening began as we introduced ourselves, and the conversation led to the differences between the American and the Briton on holiday.

"Well, the way I see it," said one man, "the Briton wants to go some place to do nothing and the American wants to go some place to do as much as possible." We all had a good laugh at that one; in fact, I've used it several times since.

Although Felmingham Hall was an Elizabethan country house originally owned by a wealthy family, today's owners, Mr. and Mrs. John Burton with their four children, are working very hard at farming and providing bed, breakfast, and dinner for their guests. I did not meet them, as it happened that Mr. Burton's mother and father were "inn-sitting" for the weekend while the Burtons went off on their own holiday. I learned that the senior Burtons had a small guest house in a nearby village, and the next morning I paid it a visit which I shall share in just a moment.

The fire burned down to a wonderful cherry red color and some of us talked well toward the midnight hour.

Before turning in, I took another short walk underneath the starry East Anglia skies and reflected that as glamorous as Felmingham Hall's past may have been, its present certainly bodes well for the future!

FELMINGHAM HALL, North Walsham, Norfolk, England NR28 OLP. Tel: (069 269) Swanton Abbott 228. An 11-room country house hotel (5 with private bath/showers), approx. 8 mi. north of Norwich. Dinner, bed, and breakfast year-round. Dinner served to non-residents. No facilities for amusing small children. Many natural scenic attractions nearby, including the sea and the Norfolk Broads, museums, churches, art galleries, theatres in Norwich and Buxton. Recreation available includes bicycles, heated covered swimming pool, color TV on grounds; golf, tennis, riding, sailing, swimming, fishing, etc., nearby. Mr. and Mrs. John Burton, Proprietors.

Directions: From Norwich, follow A140 to Aylsham. Take B1145 towards North Walsham. Turn right in Felmingham Village, before North Walsham. Go past Felmingham Church, take 2nd right. Felmingham Hall is the 2nd left on this road.

BACTON-ON-SEA VICARAGE
Bacton-on-Sea, Norfolk

"Black sheep, black sheep, have you any wool? Yes sir, yes sir, three bags full!"

I leaned against the fence at the Bacton Vicarage and counted at least fourteen of the woolly animals, the color of charcoal, and four of the most adorable little lambkins imaginable. The sun shone brightly on this April morning in Bacton-on-Sea, a village I had never heard of until about ninety minutes earlier.

It all started at Felmingham Hall where I had spent the previous night. Reverend and Mrs. Burton were "inn-sitting" for their son and daughter-in law, Mr. and Mrs. John Burton, who were off on a holiday. As I was settling my account, Mrs. Burton happened to mention that she and her busband kept a guest house which was just a few miles away, and hoped that on some future trip, I might be able to drop in.

"Future trip!" I said. "This is the time to do it. Tell me all about it and how to get there."

Her directions were unerring, so here I was at this very ancient building, which apparently had been a vicarage for hundreds of years. Both the Vicarage and the church were of the traditional flint construction which has been the signature of East Anglia since Saxon times. The exterior walls were of cobblestones which had been cut in half and imbedded in mortar. The church dated from 1300, and the Tudor rose device on the outside wall of the vicarage would give it a date of at least 1500.

The Reverend Burton, with whom I had had a long conversation the previous evening at Felmingham Hall, greeted me briefly and then left on some urgent parish business. I believe he served five different churches.

I was taken in tow by Gladys and Audrey, two very lively ladies who were in the midst of their morning chores and getting ready to "do-up" the lower hall.

I couldn't have wished for two more entertaining guides; we visited each one of the cozy bedrooms and they described almost every bed, table, and piece of furniture in the place.

They pointed out the two WCs, "one up and one down," and the fact that there was hot and cold water in each room. They invited me to observe the view of the garden and the sheepfold, and explained that Mrs. Burton did all the cooking, including such enticing dishes as Glandford trout, lamb and pork from the farm, Norfolk duckling, Norfolk turkey, and Norfolk dumplings.

"We get fruit from the neighboring farm," said Audrey, "including black currants, strawberries, raspberries, plums, gooseberries, loganberries, and apples. Mrs. Burton makes all of her own bread from locally grown wheat."

Here now, was the Reverend's office where he prepares his sermons; and there, his cello which had lovingly been placed in one corner.

While I was having that ubiquitous cup of tea, they pointed out the donkey, advising that it was traditional for all the guests to pat its head whilst having their pictures taken with it.

They sent me off in high spirits, suggesting that I follow the road along the seashore to reach Blakeney. They had one parting admonition: "Be sure and tell your readers that these are tiptop accommodations!"

"Tiptop accommodations!" I couldn't have said it better myself.

BACTON-ON-SEA VICARAGE, Bacton-on-Sea, Norfolk, England NR12 OJP. Tel: (0692) Walcott 650 375. A 4-room guest house (sharing two baths and WCs) located in a very quiet seaside village about 18 mi. from Norwich. Breakfast and dinner served every day. (See description of recreational, cultural, and scenic attractions available to guests of Felmingham Hall.) Mrs. G.R.W. Burton, Proprietor.

Directions: From Norwich take B1150 to North Walsham and Bacton. On entering Bacton, turn left at Webster and Grimes garage, follow the lane to the church. The Vicarage is next to it.

THE NORFOLK BROADS

It's hard for anyone not to suppress a smile when the term Norfolk Broads is introduced into the conversation. Double entendre *aside, the Norfolk Broads are among the greatest attractions of this section of East Anglia. These reed-fringed lagoons are thought to be the remains of Saxon peat diggings now flooded and connected by a complex network of rivers. Hidden canals link vast acreages of water drained from the local countryside offering ideal waterways by which to explore the broadlands. There are more than thirty large water areas contained in the triangular area between Norwich, Lowestoft and Sea Palling. Along with the canals, lakes, and rivers, they provide some two hundred miles of water for cruising and sailing.*

The essential character of the Broads can only be properly appreciated from a boat and there are boat liveries and tour operators in such centers as Roxham, Horning, and Potter Heigham.

One of the best ways to view the Broads by car is to take the main road between Ormesbey St. Margaret and Rollesby.

From Norwich to Great Yarmouth, the country is as flat as Holland, and like Holland, boasts windmills—five, if not more, can be seen along this stretch. In this part of the world, flat means beautiful.

THE BLAKENEY HOTEL
Blakeney, Norfolk

Elsewhere in this book I have pointed out that East Anglia, which includes the four counties of Sussex, Essex, Norfolk and Cambridgeshire, contains some of the most unusual scenic and natural attractions in Great Britain. I was seated in the residents' lounge in the Blakeney Hotel where its elevated position provides a most rewarding view of the marshlands which stretch out to Blakeney Point in the distance. These marshes are of such unusual beauty and interest that the Blakeney Hotel, in response to frequent requests, has developed a list of guides who are able to conduct ornithological tours, and will make arrangements for such a tour if you are interested.

Blakeney Point is a large sand and shingle bar which encloses the Glaven Estuary and creates a sheltered anchorage which can be approached on foot or reached by ferries which leave from the quay side. It is a protected area, being the property of the National Trust which shares its management with the Norfolk Naturalist Trust. Blakeney and Cley form a paradise for the ornithologist and

naturalist; there are many species of sea and fresh-water birds, and seals may be seen on the sandbanks off the Point. For those who seek more active leisure facilities, sailing and boating are two of the many attractions. Local boatmen are usually quite happy to oblige with regard to sea fishing trips.

I could easily see that the Blakeney Hotel was, indeed, well-situated to provide accommodations, entertainment, and food. Naturally, everything is tuned in to the view of the marshes, not only the residents' lounge where I was doing some reading about the region, but also the dining room and many of the bedrooms. It's a very comfortable seaside hotel, and has the additional advantage of having a large, heated indoor swimming pool with a transparent covering which can be opened in the summer. However, it is completely heated in the winter, and there is also a sauna. To one side of the pool are sliding doors leading to the terrace and a nearby children's play area.

The Blakeney menu reflects the availability of local game and fresh local fish, including crab and lobster in season.

The Blakeney region's history includes connections with Lord Nelson, and the Granary, which today is used as an annex to the hotel, is reputed to have been used in Nelson's day for victualling ships. The area was also the scene of the first landing made by the Norseman in England, and there is quite a bit of archaeological interest in the area, as well.

The Norfolk coastline, the Blakeney Marshes, and the Blakeney Hotel provide a different, off-the-beaten-track holiday experience.

Next time, I am going to bring my binoculars and bird list. However, it is doubtful that I would sight very many of that rare species: *the American tourist.*

THE BLAKENEY HOTEL, Blakeney, Norfolk, England NR25 7NE. Tel: (0263) Cley 740 797. A 53-room seaside hotel 25 mi. from Norwich. Blakeney is in the center of Britain's outstanding coastal and marshland bird sanctuaries. Morning coffee, lunch, tea, and dinner served to non-residents. Open every day. Heated indoor swimming pool, sauna baths, and game rooms in hotel. Shooting, fishing, riding, golf, tennis, bird watching, walking, sea and river fishing nearby. Ralph Murfitt, Chairman

Directions: Follow the A1 to Peterborough, then the A47 to King's Lynn. Then A148 to Holt and follow signposts to Blakeney.

BURY ST. EDMUNDS

Shall I risk saying it at least once more? The traveler to Britain who goes from London to Stratford-on-Avon and on to the Lake Country and then to Edinburgh has really experienced about five percent of this enchanted isle. Witness East Anglia in general and Bury St. Edmunds in particular.

Bury St. Edmunds is the crown of East Anglia. Here in the vast Norman Abbey were buried the remains of King Edmund, martyred in 869 A.D. by heathen Danish invaders.

For centuries the town was a premiere center for pilgrimages and it may come as a surprise to know that at the Abbey high altar, twenty-five barons of England swore on the 20th of November, 1214, that they would enforce the observance by King John of the Magna Charta.

The main attraction of the town today is the Abbey of St. Edmund, whose history is much too complicated for me to even attempt here. Suffice to say that it is one of the great ancient monuments of England and even though its architecture, reflecting over a thousand years of renovations and changes, is confusing, nonetheless it continues to attract travelers from all parts of the world.

THE ANGEL HOTEL
Bury St. Edmunds, Suffolk

The place to stay at Bury St. Edmunds is the Angel Hotel, on the market square directly across from the great Abbey gatehouse. It so delighted Charles Dickens that he resided there twice when giving readings of *David Copperfield.* His room, number 15, is preserved today exactly as it was more than a century ago.

The first thing of note about the Angel Hotel is the really impressive vine-covered facade. It must have taken years for this foliage to completely embrace the front of the hotel.

Behind this facade is a very pleasant, traditional hotel with attractive dining and public rooms, and conventional hotel bedrooms. One or two, I believe, have four-poster beds.

Travelers on their way to or from the engaging wool towns and eastern seacoast of East Anglia would do well to stop at the Angel for some refreshment, a meal, a visit to the great Abbey, and even an overnight stay.

THE ANGEL HOTEL, Bury St. Edmunds, Suffolk, England. Tel: (0284) 3926; Telex: 81630 (Angel G). A 40-bedroom (mostly private baths) in the center of town just a few paces from the famous Norman Abbey. Breakfast, lunch, and dinner served daily. Conveniently located for access to the east coast ports and ferries in less than two hours. Cambridge and the race course at Newmarket is nearby. Rooms have radio, telephone, color television, and central heating.

Directions: Once in Bury St. Edmunds, make inquiries for the Angel Hotel.

SLEPE HALL HOTEL AND RUGELEY'S RESTAURANT
Ramsey Road, St. Ives, Cambridgeshire

"St. Ives has many interesting events in its past, present, and future," commented Peter Scott, as he and his attractive wife Maggie and I paused for a moment to peruse a map which showed the distances from St. Ives to all of the many cultural and recreational attractions in this area. They were taking me on an informal tour of Slepe Hall.

"Of course, the principal attraction is Cambridge and the colleges," said Maggie. "This would occupy a visitor for several days. However, St. Ives, itself, has many intriguing features. King Henry I granted St. Ives the right to hold a fair in 1110, and the town grew up around the fairgrounds and it is still one of the largest fairgrounds in England. Overlooking the marketplace is a statue of Oliver Cromwell who was a farmer nearby. We also have a narrow six-arched bridge over the river Ouse, built in 1415, with a chapel in the center."

They both went on to describe the dozens and dozens of tricky little back roads that go over the famous fenlands. Within the

confines of St. Ives, the visitor may enjoy watching bowling on the village green, cricket, and football. There's also good fishing on most of the rivers, and there are many nearby golf courses.

Peter and Maggie are young, attractive, and energetic. They came to Slepe Hall in 1970, and have been working hard making improvements and establishing a reputation for not only friendly, quiet, comfortable hospitality, but for good food, as well.

Among the menu specialties are Slepe Smokies, fluffy mushroom flan, Cromwellian pork loin, traditional roast joints carved from the trolley, steak and venison pie, fresh Scotch salmon, grouse, pheasant and partridge, and quite a few lobster dishes.If I haven't mentioned this elsewhere, Slepe Hall, as well as most of the other hotels and inns, at various times of the year has special rates for two people in a double room with dinner, bed, and breakfast at an appreciable savings over the regular rates.

There are fifteen bedrooms at Slepe Hall, most of which have private WCs and either bathrooms or showers. The building is centrally heated and each room has a TV, a telephone, and a radio. On the whole, they are of quite a comfortable size, and each bed has a feather-filled comforter.

"I think we're tuned into the idea of the American traveler," said Peter. "Some of them become so engrossed in the attractions of the nearby countryside that they suddenly find the dinner hour is waning. That's why we take last orders as late as 9:45 p.m., and even if they do arrive late, if they phone ahead, we can make certain that there will be something for them here when they arrive."

SLEPE HALL HOTEL AND RUGELEY'S RESTAURANT, Ramsey Rd., St. Ives, Cambridgeshire, England PE17 4RB. Tel: (0480) 63122. A 15-room hotel (9 with private baths) and restaurant, 12 mi. from Cambridge. Open all year except Dec. 24-26. Breakfast, lunch, tea, dinner served to non-residents. Near River Ouse and many waterways for sailing and fishing. Also the historic fens, the Oliver Cromwell museum and birthplace, Fitzwilliam Museum and Art Gallery, and other Cambridge cultural attractions. Tennis, golf, swimming, riding, boating, fishing, walking, available nearby. Peter Scott, Resident Owner

Directions: From London: take A1 north to Huntingdon Exit. Proceed around Huntingdon Ring Rd. and take St. Ives Rd. (A141/A1123). Turn right at traffic lights on reaching St. Ives. Slepe Hall is 300 yd. on left. From Cambridge: take A604 north 10 mi. Take St. Ives turn-off on A1096. Proceed around the Bypass (the 15th-century bridge can be seen clearly over to the left as you cross the new road bridge) and make for Huntingdon until you come to some traffic lights (the only ones) next to a filling station called Hunts Motors. Turn left towards "Town Centre, Recreation Centre"; Slepe Hall is 300 yards on the left. (If lost, take directions or follow signs to "Recreation Centre"; Slepe Hall is near, next to the Fire Station.)

CAMBRIDGE AND THE FENS

Cambridge is a city of colleges and bridges. Clare Bridge, Trinity College Bridge, and the Bridge of Sighs span the river on the Backs, those picturesque banks of the Cam, with their peaceful green lawns running down to the river, shaded by willows, and carpeted with daffodils in the spring.

Cambridge University was founded in the 13th century and now consists of several different colleges, some of which are well-known including Emmanuel, Jesus College, Magdalene College, and Trinity College. Much to my surprise, I discovered that I was not the first writer to visit Cambridge, and that several of my predecessors, including Michael Drayton, wrote about it in 1622; Daniel Defoe had some comment about scandalous assemblies at unseasonable hours; Charles and Mary Lamb visited the town and the University, and Mary wrote about the excessive amount of walking that was necessary. Henry James spoke of the "loveliest confusion of Gothic windows and ancient trees, grassy banks, and mossy baluastrades, of sun-checquered avenues and groves, of lawns and gardens and terraces, of single-arched bridges spanning the little stream."

North of the elegant landscaping of Cambridge's gardens and parks lie the Fens, an expanse of flatland now farmed and yielding cabbages, potatoes, carrots, sugar beets and every other green and root crop. They proliferate in the rich black peat soil. There have been attempts to drain this land as far back as the Roman occupation, but it remained for a rather improbable figure in history, Charles II, to institute a scheme to drain large areas with the aid of Dutch experts. Now the water is confined to innumerable drains and rivers, many of which are higher than the shrunken peat land around them.

Cambridge and the Fens have many historic buildings, museums, Cromwell memorabilia, cathedrals, archaelogical sites, wildlife, nature trails, windmills, and sports. As far as I know, it is also possible to hire a punt, a romantic way to see Cambridge from the river.

SWYNFORD PADDOCKS
Six Mile Bottom, Newmarket, Suffolk

I awakened on a gentle April morning to the sound of the drumming of hooves and the neighing of horses. I sprang from my bed at Swynford Paddocks to be greeted by the truly breathtaking sight of several gorgeous thoroughbred horses galloping freely across the turf, their manes flying and eyes flashing. Just when I thought they were going to crash into the fence, they swerved and continued their gallop, now disappearing out of sight.

Besides being a very sophisticated country house hotel, Swynford Paddocks is also a horse farm where thoroughbreds are bred and raised. It has been a horse farm since 1920, and one of the English Derby winners was bred here a few years ago. I had spent some very pleasant hours the previous afternoon wandering through the stables enjoying the feel of the splendid posts and bars, and that wonderful smell of hay and horses. There were chickens following me around, and I made the acquaintance of a brand-new foal.

Ian Bryant is the proprietor and guiding spirit of this unusual accommodation. Incidentally, he joined several of the *CIBR* North

American innkeepers at a meeting we held in the bluegrass country of Kentucky in November, 1979.

Appreciation of both bloodstock horses and the good things in life has extended itself into the decor and furnishings of Swynford Paddocks, with photographs and paintings, and a collection of horse and racing memorabilia in the main lounge.

All of the bedrooms are unusually large, beautifully furnished, with amenities bordering on the luxurious. For example, my bathtub was the longest and deepest I've ever enjoyed, and the warm bath towels were big enough to wrap around twice—even bigger than the ones supplied at the paradores in Spain.

Early morning tea includes a newspaper and a full English breakfast served in the room, if desired.

The menu included a house specialty with a French name that translated into a freshly baked pastry case in the shape of a fish filled with scallops, prawns, mussels, and white fish, cooked in a white wine and cream sauce. It also included a large pink Norfolk trout poached with herbs.

A close-up view of British racing at Newmarket is afforded interested guests by a small program of racing holidays, during which guests are accompanied to racing stables, studs, the Jockey Club, an equine pool, and to see the early morning workout on the heath. Naturally, during the racing dates, accommodations at Swynford Paddocks are highly prized.

As if all of this were not enough, the house has an intriguing and scandalizing past. In 1807, it became the home of Colonel Leigh and his wife Augusta, who was Lord Byron's half-sister. Leigh apparently spent a great deal of time away from home, either racing or gaming, and Augusta, becoming bored and dissatisfied at being left behind, apparently entered into some kind of relationship with

her half-brother, who was not only a great poet at the top of London society, but also a very handsome man. It may never be known for certain whether Medora, born to Augusta shortly thereafter, was really Byron's daughter, but most historians claim she was, and she always insisted that Byron was her father.

A rather unusual place, Swynford Paddocks.

SWYNFORD PADDOCKS COUNTRY HOUSE HOTEL, Six Mile Bottom, Newmarket, Suffolk, England CB8 OUQ. Tel: (063-870) Six Mile Bottom 234.

[*Since the first printing of this edition of this book, the above inn has had a change in ownership (one of the built-in dangers of guidebook writing). In all but the most exceptional circumstances, it is my policy not to continue to list an accommodation that has changed hands unless I have had the opportunity to meet the owners/managers personally and to ascertain the prevailing conditions and policies.*

Therefore, I am unable to recommend this hotel at this time; however, should you decide to give it a try, I would appreciate any comments you might have about your stay.]

MORRIS DANCING IN THE BERKSHIRES

On the last day before this book was sent to the printer, I was having lunch with some of my friends at the Red Lion Inn in Stockbridge, Massachusetts, when we noticed a group of about twenty young people wearing white trousers, red vests, and yellow hats decorated with flowers making their way across the street to the inn, and we could hear the jingle of the bells that were attached to their arms and legs.

These were the Marlboro (Vermont) Morris Dancers who were here to help celebrate the coming of spring in the Berkshires. The innkeeper at the inn, Betsi Holtzinger, hosted this group for lunch, and following the noon meal, they performed an impromptu series of dances in the pub of the inn, to the edification of the patrons.

Afterwards we all went outside where the dancing and playing began in earnest. The musical accompaniment consisted of a fife, drum, a concertina accordion, and a violin.

Some of the dancers seemed to float through the air almost as though they were suspended by wires, with their feet barely touching the ground performing all kinds of extra little kickshaws.

Oddly enough, I was taken back to a similar afternoon of country pleasures in a small village near the town of Stockbridge, England. It, too, took place next to a village inn and the two scenes could have easily been interchanged because the onlookers looked pretty much the same. The English people in Hampshire were arrayed a little more formally with tweed jackets and ties for the men, and tweed skirts and sweaters for the women. The Americans in Stockbridge were wearing various types of blue jeans.

It was a very gay and happy sight to see these colorfully dressed and happy people in America, dancing just for the sheer joy, the same dances that have been performed in the Cotswolds for hundreds of years.

THE COTSWOLDS AND THE HEART OF ENGLAND
Counties of Gloucestershire, Hereford, Worcester, and Warwickshire.

Sometimes known as the West Midlands, this area extends almost the full length of the Welsh border and spreads eastward to include the counties at the very heart of England.

Here is the land of Shakespeare, the Cotswolds, and the Shropshire Lakeland.

In Gloucestershire, which embraces the largest portion of the Cotswolds, are restful landscapes and gentle hills, clear rivers, shallow trout streams, and houses built of butter-colored limestone. It includes Cheltenham, Cirencester, Stroud, Chipping Campden, and Stow-on-the-Wold.

Herefordshire lies against the Welsh borders and has lush green meadows, apple orchards, and hop fields; manor houses, castles, and an excellent collection of Elizabethan timber-framed buildings. This is excellent walking country.

The peaceful towns of Shropshire were once outposts on the grim frontier with Wales. Now ponies and grouse share the lonely heather-cloaked heights, and walkers carry A.E. Houseman in their kit bags.

Stratford-upon-Avon, in Warwickshire, Shakespeare's birthplace, attracts thousands of visitors every year.

The AA Touring Guide To Britain *lists three tours in the Heart of England.*

COTSWOLDS AND HEART OF ENGLAND

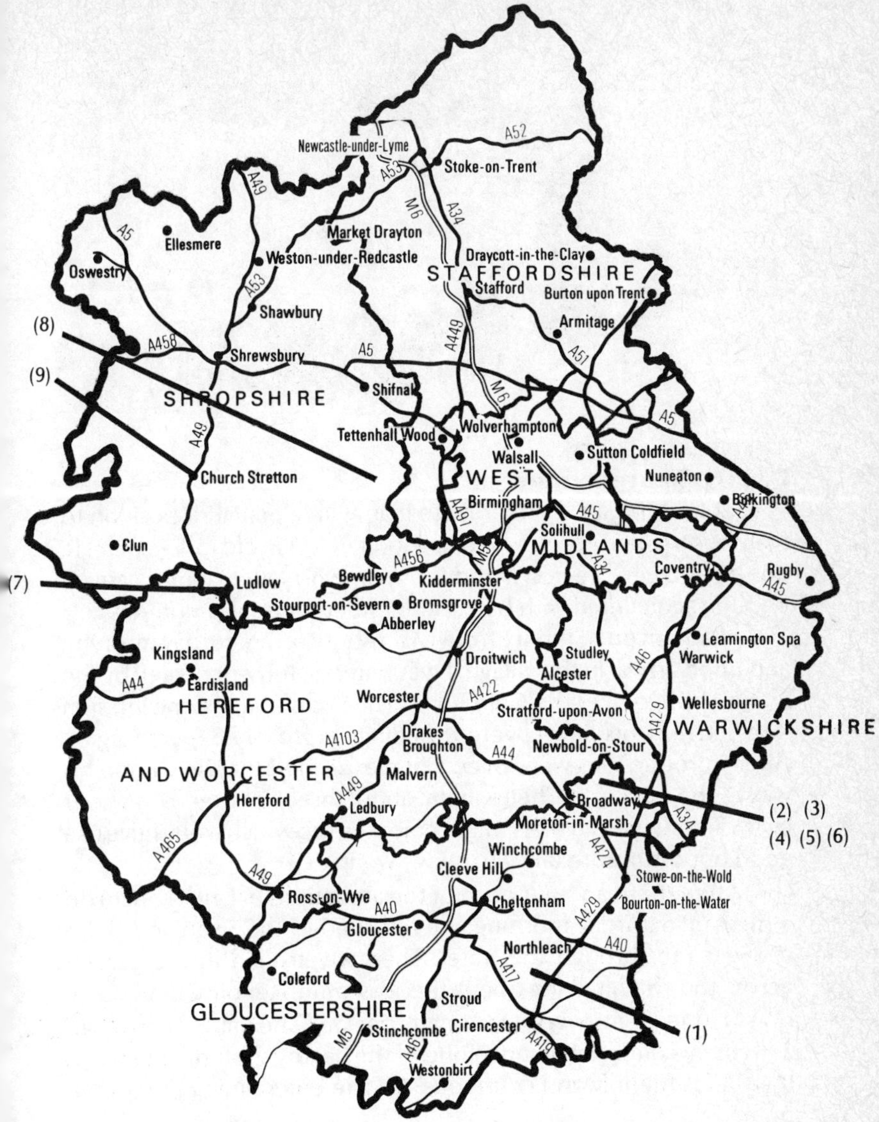

(6) MANOR HOUSE HOTEL, Moreton-in-Marsh, Gloucestershire, 102

(7) THE FEATHERS, Ludlow, Shropshire, 103

(8) OLD VICARAGE HOTEL, Bridgnorth, Shropshire, 104

(9) RECTORY FARM, Church Stretton, Shropshire, 106

THE SWAN HOTEL
Bibury, Gloucestershire

Colin Morgan, a rather large man with a genial disposition to match, is the perfect picture of a debonair Cotswold innkeeper. He possesses a very keen wit and is a man who laughs quite easily. I became acquainted with him under rather unusual circumstances.

I had driven to Bibury from Malmsbury on a Saturday morning and upon arrival in the village, I was immediately enchanted by the arched bridge over the Coln River. The Swan's handsome inn sign directed me to its vine-covered buildings and to innkeeper Morgan. After introductions were over, Colin explained that he was on his way to the market at Cheltenham, about three-quarters of an hour away, and suggested that I might enjoy the trip which would give us a good opportunity to talk. So, off we went.

After about an hour or so of the attractions of Cheltenham on a pleasant Saturday morning, we returned to the Swan and Colin showed me through the hotel. Then we strolled in the garden across the road, talking about the joys of innkeeping in general.

"I think I'm a very fortunate person," he said. "I have an extremely comfortable inn in one of the beauty spots of Britain and the staff is friendly and courteous. It's like entertaining in my own home."

At this point, we were joined by Bob, a lovable English sheep-dog, whose size made him a perfect companion for his master. "In addition to all that," he continued, patting Bob on his woolly head, "here I am situated on the banks of this lovely river in the center of one of Britain's prettiest villages. We are just a few miles of very pleasant driving from Cirencester, Chedworth, Cheltenham, and all of the picturesque villages of the Cotswolds."

Our stroll took us to one end of the gardens to a trout pool which was fed by a spring. We walked up to the very edge. "These are our own trout," he said. "The guests like to look at them because the water is so clear. Later, they appear on our menu either poached or grilled and served with a special cucumber sauce. I do hope that you'll come next time for our Sunday lunch when we always have a large sirloin of beef which I carve at the table. It's the time when many residents from the surrounding area join us."

The public rooms and lodging facilities at the Swan are done in quiet good taste, and I could see that Colin had an appreciation for the prints of Hogarth and Thomas Rowlandson. The Swan is a beautifully mellowed old stone building set against a low hill with swaying trees. Most of the lodging rooms look over the river and gardens to the adjacent wildlife refuge.

Yes, I quite agree with Colin Morgan. He is, indeed, a very fortunate man.

THE SWAN HOTEL, Bibury, Gloucestershire, England. Tel: (028 574) 204. A 24-room Cotswold inn 8 mi. from Cirencester. Breakfast, lunch, tea, and dinner served every day in the year. All of the many scenic and cultural attractions of the Cotswolds are within a short distance. Fishing on the grounds; golf and other sports available nearby. Colin Morgan, Innkeeper.

Directions: From London take the M4 motorway to Exit 15 (Swindon). Follow A419 to Cirencester, then A433 to Bibury.

EXCURSION TO CHELTENHAM

When Colin Morgan, the proprietor of the Swan, suggested that I come along to Cheltenham while he did some marketing, I jumped at the opportunity. With his expert hand at the wheel, we negotiated the narrow Cotswold roads in short order and he soon dropped me off in the center of town, making arrangements to meet me an hour later.

As Colin disappeared around the corner, it occurred to me that I would be in a sorry plight, indeed, if by some chance he forgot to return. I hadn't the foggiest notion of Cheltenham's location, much less of how I would find Bibury where I had left my automobile.

I walked the tree-shaded streets of the town and paid visits to several stores. Here are some random tape-recorded notes:

. . . A green grocer's, sometimes known as the fruit or produce market in North America . . . A small box of fresh strawberries—$1 . . . grapes—$1.75 a pound . . . pineapples—$1 . . . nectarines—

30¢ . . . fresh lettuce—50¢ a head . . . Lavish displays of radishes, rhubarb, cauliflower, and carrots.

At bookstores, shelves equally divided between current and second-hand books . . . Men's clothing shop—blue blazers are $100 . . . traditional flannel trousers—$60 . . . Many boutiques and gift shops, and many people browsing and looking. I keep seeing and nodding to the same people again and again.

At a little sidewalk grill a man cooking sausages and hamburger patties spotted me as an American. "Would you like to have a sample. I'm sure you don't get things like this in America," he said with a wink.

At a rather fancy supermarket that had Spanish bullfighting posters: Heinz baked beans—30¢ a can . . . packages of frozen mince meat—60¢ a package . . . fruit cocktail—60¢ a can . . . Lots and lots of biscuits.

In the center of the town, a large park with many flowers and everyone sitting around on benches enjoying themselves in the sun . . . A striped tent in one corner has snacks which can be eaten at the benches, on the lawn, or underneath the gay umbrellas on the terrace.

. . . Here's a W.H. Smith store selling just about everything but food, including posters of the Fonz side-by-side with Toulouse-Lautrec and Elvis . . . Jigsaw puzzles, models, books, paperbacks, and records . . . the continuous barrage of rock music on the PA system. At first everything appears all jumbled up, but really is very orderly . . . Here are books on travel . . . more than I'd ever dreamed existed . . . Even found a copy of Country Inns and Back Roads, North America *. . . Many books about the Cotswolds.*

The record department has Emmy Lou Harris, Billy Jo Spears, and Art Garfunkle sharing shelf space with Neville Mariner and Leonard Bernstein.

Back at our meeting point . . . a triangular sign lists a great many nearby attractions in the Cotswolds as well as all the National Trust properties in the area . . . Everywhere flowers and large chestnut trees arching overhead, heavy with blooms . . . A wonderfully festive air on this Saturday . . .

Ah, there is Colin Morgan, a welcome sight, indeed. He didn't forget me . . .

THE OLD BAKEHOUSE
Stanway, Cheltenham, Gloucestershire

I was totally and completely lost in the Cotswolds one Sunday afternoon, and at teatime I stopped at the sign for the Old

Bakehouse, because there was another little sign underneath that said: "Teas." Months later, I tried to find Stanway in the *AA Motorist's Atlas of Great Britain.* It took me at least fifteen minutes.

The tea was just what I wanted—an assortment of cakes and a bottomless teacup. I had a nice chat with the proprietess, Mrs. Rita Wynniatt, who showed me through the rest of the house which included two double rooms with a shared bathroom, and a residents' lounge boasting a TV.

The Old Bakehouse is a farmhouse constructed of that wonderful yellowish Cotswold stone. There were quite a few chickens in the dooryard and a tiny, carefully tended kitchen garden. Teatime attracted an assortment of cars including a sporty Fiat and a Jaguar.

Britain is dotted with these "B & Bs." Most of them are very unofficial and are not listed in any guidebooks. For the adventuresome traveler, it's possible to stay in them throughout the U.K., but (and this is a *big but*) the "drop-in" traveler has no way of knowing in advance whether or not the rooms are comfortable, the beds sleepable, and the breakfasts digestable. They can be disappointing.

I tested Mrs. Wynniatt's beds, enjoyed her tea, and I must say that the dining room and lounge seemed very comfortable. I did not eat breakfast, but I would hope for the sake of our readers that it would have been a good one. Not everyone can boil an egg, including me.

I'm sure you'll enjoy the Old Bakehouse and most of the B & Bs in the U.K. In high season, don't wait beyond three o'clock in the afternoon to start looking.

THE OLD BAKEHOUSE, Stanway, Cheltenham, Gloucestershire, England. Tel: (038643) Stanton 204. B&B with two double rooms sharing a bath. Open from March to end of October. Mrs. Rita Wynniatt, Proprietress.

Directions: Stanway is on B4077 which crosses A46, the main road between Cheltenham and Broadway. There's a small village at the crossroads called Toddington.

COLLIN HOUSE HOTEL
Broadway, Worcestershire

"I believe we are here to entertain people and to offer them a whole experience, and I don't like to impose my ideas of food on anyone. We try to offer our guests a selection of food that I hope they will find interesting and enjoyable. After all, everyone has different tastes and, therefore, many things have to be taken into consideration. I take my time seeking out good food, including the duckling, excellent steak, fresh vegetables, and I develop a menu from that point. I think we are quite extraordinary. We've got Chinese, French, and basic English food. We have an incredible dessert menu. But underneath it all, the only thing that I would hope to achieve is meals that are reasonably well balanced—main courses not loaded with cream; and I deliberately keep a fairly large selection of what I call 'light meals'."

Judith Mills of the Collin House was explaining some of her deeply felt convictions about not only cuisine, but also hospitality. We were in a very snug sort of tavern room with a large Inglenook fireplace and, along with other diners, were making our menu selections before going in to dinner.

This was my second visit to Collin House, and I must say that the new proprietors, John and Judith Mills have really done a marvelous job of establishing a lovely country house hotel. It is a 300-year-old Cotswold farmhouse on eight acres, with lots and lots of gardens. All of the bedrooms include bathrooms and are furnished with a lighthearted air. The rooms have been named after plants and flowers.

Although at the time of my visit the beautiful fireplace was flanked with flowers, during many of the other months a large fire blazes here and makes it even more cozy.

One of the engaging things about Collin House is the unusual art collection assembled by John Mills, who has quite a bit of experience in this field. John has prepared a very useful directory of castles, manor houses, bird sancturaries, walking tours, and back road drives for the guests. His knowledge of such things is incredibly wide.

Our orders had been taken, and while we were being shown into the dining room, where John would be joining us, I couldn't help but think that Judith's comments about the food were reflected in the menu, which included grilled trout with a sherry and almond sauce, pan-fried prawns with a Mediterranean sauce, sirloin steak with a horseradish sauce, and a crispy half duckling served with a bacon and walnut stuffing.

"Well, what plans do you have for tomorrow?" asked John, with a twinkle in his eye.

"Well, you are an expert on the Cotswolds and I was going to put myself entirely in your hands."

"That's a pleasure," he said, and immediately produced a wonderful map of the Cotswolds that included all of the famous villages and attractions. "By the way, you might tell your readers that this is a lovely place to visit in the off-season and we are open every day except Christmas and Boxing Day. Now, do you want to go by car or will you try the walking route?"

A walk in the Cotswolds. It's hard to imagine anything more idyllic.

COLLIN HOUSE HOTEL, Broadway, Worcestershire, England WR12 7PB. Tel: (0386) 858354. A 7-bedroom (private baths) farmhouse-cum-inn in the heart of the Cotswolds. Breakfast, lunch, and dinner served except for Christmas and Boxing Day. Open all year. Swimming pool. Conveniently located to enjoy all of the scenic, literary, and recreational attractions of the Cotswolds. Many palaces, castles, and glorious countryside drives and walks nearby. Mr. and Mrs. John Mills, Proprietors.
Directions: One mi. from Broadway on A44 toward Evesham. Turn right at signpost for Willersey. Entrance 300 yds. on right.

LYGON ARMS
Broadway, Worcestershire

Guests at the Lygon Arms are presented with a brochure which offers a brief history of the inn since 1535. I mention this to emphasize just how much history has taken place in this inn over the centuries.

The brochure makes fascinating bedside reading and I am certain that many guests at the inn find it most appropriate. For several centuries it was known as the White Hart Inn and as the brochure notes, "It is of interest that in a four-foot-thick wall in one of the old bedrooms there is a fireplace that appears to be 14th-century work, and one of the mullioned windows in another bedroom has dates from 1586 to 1640 cut in it."

There is a room on the first floor in which Oliver Cromwell is said to have slept before the Battle of Worcester which took place on the 3rd of September, 1651. It has a carved Elizabethan fireplace and an early 17th-century plaster-enriched ceiling and frieze. There were other manor house ceilings in this part of England which were also decorated in the same manner and so it is believed that a group of traveling artisans did the work on their way through.

Another room has the original 17th-century oak paneling and oak spiral staircase. Charles I, who is known to have passed through Broadway at least five times, may have met some of his local supporters at the inn.

Henry Ford came here and wanted to ship the Lygon Arms over to Greenfield Village in Michigan stone by stone. Apparently

something interfered, so he shipped another nearby manor house.

A highlight in the inn's career in recent years took place when the Duke of Edinburgh lunched at the Lygon Arms in March, 1968.

A somewhat modern touch is the bell of the *USS Hunter* which was given to Britain during World War II and renamed the *HMS Broadway.* The new year is rung in with this bell at midnight on January 1st.

Today, the Lygon Arms is a large country hotel with many luxury features. The atmosphere, particularly in the front part of the inn, is definitely "old world." Low ceilings, lots of well-polished wood beams and panels, old fireplaces, and antique wooden chairs and tables are a thrust backward in time.

Every room in this section has an individual color scheme and fine antique furniture. I'm told that this is one of the finest collections of old English furniture in England.

Because the Lygon Arms and Broadway are very popular with American tourists, new wings have been added at the rear with lodging rooms that have modern furniture and decorations.

When I was there in the height of the season in August, the main street of Broadway on which the inn is located was a very busy place. Therefore, the garden area including some very natural fields and orchards to the rear was most welcome. There was also a good tennis court.

LYGON ARMS, Broadway, Worcestershire, England WR12 7DU. Tel: (0386) 852255. A luxurious 67-room hotel in Shakespeare country about 40 mi. from Birmingham. Breakfast, lunch, tea, dinner served to non-residents. Open all year. Royal Shakespeare theater, many stately homes or gardens, golf course, fishing and riding nearby. Adjacent to attractive Cotswold villages and countryside. U.S.A. reservation tel: 212-751-8915. Kirk Ritchie, Managing Director.

Directions: From London take A40 through Oxford to Burford. Follow A424 through Stow-on-the-Wold to Broadway.

THE MANOR FARM
Broadway, Worcestershire

The village of Broadway is unquestionably a highly popular area. With its village green and world-famous High Street, it is one of the most beautiful of British villages and is right in the center of the Cotswolds.

The Manor Farm, a lovely old Cotswold farm building, is on a road parallel with High Street, right across from what would be called in Vermont a "mowing." While I waited at the front door I watched three horses grazing in the field. Soon Tricia Hughes appeared, and she proved to be a very amiable and considerate hostess.

I followed her up a winding staircase, with some pleasant prints on one wall, and we stepped into a most attractive front bedroom with a double bed and a view of the mowing.

"This is the bedroom that includes a bathroom and tub," she remarked. There was also a beautiful, carved, half-tester bed, and I wondered whether Cromwell might have slept in it at an earlier time.

There are four other bedrooms both extremely well furnished with lovely flowered wallpaper and pleasant views.

Although a great many people can be found on High Street in Broadway in all seasons of the year, fortunately, the Manor Farm is well away from that hustle and bustle. One might say that it is "in Broadway" but not "of" it.

THE MANOR FARM, West End, Broadway, Worcestershire, England. Tel: (0386) 858894. A 5-bedroom (mostly shared baths) bed-and-breakfast home located in one of England's most popular Cotswold villages. Breakfast only meal served. Open all year. Conveniently located to enjoy the cultural, historical, and recreational attractions in the Cotswold countryside. Tricia Hughes, Proprietress.

Directions: From London take A40 to Burford; A424 to Moreton-in-Marsh; and A44 to Broadway. Continue through the village and turn left on A46, signposted Cheltenham. Manor Farm is the first left.

MANOR HOUSE HOTEL
Moreton-in-Marsh, Gloucestershire

Moreton-in-Marsh is an ancient Cotswold town situated on the Roman Road (Fosse Way) that runs from Seaton to Lincoln. It's an attractive place with a wide main street lined with shops and houses built for the most part in the pleasant local stone. The Market Hall and Curfew Tower date back to Tudor times.

Near at hand are the delightful Cotswold villages, including the Swells, the Slaughters, Bourton-on-the-Water, and the towns with their great 'Wool Churches,' built and enlarged by merchants over the centuries.

The Manor House Hotel is from three to five hundred years old and new editions have been made with great care to match the colors and textures of the original mellowed stone. As in the Mermaid Inn in Rye, there is also a priest's hiding hole, a secret passage, and a bedroom reputed to be haunted.

The bedrooms in the old buildings are furnished in traditional style, but with modern services.

English people all love gardens and the Manor House garden is really exceptional. The buildings of the inn and the long high walls keep the noise of the outside world from intruding into its tranquillity. There are many varieties of flowers, including roses, and a considerable number of happy song birds. The old church in Moreton-in-Marsh is off one corner of the garden and the ancient font which was used in the church is now the center of a quiet reflecting pool.

On my most recent visit, I was delighted to find that there are many new diversions for enjoying a longer stay at the Manor House

Hotel, including horseback riding from the inn's own stables. There is also a new indoor swimming pool, a spa bath and a sauna.

MANOR HOUSE HOTEL, Moreton-in-Marsh, Gloucestershire, England GL56 0LJ. Tel: (0608) 50501. Telex: 837151. U.S. reservation: 800-223-9868. A 40-room in-town hotel on the main street of a bustling Cotswold village, 27 mi. from Oxford. Open all year. Breakfast, lunch, and dinner served to non-residents. Horseback riding, indoor swimming pool, spa bath and sauna on premises. Excellent walking and splendid backroading nearby. A short distance from Stratford-upon-Avon. Mr. and Mrs. M.H. Fentum, Directors.

Directions: From Oxford take the A34 to Woodstock and then on to Chipping Norton and Moreton-in-Marsh on the A44.

BACKROADING IN THE COTSWOLDS

Some of the best roads are not on the map, and don't even have numbers. These can be the most exciting, with surprises like pheasants in the fields, foxes—a blur of fur streaking across the road in front of the car, and flocks of birds swooping down to settle in the trees.

It's May in the Cotswolds, and on a sunny day the great rolling fields are separated by hedgerows and trees, and the greenness of the fields is blended with the blue-green of the sky. Ah, the skyline . . . sometimes a row of trees, sometimes a solitary tree . . . or the chimneys and roofs of an old Cotswold farmhouse.

Now, a family playing badminton without a net . . . a weekend mason mending his stone wall. . . . Here and there frequent picnickers.

At the crossroads there's always a pub, a B&B, and stopped automobiles with people bending over maps and peering at signposts . . .

THE FEATHERS
Ludlow, Shropshire

I'm sure that many of our readers have seen photographs of the facade of the Feathers Hotel. It was featured for a few months on the television commercials for a popular credit card. In fact, its half-timbered, ornate, Jacobean exterior is one of the best-preserved examples in all of the United Kingdom.

The lobby and reception area have the wonderful patina of antiquity and the public rooms, some named after former reigning monarchs, have carved mantelpieces, stone arches, outstanding panelling, and exceptional decorations.

The hotel has a history dating back to 1603 and, like the town of Ludlow, has had many periods of feast and famine. It is the site of the Ludlow Festival, held during the last part of June through the first ten or eleven days of July with concerts, quartets, jazz bands, popular entertainers, and theatre. I doubt very much if one could get a room at the Feathers at that time without reserving at least a year in advance.

Behind the facade and above the first floor, the Feathers resembles a contemporary American city hotel or motel. The furniture is much the same and the amenities include color TV, glass tops on the dressing tables, and serve-yourself-coffee with non-dairy creamer. I'd describe the bedrooms as conventional, but certainly comfortable.

THE FEATHERS, Ludlow, Shropshire, England SY8 1AA. Tel: (0584) 5261. A 35-bedroom inn (all private bathrooms) near the border between England and Wales. Open all year. Breakfast, lunch, and dinner served. Quite convenient to enjoy excursions into the Shropshire and Wales countryside. Reservations needed considerably in advance for stays during the Ludlow Festival, late June and early July. Mr. and Mrs. Peter Nash, Managers.

Directions: Ludlow is located on A49 between Shrewsbury and Hereford.

THE OLD VICARAGE HOTEL
Worfield Bridgnorth, Shropshire

Christine and Peter Iles and I were enjoying a cup of tea in front of the fireplace in the drawing room of the Old Vicarage Hotel. Although I had visited Shropshire fleetingly on an earlier visit, this was the first time I had been able to talk with anyone acquainted with its many virtues. There was one prime question in my mind and I put it to them. "What is the Ironbridge Gorge Museum?"

Peter stirred another half lump of sugar into his tea and his eyes took on the look of a man fascinated by history.

"Actually, the Severn Gorge was the scene of the remarkable breakthrough which led Britain to become the first industrial nation and workshop of the world," he declared. "Here the iron master Abraham Darby first smelted iron using coke as fuel. This paved the way for the first iron rails, iron bridges, iron boats, iron aqueducts and iron-framed buildings. The museum itself has actually been created around a unique series of industrial monuments and spreads out over six square miles of the Gorge.

"It actually takes more than half a day to really see and understand everything, but as an educational and entertaining experience it compares with almost anything in its class. Most of our guests take the time to visit it."

In the course of my short visit with Peter and Christine I found that the entire area had much to recommend it, with a wealth of museums, castles, historic houses, abbeys, archaeological sites, and associations with such famous people as Charles Darwin and Charles Dickens.

The Old Vicarage provides an excellent base for both the tourist and the businessman visiting the West Midlands. It is a very handsome Victorian house, built around the turn of the century on two acres of well-cultivated grounds. It is on the edge of a conservation village which has changed little since the 13th century.

I was quite taken with the elegant good taste of the bedrooms, which are named after the local Shropshire villages, and the warm hospitality of the house.

We talked extensively about the à la carte menu, which featured pork filets, venison and red wine, trout with celery and walnut stuffing, steak and kidney pie, and scalloped veal with Gruyère cheese.

Peter pointed out to me that the Vicarage had been featured in *One Hundred Great British Weekends* and also in a recent article in *Ideal Home* Magazine. "We do have very excellent value weekend rates," he said.

THE OLD VICARAGE HOTEL, Worfield Bridgnorth, Shropshire, England WV15 5JZ. Tel: (07464) Worfield 498. An 11-bedroom (private baths) country house hotel located in the Shropshire countryside. Breakfast, lunch, and dinner available. Open all year and all holidays. Most conveniently situated to enjoy the cultural, historical, and recreational attractions of the Severn Gorge, the Clee Hills, Shrewsbury, Ludlow, and Hereford. Also convenient to visit nearby Wales. Peter and Christine Iles, Proprietors.

Directions: First locate Bridgnorth, west of Birmingham. Avoid going to Birmingham and Wolverhampton, and take the other roads to Bridgnorth. The hamlet of Worfield is north on A454, which runs between Bridgnorth and Wolverhampton; turn north at the Wheel Pub. Take the first left fork and go to top of hill.

RECTORY FARM
Woolstaston, Shropshire

The road over the Shropshire hills from the Old Rectory Hotel in Worfield to Rectory Farm in Woolstaston was a joy. It was a quiet Saturday afternoon and there was hardly another automobile on the road, most of which winds across the tops of limestone ridges. There are dozens of ways to make this trip and rather than get too involved, I'll just say that even if you get lost, it's a pleasure. Incidentally, I found in many years of traveling in Britain, some of the most common directions include making turns at one or another of the many well-known pubs.

This part of Shropshire is really lovely and is just a few miles from Wales, to the west. I came upon the sign for Woolstaston, pointing west from A49. It is half-concealed by bushes, so have a care. I turned up the narrow passage road and I must say I had some misgivings when I passed a few piles of red gravel along the side of the road, presumably to be used in case of icy conditions. It was a sunken road, centuries old I'm sure, and I had the feeling of traveling in a sort of green tunnel, open at the top, similar to the sunken roads in Dorset and Devon. The afternoon rain had given way to fluffy white clouds and I soon arrived at the village. I quickly found Rectory Farm, a beautiful, half-timbered house with a splendid view of the rolling countryside. It has a very attractive garden, with surrounding fields where Hereford beef cattle and Friesan milking cows graze.

I knocked, stepped inside, and hearing voices in the distance, called out in what I hoped were well-modulated, but carrying, tones. Mrs. Davies soon appeared, and she remembered Mrs. Jane MacDonald, who had recommended Rectory Farm to me originally.

There followed a splendid tour of this long farmhouse with suites and bedrooms overlooking the landscape. The house was built in 1620, and there is a definite slant to some of the floors and stairways; I was pleased to see the exposed timbers and the wonderful, pristine white plaster.

The common room, occupying one end of the house, has a cathedral ceiling with exposed beams, very pleasant furnishings, and a friendly fireplace.

Rectory Farm was just as Jane MacDonald described it: "A fantastic, super, wonderful farmhouse run by a terrific woman named Mrs. Davies. She is young, energetic, lots of fun, and her house is gorgeous. We had our own wing, complete with mahogany antiques, needlepoint, brass and copper everywhere, and tea and biscuits served at 10 p.m."

RECTORY FARM, Woolstaston, Church Stretton, Shropshire, England TF8 7AW. Tel: (069-45) Leebotwood 306. A 4-bedroom (private baths) bed-and-breakfast home on a farm in the lovely Shropshire country. Breakfast the only meal served. Open from Mar. to Oct. Splendid walking country. Within a most convenient distance of the many recreational, cultural, and scenic attractions in Shropshire and Wales. Not suitable for children under twelve. Mrs. J.A. Davies, Proprietress.

Directions: On the A49 between Shrewsbury and Hereford, look for signpost pointing west to Woolstaston; continue (as above) 1½ mi. to Rectory Farm.

WALES

Wales is utterly fascinating and to me quite mind-boggling. The people are friendly and accommodating; the scenery runs the gamut from beaches to great mountain peaks; the numerous castles are all history-laden; and the varied opportunities for a holiday are literally uncountable.

Wales has three impressive national parks, including Snowdonia Park, which is the haunt of intrepid mountain climbers and holiday seekers. Brecon Beacons Park is perfect for pony trekking and walking.

Llangollen is the home of the world-famous International Musical Eisteddfod in July. Wales contains several opportunities for amusement, riding on what is referred to as "the great little trains."

Just a word about the Welsh language: Unbelievable. I say that to give encouragement to anyone who has tried to pronounce the "lls," "ffs," and a few of the totally unfamiliar combinations of consonants. Fortunately, the Welsh people have a good sense of humor and are probably adjusted to the mangling of their native tongue. Give it a try, it's part of the fun, and the Welsh give "A" for effort.

List of common Welsh words and some meanings in English:

Aber— mouth of a river
plas— mansion
llyn— lake
bedd— grave
newydd— new
bryn— hill
coed— woods
caer— fort
eglwys— church

From the mountains, lakes, and seacoasts of Wales have come such notables as David Lloyd George, Sir Henry Morton Stanley (of Stanley and Livingston fame) Dylan Thomas, Richard Burton, and Merlin, King Arthur's wizard.

Wales is filled with stories of bards, poets, and heroes. The AA Touring Map of Britain outlines twenty-one tours in all sections of Wales, and some of the accommodations that I've listed are located on many of these routes. No one can possibly understand and fully appreciate Wales in just one visit.

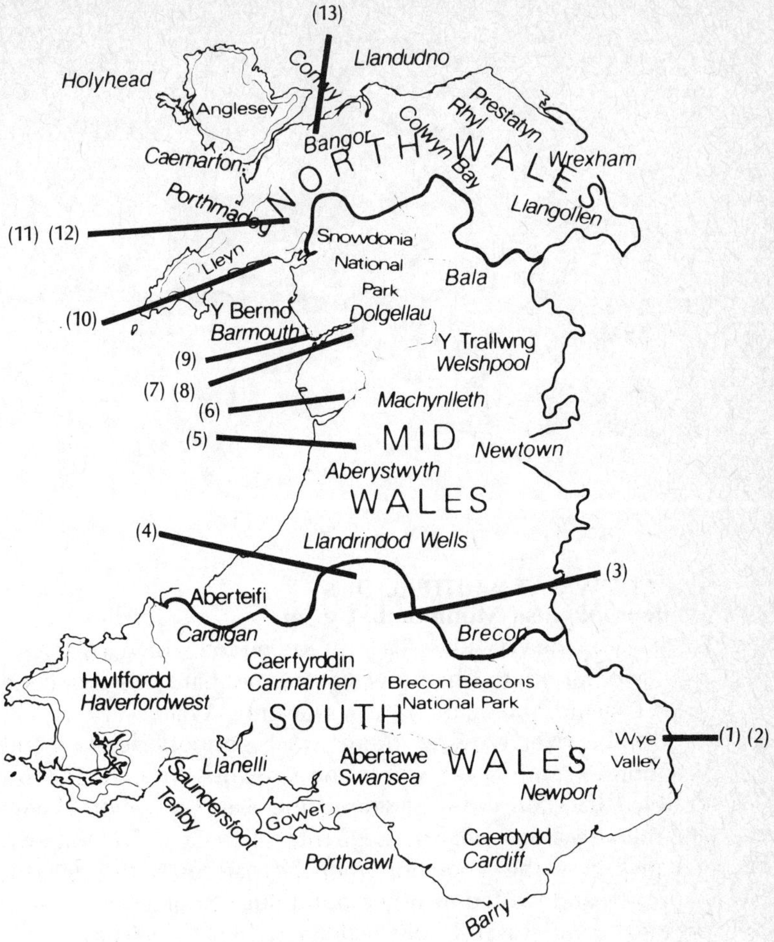

WALES

(1) CROWN AT WHITEBROOK, Whitebrook, Gwent, 110
(2) KING'S HEAD HOTEL, Monmouth, Gwent, 111
(3) TY MAWR, Brechfa, Dyfed, 112
(4) Y NEUADD (B&B), Pentretygwyn, Dyfed, 115
(5) MRS. ROWLAND'S B&B, Taliesin, Gwynedd, 117
(6) TYN-Y-CORNEL HOTEL, Talyllyn, Gwynedd, 118
(7) GOLDEN LION ROYAL HOTEL, Dolgellau, Gwynedd, 119
(8) BONTDDU HALL, Bontddu, Gwynedd, 121
(9) PLAS MYNACH CASTLE, Barmouth, Gwynedd, 122
(10) BWLCH-Y-FEDWEN, Penmorfa, Gwynedd, 124
(11) FFRIDD UCHAF (B&B), Rhyd Ddu, Gwynedd, 126
(12) SYGUN FAWR HOTEL, Beddgelert, Gwynedd, 127
(13) RHIWIAU RIDING CENTRE, Llanfairfechan, Gwynedd, 128

THE CROWN AT WHITEBROOK
Whitebrook, near Monmouth, Gwent

I was in the Wye River Valley traveling south on A466, the road from Monmouth to Chepstow. On the east bank, it's Gloucestershire, England, and on the west, it's Gwent in Wales.

At the river crossing, there was a signpost clearly marked Whitebrook, the village where the Crown is located. The road doubled back on the west side of the river for a short distance and then became a single passage route. I began to feel somewhat tentative about the expedition when the road passed through some barnyards and twisted its way around huge boulders; however, I pressed on and was rewarded with the sight of the village.

The Crown proved to be a very jolly place, a traditional village inn (as opposed to a country house hotel), which probably dates back to 1680. My hosts were John and David Jackson. John grabbed a fistful of keys and we took a quick tour of most of the eight bedrooms, all of which have either a bath or a shower. (Sometimes inns and guest houses have WCs and baths down the hall.) These rooms have been modernized with intercommunications systems and built-in radios.

The two brothers have most interesting backgrounds. Until about twelve years ago, they operated a family-owned restaurant in Weston-Supermare. John then went off to Bermuda for about six years after which he returned to London, working in some of the famous restaurants.

On the other hand, David went to Nigeria where he met and

married Colette, a very attractive Irish girl. Now the brothers are united, and view the Crown as a family venture.

The menu at the Crown is predominantly French, including several Continental dishes, for which David is gaining a most commendable reputation. He finished very high in the Chef of the Year competition, recently reaching the regional finals.

On the other hand, John is a Master Sommelier, one of the very few wine waiters to pass this examination run by the Worshipful Company of Vintners in the city of London. Their respective qualifications provide guests with the best possible assurance of quality and professionalism.

I'm happy to say that John was able to join a group of almost one hundred *CIBR* innkeepers from North America, Britain, and Europe at a most enjoyable seminar in the state of Arizona. John's talk on wines and wine service was one of the highlights.

The Crown is situated in the hills next to a brook flowing into the Wye through the steep wooded valley which is on the edge of Tintern Forest. It reminds me a great deal of parts of New England and North Carolina. There are many roses, rhododendrons, iris, pansies, and other flowers, as well as oak, ash, and beech trees which provide homes for nightingales, owls, and magpies.

For many travelers, the Crown may provide an introduction to Wales, and I'm sure the Jackson family will make it a cordial stay.

THE CROWN AT WHITEBROOK, Nr. Monmouth, Gwent, Wales, NP54TX. Tel: (0600) Monmouth 860254. An 8-room village inn in the true inn tradition, located approx. 4 mi. from Monmouth and about 2½ hrs. from London. Breakfast, lunch, tea, and dinner served every day. Walking in the Tintern Forest, fishing for salmon in the River Wye, and golf in the three local courses provide interesting recreation. The Jackson family, Innkeepers.

Directions: Traveling west on M4, take the first exit after crossing the Severn Bridge, follow signs for Monmouth (A466) through Tintern and Llandogo. At Bigsweir Bridge, turn left for Whitebrook. The Crown is 2 mi. up a narrow country lane.

THE KING'S HEAD HOTEL
Monmouth, Gwent

The King's Head Hotel is aptly situated in Agincourt Square. It is a historic 17th-century building that has been tastefully and imaginatively modernized to meet the needs of the 20th-century traveler. It owes its name, perhaps, to Henry V, but Charles I often visited the hotel in the early part of his reign, and it is said that the royalist landlord of the period set up a large plaster panel of the king's crowned head and shoulders in what is now the hotel bar. This cozy old-fashioned room has a curious plaster ceiling heavily molded in a design of wreaths of fruit.

All bedrooms have private baths and color TV.

Monmouth is an ideal touring center for the Wye Valley and the Royal Forest of Dean. The surrounding countryside abounds with magnificent viewpoints, picnic places, ancient castles, churches, and abbeys, and offers fishing, sailing, horseriding and walking.

THE KING'S HEAD HOTEL, Monmouth, Gwent, Wales. Tel: (0600) Monmouth 2177. A pleasant in-town hotel open year-round.

Directions: Monmouth is a few miles north of Chepstow, the M4, and the Severn Bridge.

TŶ MAWR COUNTRY HOUSE HOTEL
Brechfa, Dyfed

Except for the distinctive Welsh signposts, I might well have been in Vermont. The road and surroundings—the rushing brook, the boulders and the fir trees—reminded me of the back way between Wells and Cambridge Springs, Vermont. This area is right on the border of the Cambrian Mountains, some of the most remote upland country in southern Wales. There are large tracts with no roads to cross.

Now following Cliff Ross's simple directions, I arrived at the village of Brechfa, which is hidden in the valley and steep rolling hills surrounding the River Cothi. I spotted Tŷ Mawr almost immediately—a restored 16th-century house which stands on the banks of the Marlais, a smaller stream.

My feeling of being in Vermont was heightened even more when I stepped inside the front door. Except for the very old building, I might well have been in a Vermont ski lodge. The interior walls were of stone and heavy supporting beams, brightened by a generous use of colorful draperies and wall hangings. It had a modern, contemporary look, but at the same time, I sensed a keen appreciation of the past.

Tŷ Mawr is a dream come true for hoteliers Cliff and Jill Ross. Cliff is a Scot and Jill is originally from Lincolnshire. "When we discovered this place in 1973," said Jill, "it was almost in ruins. However, the combination of the simple beauty of the building and the location here in the village won us over immediately. The first thing we had to do was to rebuild, so we pitched right in with the workmen helping to lay the brick and stone. This made a great deal of difference in the design, because we appreciated the original simple statement made by the building."

We were seated in the attractive residents' lounge where three of the walls were done in massive stone, and a fire crackled merrily in the fireplace. The combination of the old and new was highlighted by the contemporary furniture and the colorful prints which Jill had hung on the walls. I noted quite a few familiar-looking American and British magazines.

Cliff and Jill were easy to talk to and the three of us carried on an animated conversation, with ideas flying thick and fast. It was close to dinnertime before we knew it, so Jill took me on a quick tour of the house and we agreed to meet in the dining room a bit later.

There are five double bedrooms at Tŷ Mawr, one with twin beds, and all with private bathrooms. They are furnished, as is the rest of the house, with an eye toward blending the furniture and draperies with the stone walls and oak beams.

Jill is in charge of the kitchen and, I gather, does a great deal of the cooking herself. She specializes in Cordon Bleu cooking and uses fresh local produce when possible. There's plenty of fresh salmon, sea trout, sewin, venison, guinea fowl, duckling, and veal.

After dinner, over coffee, Cliff filled me in on this rather remote village. "Brechfa is a truly rural Welsh-speaking area and throughout the year there are always local farming and social events, such as sheep shearing, horse sales, haymaking, pony racing and trotting, village fêtes, and the Eisteddfodau. It is really quite natural."

Jill was not to be denied. "There's so much for guests to do here. A great many of them come for one night and then return for a longer holiday. The sea is within a half-hour's drive, and there are many beaches along the Pembroke and Cardigan coasts which are just a short distance away. We have lots of ancient castles to explore, as well as the Roman gold mines, the woolen mills and Brecon Beacons National Park. There's lots of good fishing—salmon, sewin, or trout. We can make arrangements here.

"There are golf courses in the area and over three hundred acres of farmland with plenty of cover for rough shooting. Lots of our guests go horseback riding or pony trekking."

As we were going upstairs for the night, Cliff pointed out that Brechfa is a reasonable drive to Fishguard, which is the place to catch the ferries to Rosslare and Cork in Ireland.

A bit of Vermont in Wales. This is a sort of reverse exchange, because years ago a great many Welshmen and their families immigrated to Vermont's slate-quarrying hills and valleys near Wells and Poultney. The choirs in Vermont's small country churches are swelled with the rich Welsh voices. There are still strong connections with the rugged Welsh homeland.

TŶ MAWR COUNTRY HOUSE HOTEL, Brechfa, (Nr. Carmarthen) Dyfed, Wales. Tel: (026 789) Brechfa 332. A small 5-room country house hotel and restaurant 12 mi. from Carmarthen. Closed last 2 wks. in Feb. and last 2 wks. in Oct.; 30 min. from beaches on the Pembroke and Cardigan coasts. Ruined castles, Roman gold mines, woolen mills, picnic areas, Brecon Beacons National Park and nature reserves nearby. Fishing and horse riding on the grounds. Rough shooting, golf, walking nearby. No credit cards. Clifford D. Ross, Director.

Directions: Follow A40 from Llandeilo to Carmarthen. Watch for B4310 on the right and follow 6 mi. to Brechfa.

TRAVELING IN WALES

The roads are all paved, even those that look like little single yellow or blue lines on the map. Even the roads marked in red with three numbers, such as A485, are inclined to be narrow; four-number roads can become single passageways every so often, but not the three-number variety. I found the four-numbered roads basically more fun.

On checking the routes, I discovered that the center of the town was a key point. This is where the signposts are located, and once out in the country there are very few reassuring route numbers until the next crossroads. The villages all have Welsh names and this can be confusing, especially with a two-worded village name where none of the letters are vowels. I gave up trying

to pronounce them, because I realized I was trying to associate them with English sounds and not with Welsh sounds.

I found the best way to go from point to point was to stop at the crossroads and check the signposts, even though I might not be able to do anything except look at the name of the village. People of whom I inquired directions were most accommodating, and in some cases I had to go into the pub with the map rather than trust myself for any pronunciation. My approach was, "Oh pardon me, sir, can you show me where we are on this map?"

Counties are not mentioned as much in Wales as they are in England, but people are very proud to be from North Wales or from Mid-Wales or South Wales.

Just as April is an ideal time to be in the south of England, May is an excellent time for traveling in Wales. School is still in session and there aren't as many travelers on the road, especially in caravans (known as trailers or mobile homes in North America).

Whenever I asked someone in Britain about the length of time it takes to get from point to point, I found that it was a good idea to double the estimate. Britons drive much faster than North Americans, besides which they are used to the narrow-passage roads.

Quite frequently I found myself on the top of a hill in a brief shower looking down into the valley or hill beyond, which was bathed in sunshine.

Instead of wearing traditional blue jeans or something similar, Welsh farmers running tractors in the fields generally wear suit coats, and sometimes a shirt and a tie. Men wear a variety of hats and caps here. A deerstalker hat is quite popular with many different men. There are also wool caps of varied designs. On Sundays, gentlemen are turned out in very good sport jackets with either grey or fawn-colored trousers and suede shoes.

Y NEUADD (Mrs. Wanda Morgan's B&B)
Pentre-Ty-Gwyn, Llandovery, Dyfed

It was nice and warm in Wanda Morgan's kitchen. I was savoring what I am sure is one of the most sumptuous teas served anywhere in Britain. There were at least five different kinds of cakes and breads, plenty of whipped cream, jam, and butter, and a pot of tea under a tea cozy.

Wanda was very busy moving between the oven, the cupboard, and the table preparing several additional plates and trays of these delicious concoctions. She paused for a breath for a moment and insisted that I take two or three more small cakes. When she wasn't looking, I put them into a paper napkin and dropped them into my pocket.

About 45 minutes earlier, already running well behind schedule, I was cruising along the A40 between Brecon and Llandovery when my attention was drawn to an unusual statue on the side of the road. It turned out to be a well-known local monument called, "The Drunken Coach Driver." It was then that I noticed the sign for Y Neuadd, a B&B and Tea House located in the village of Pentre-Ty-Gwyn, which was located about a mile up a stony road.

"Y Neuadd means 'the hall' in Welsh," said Wanda, as she passed me another tray of scones and a pot of honey. "It means the minister of the church used to live here. Even though we seem very quiet and remote, we're only three miles from Llandovery. We have three double and two single bedrooms and the double rooms have private WCs and a shower.

"Most of our food is home-produced—we bake all the bread and make our own preserves, and the milk and cream comes from Amber, our Jersey cow, and the lamb, beef, poultry, and eggs from right here on the farm. We serve dinners on request and, of course, a good Welsh breakfast for our overnight guests.

Gethin Morgan, who had been busy serving the teatime guests, returned to the kitchen and the three of us sat around the table while they filled me in on what was for both of them a second career. "I used to be in business," explained Gethin, "but Wanda and I decided that we'd like to try something else. This is what happened and we are both very happy." I said that it was a familiar theme I had heard from many innkeepers in North America.

Finding Wanda and Gethin and their pleasant little guest house was indeed a lovely happenstance. Just watch for the monument on the left-hand side of the road and look for the sign on the right saying Pentre-Ty-Gwyn. Even if, like me, you can't pronounce it, you'll certainly have a warm welcome at Y Neuadd.

Y NEUADD, Pentre-Ty-Gwyn, Llandovery, Dyfed, Wales SA20 0RN. Tel: (0550) Llandovery 20603. A 5-room guest house approximately 3 mi. east of Llandovery on A40, the main road from Oxford to Fishguard. Bed and breakfast offered every day from March 1st to October 31st. Dinner is available upon request. Tea is served daily to non-residents. Located in the mid Wales mountains. Credit cards not accepted. Gethin and Wanda Morgan, Proprietors.

Directions: From the Severn Bridge, travel to Usk on the B4235 and to Abergaveny on the A471. On to Brecon on the A40. Watch for monument of Drunken Coach Driver 3 mi. to the east of Llandovery and look for the sign to the village of Pentre-Ty-Gwyn on the right. Y Neuadd is 1 mi. in on a country road.

MRS. ROWLAND'S BED & BREAKFAST
Route A487 between Machynlleth and Taliesin, Powys

I've included Mrs. Rowland's B&B because it's somewhat typical of other Welsh and English B&Bs.

Mrs. Rowland's looks like a pretty active farm with all kinds of rusty farm machinery and a lovely old stone house. Roosters were crowing in the background, and lambs were wandering about. I parked and went to the wrong entrance through the farmhouse kitchen where there was some laundry drying. Mrs. Rowland made it amply clear to me that most of the guests use the front gate!

The rooms I saw were very nice, quite large, and rather gaily done up. If I gave out stars for accommodations—which I don't—on a basis of four, I believe I would give Mrs. Rowland about one-and-a-half stars based on her bright bedrooms with their good views of the countryside.

Mrs. Rowland belongs to that legion of Welsh farm wives who also take in bed-and-breakfast people, and I think it would be an interesting experience to stay here for the night just to see what it's like in a real Welsh farmhouse. Certainly the price is right.

The charge is four dollars per night per person including breakfast, and the evening meal is served on request.

It's about eight miles south of the village of Machynlleth, and a small sign on the west side of the road simply says, "Bed and Breakfast." I can well imagine that in the high season cars could be very numerous on A487, which is one of the principal routes through this portion of Wales.

I'm not certain what kind of food is served for dinner. Breakfast is pretty much the same everywhere, but dinners can vary. Probably it's good wholesome food: potatoes, lamb, beef, perhaps in a stew, a pot pie, or something similar.

I'd like to hear from anyone who stops at Mrs. Rowland's. I'm sure she doesn't remember me, but I'll never forget her.

MRS. ROWLAND'S B&B, Route A487 just north of the village of Taliesin, near Machynlleth. Tel: Glandyfi 284. 4 rooms share 1 WC and bath.

TYN-Y-CORNEL HOTEL
Talyllyn, Towyn, Gwynedd

I was cruising north on the A487 through the gorgeous mountain country in Wales. It reminded me of several similar places in other parts of the world, such as the beautiful valleys in northern New Hampshire and mountains of northern Italy. One notices small white dots lost among the green mountain-side fields, which become on closer inspection the ubiquitous Welsh sheep. The houses in the villages are of stone typical to the area which runs from greyish-green to black. The corners of the steep roofs are decorated with little ornamental figures.

The road to the village of Towyn turned off to the left of A487 and the Tyn-Y-Cornel Hotel was located in the smaller village of Talyllyn which is en route to Towyn. (Signposts in Britain usually indicate the farthest village from the turnoff point.) The road dropped down through evergreen forests and alongside a lake which is tucked in between two steep mountains. The scene was idyllic to say the least. Fortunately, the sun had come out and the clouds had broken, and everything was bathed in golden light. I could see the hotel at some distance down the lake with the mountains behind it.

Subsequently, I met Clive and Shirley Thompson, the directors of the hotel, and learned that the lake was owned entirely by the hotel and was noted for trout fishing which was reserved for residents staying in the house. "We only allow fly fishing and we have a strict nine-inch limit," explained Shirley.

"And flies and casts are kept in stock at all times," added Clive. "The best fishing months are April, May, June, and September."

"Our guests are always delighted with the unusual number of birds we have," said Shirley. "We have swans, cormorants, wild ducks, and great crested grebes on the lake. Our garden is a meeting place for all the wild birds in the vicinity, as well."

I remarked on the similarity of the scenery to the fjords in Norway, and both of them said that many of their guests had already noted the resemblance. "It is because the sides of the mountains are so steep next to the lake."

The hotel, besides having such a marvelous view of the lake and the mountains, proved to be a most comfortable and pleasant place. There are bedrooms in the main house and also some newer bedrooms in converted farm outbuildings. The latter all have a very beautiful view of the lake and have telephones, central heating, and radios.

"Each room is provided with a hot water bottle," said Shirley.

"Sometimes they are most welcome, indeed. We are open weekends in the winter. During the rest of the year we're here throughout the week.

"We have some excellent walking and driving here in the Welsh mountains," Clive remarked. "It's a very pleasant place to stay for touring the Cambrian Coast and the Snowdonia National Forest. We can arrange pony riding on the slopes nearby and it's quite surprising how many of our guests enjoy it, even though it may be their first time astride a horse."

One of the other interesting attractions in this part of Wales is the Talyllyn narrow-gauge railway which runs down the valley to the coast. There are several of these small Welsh railroads. I understand that this one is the most picturesque and unusual. There are also three golf courses within a short drive of the hotel.

All in all, it sounds like a wonderful place to stop for two or three days just to take in the marvelous Welsh scenery.

TYN-Y-CORNEL HOTEL, Talyllyn, Towyn, Gwynedd, Wales, LL369AJ. Tel: (065477) Abergynolwyn 282. A 17-room lakeside hotel in the beautiful mountains of western Wales approximately 60 mi. from Chester and Shrewsbury and 10 mi. west of Dolgellau. Open Easter to November. Breakfast, bar lunch, and dinner served to non-residents. Fishing on grounds. Riding and pony trekking, golf, swimming, walking nearby. Clive and Shirley Thompson, Directors.

Directions: Locate Shrewsbury on a map of Wales and follow routes A458 almost due west to its junction at A470. follow A470 to a point near Dolgellau and then south on A487 just a few miles, with an eye out for the road to Towyn which is off to the right. Follow this road to Tal-y-llyn.

GOLDEN LION ROYAL HOTEL
Dolgellau, Gwynedd

Dolgellau is one of the many towns on the western shores of Wales linked by the coast road which starts at St. David's in South Wales and runs through Fishguard, Cardigan, Aberaeron, Aberystwyth, and Barmouth to points on the North Wales coast.

Coming from the south, the road doubles inland a few miles to accommodate the famous Mawddach Estuary. This stretch of road, with Cader Idris Mountain towering above all, is one of the most breathtaking in Britain. It drops down into Dolgellau, whose twisted streets are reminiscent of some of the twisted place-names of Wales.

The Golden Lion Royal Hotel is situated on one of the quiet

streets of the town, and has been for more than half a century under the watchful eye of a single family who, today, is represented by Mr. and Mrs. Gilbert Hall, the proprietors.

One patently obvious fact when entering the hotel is that Mr. Hall is a collector of things military, including sabers, medals, recruiting posters, prints of military uniforms, and actual military uniforms on life-sized dummies.

These and many other memorabilia are tastefully displayed throughout the several public rooms, lounges, and dining rooms, creating a very comfortable and pleasant Victorian atmosphere. A table in one of the lounges had coffee and tea available throughout most of the day, and this was one of the gathering points for hotel guests.

The resourceful Mr. Hall has also provided an adjacent area known as the Lion Yard, a popular meeting place for visitors and locals.

The hotel menu has local salmon, grouse, lobster, venison, and oysters.

All 30 bedrooms have hot and cold running water, and 13 have private bathrooms. There are 6 main bathrooms to serve the remainder.

Wandering at random through the hotel, I discovered that one of the sabers was sent from Chelmsford, Massachusetts, and was used by a soldier of the Union Army during the American War Between the States. I'm certain that Mr. Hall has many such gifts. Having spent some time in India, I took particular notice of the souvenirs and uniforms from both British and Indian regiments serving there.

I found it very interesting that the brochure for the hotel contained a "knock" among the many boosts. It appears that the hotel was mentioned in some chronicles by a poet, reputed to be Wordsworth, who wrote:

"If ever you go to Dolgelley
Don't stay at the 'Lion Hotel,'
There's nothing to put in your belly,
And no one to answer the bell."

Ah, Wordsworth, or whoever you are, things have really changed at the Golden Lion Royal Hotel.

THE GOLDEN LION ROYAL HOTEL, Dolgellau, Gwynedd, North Wales. Tel: (0341) 422 617. A 26-room traditional hotel (13 with private baths-shower), 60 mi. from Chester. Closed Dec. 20 to Jan. 4. Breakfast, lunch, tea, and dinner served to non-residents. Dolgellau is convenient to some of the most beautiful scenery in North Wales including Snowdonia National Park. Fishing, walking, climbing, pony trekking are all available nearby. Mr. and Mrs. Gilbert Hall, Resident Owners.

Directions: From Chester take A5104 through Hawarden. Llandegla Moors, Bala Lake to Dolgellau.

BONTDDU HALL HOTEL
Bontddu, near Dolgellau, Gwynedd

I was enjoying what the British call a "good tea" in the Green Room at the Bontddu Hotel on an afternoon whose mood was alternately sunny and stormy. The magnificent view of the Mawddach Estuary and Cader Idris range of mountains was alternately spectacular and clear or quickly obscured by fog or a hail storm. This view, which is above all else the distinguishing feature of the hotel, is an unforgettable blend of water, mountain, and wood—one of the most splendid in the highlands of Wales.

All of the drawing rooms and the dining room are situated on the view side of the hotel, as are most of the guest rooms.

The Bontddu Hall was the only three-star hotel that I visited in Wales, and it had all of the unmistakable accouterments of a luxury resort. There was a very impressive entrance hall, much wood paneling, and the high-ceilinged public rooms had rich-looking furniture and draperies. The dining room was decorated with a most unusual collection of shining cavalry helmets, resplendent with horsehair plumes.

There are twenty-six lodging rooms, most with private bathrooms, and these include a newer section of a more modern design.

Although I could not stay for dinner, there was an obvious emphasis on food, since one of the dining rooms is called the

Gourmet Room. This might be because *Gourmet Magazine* gave a most favorable review of the hotel's menu a number of years ago, making particular mention of the North Wales lamb, lobster, salmon, smoked trout, paella (I never learned how this Spanish dish appeared on the menu), and pheasant-and-bacon pie.

This is really a most impressive area of Wales, quite convenient for a holiday of longer duration. Guests may play golf at several famous courses nearby, and there is fishing, walking, or swimming on the sandy beaches.

Incidentally, Bontddu has won the "prettiest village in Wales" title three times. It is pronounced "Bon-thee" in Welsh.

BONTDDU HALL HOTEL, Bontddu, nr. Dolgellau, Gwynedd, North Wales. Tel: (034149) Bontddu 661. A 26-room luxury hotel 5 mi. from Dolgellau. The hotel has an inspiring view of the famous Mawddach Estuary and the Cader Idris range of mountains near some outstanding golf courses. Open from May-Oct. Breakfast, lunch, tea, and dinner served to non-residents. May be reserved from U.S. by travel agents through Dial Britain. Tel: 800-424-9822. W.S. Hall, Proprietor.

Directions: Use Exit 12 from M6 and go left on A5 towards Shrewsbury. From Shrewsbury take A458 to Dinas Mawddwy, then follow A470 to Dolgellau and A496 toward Barmouth.

PLAS MYNACH CASTLE COUNTRY HOUSE HOTEL
Barmouth, Gwynedd

The sign said "Plas Mynach Castle Hotel" and since it directed me under a very fancy stone archway, I decided to investigate. A short distance farther along a curving road through gardens and woodland I came to a very formidable castle-like building with a splendid view of Cardigan Bay. Venturing through a massive oaken door, I stepped into a most impressive reception and lounge area that was paneled from floor to ceiling. A fire was expectantly laid at one end and a large window provided a view of the mountains.

I heard a step on the stairs and turned to see a tall, rather imposing-looking man descending the curving staircase. It was the owner of Plas Mynach, Brian Devereux.

Although my arrival, just a few minutes before teatime and dinner preparations, was not announced, he could not have been more convincingly cordial. While we were getting acquainted and taking a short tour of the premises, I learned that he had been in the film business in other parts of the world for quite a number

of years, but now was devoting his time to this Welsh country house hotel.

In the main drawing room some of the houseguests were playing cribbage and watching a television set discreetly placed in a quiet corner. Brian commented, "We have many friendly board game competitions here; for example, Scrabble, checkers, and chess. We even have modest prizes, just to keep the competition keen. On the other hand, I think we provide a balanced selection of sporting facilities and amusements, because we have fifteen acres of rough shooting available and also archery and skeet shooting.

"I guess that we are particularly known for having outstanding walking and Barmouth is well-known for its sea bathing and miles of fine, safe, sandy beaches. By the way, we have a private path which leads from up here on the cliff down to the Promenade and the beach."

After a very satisfactory tour of the lodging rooms we returned to the reception hall, where Brian started a fire, and in no time at all we had a very cheery blaze and, as if by magic, the tea tray appeared. Brian relaxed for a moment, commenting upon the life of a hotelier, "It's been a departure from the things that I have done all my life, but I wouldn't give it up for anything in the world. I have been a filmmaker and also a lighting designer. By the way, since you are a publisher, perhaps you would be interested in my manuscript?"

I enquired as to the book's title and was prepared for almost anything in the world from a romantic novel to a discourse on

British film. Brian really surprised me by saying that the title of his book is "How Not To Die of Snake Bites."

At first I thought he was putting me on, but he was indeed serious. Before we could go further into the subject he had to excuse himself to supervise things in the kitchen.

This was my cue to make a reluctant departure and he walked with me out to my car, calling my attention to the wonderful display being created by nature where the many textures and colors of clouds, mountains, and sea were dramatically lit by the bars of late afternoon sunshine.

"I'm so glad you came by," he said, "and when I come to North America, I'm going to be sure to visit some of your inns."

As I drove back down the curving driveway to the main road I was still puzzled as to how a former filmmaker and lighting designer, now hotelier in North Wales, came to write a book about snake bites.

PLAS MYNACH CASTLE, Barmouth, Gwynedd, Wales, Tel: (0341) 280252. A 14-room country house hotel approx. 70 mi. from Shrewsbury. Open from March through Nov. Breakfast, lunch, tea, and dinner served daily to non-residents. Ideally situated for visitors to Merioneth to enjoy the seaside town of Barmouth and the Cader Idris and Snowdon Mountain ranges. Harlech Castle, Shell Islands, and the Roman Steps are within a short distance. Golf, riding, fishing, shooting, boating, and bathing are available. Brian Devereux, Owner.

Directions: From Shrewsbury follow the A458 to Dolgellau and then the signs onto Barmouth. Proceed through the town on the road to Harlech. The hotel is 1 mi. out of town on the left.

BWLCH-Y-FEDWEN COUNTRY HOUSE HOTEL
Penmorfa, Porthmadog, Gwynedd

I leaned against the door watching Gwyneth Bridge prepare my breakfast, cooking the eggs exactly as I ordered.

"This is a coaching inn dating back to 1664," she said, deftly sliding two sunnyside-up eggs onto a warm plate and then adding a rasher of bacon and a few small sausages. "Arthur and I have been here for three years and I think we have finally gotten things in order." This selfsame Arthur Bridges, he of the ready smile and fierce beard, joined us in the kitchen at that precise moment.

"Good morning," he boomed. "I hope you slept well. I see that you were out early this morning on a walk and I am glad that we had some of our usual beautiful weather for you." His eyes twinkled as he picked up the waiting breakfast plates and disappeared into the dining room.

"Arthur is really awfully good with the guests," said Gwyneth, as she bustled about preparing still more breakfasts. "He's very well informed about Wales and has some of the greatest stories."

Bwlch-y-Fedwen is situated in the middle of Penmorfa village, two miles from Porthmadog, and one mile from Tremadog.

The hotel has now been fully modernized in a warm and homey manner, at the same time retaining its original character. Antique furniture, oak beams, stone walls, and huge open fireplaces and candlelight in the dining room and bar create a very friendly and warming atmosphere.

During a lull in the kitchen activities I asked Gwyneth about the evening meal. "Well, our local lamb is really our specialty," she replied. "And of course we have local salmon in season. Our guests all seem to enjoy my sweets, including the "Queen of Puddings," which is another of our specialties. I also enjoy making meringues."

My bedroom was most comfortably furnished, with a view of a little garden in the rear and then down across the valley to some of the North Wales mountains.

I must add a word about the spic-and-span appearance of the Bwlch-y-Fedwen. Cleanliness is one of the virtues highly prized by Britons everywhere, but this particular hotel has to get the lifetime "Mr. Clean Certificate" for neatness. Not only were the bedrooms and public rooms most tastefully decorated, but nothing, and I mean *nothing,* was out of place.

Gwyneth and Arthur . . . you're terrific!

BWLCH-Y-FEDWEN COUNTRY HOUSE HOTEL, Penmorfa, Porthmadog, Gwynedd, Wales, LL49 9RY. Tel: (0766) Porthmadog 2975. A 6-room hotel, approximately 70 mi. from Chester in North Wales. Open from April to October. Meals are served to residents only. Within a short distance of the mountains of Snowdonia National Park, and within an easy drive of the many castles, railways, and other attractions of North Wales. Walking, climbing, fishing, golf courses, and sailing available nearby. No credit cards. Mrs. Gwyneth Bridge, Proprietor.

Directions: From Chester follow A55 to Mold, then Ruthin. Here, use A494 to Cerrigydrudion. Take A5 to Betys-Y-Coed and Capelcurig. Turn left on A4086 and then A498 for Beddgelert to Tremadog. Follow A487 to Penmorfa. This road leads through some of the most spectacular mountain scenery in Wales. I also realize that these are most confusing directions. May I suggest that having a map of Wales in advance and tracing the road under more leisurely circumstances would be an excellent idea.

FFRIDD UCHAF FARM (Mrs. Wynne-Robert's B & B)
Rhyd-ddu, near Beddgelert, Gwynedd

Because Beddgelert, located in the Snowdonia region of Wales, is a very popular resort village, I thought it would be fun to include a B & B, as well as the Sygun Fawr Country House Hotel.

The Ffridd Uchaf Farm, sitting at the top of a little hill, turned out to be tiny, but terrific, and the proprietress was a very, very energetic and attractive woman named Mrs. Wynne-Roberts. I had dropped in on her totally unexpectedly, but after she became convinced that I was legitimate, we had a very animated and rewarding conversation over a cup of tea.

Mrs. Wynne-Robert's husband's family has been in this house on this 800-acre farm since 1700, and it's a good example of a working farm in the mountains. They raise Welsh black cattle and sheep. The view from the farmhouse is like being in the middle of a bowl-shaped meadow in a circle of mountains. While we were talking, a group of young backpackers walked through the barnyard, following the path over the low hill behind the farmhouse.

Mrs. Wynne-Roberts explained that in addition to her two rooms, she also has "self-catering holiday flats" available. "Guests can buy things down in the village and they can get their evening meal in their flat as well."

The rate is ten dollars per person for bed and breakfast, and a bath is twenty pence extra.

It is possible to telephone from London for a reservation, and perhaps when phoning B & Bs, it would be a good idea to mention the choice had been made from a book by Norman Simpson—this would give the traveler more identification.

As I drove away I could see little lambs gamboling in the rocky pasture, and I made sure to close the big iron farm gate behind me.

FFRIDD UCHAF FARM (Mrs. Wynne-Robert's B&B) Rhyd-ddu, Nr. Beddgelert, North Wales, (post office address: Caernarvon, North Wales). Tel: (076-686) Beddgelert 253. A 2-room B&B about 2 mi. from the village of Beddgelert. Probably open year-round. Convenient to all of the Snowdonia National Park attractions. No credit cards. Mrs. Wynne-Roberts, Proprietress.

Directions: From Beddgelert follow the road to Caernarvon (A4085) about 2 mi. and look for sign on right-hand side of road.

SYGUN FAWR COUNTRY HOUSE HOTEL
Beddgelert, Gwynedd

I well remember the day. I was absolutely exhilarated. I had spent the previous night at the Bwlch-y-Fedwen, at Penmorfa, and as a result of hearing about the beauty of the Mount Snowdon area had decided to drive into this section of Gwynedd in Northern Wales although it was not on my original itinerary. The way led upward through some beautiful mountains to the village of Beddgelert. The morning was beautiful with the sunlight sparkling on the river. Reaching the village center, I followed the A498 up the valley toward the pass of Llanberis.

On my way out of Beddgelert I saw the sign that pointed over the river and said "Sygun Fawr Country House Hotel." I just couldn't resist it. And what a happy impulse that was. For one thing, it directed me to this very attractive 17th-century Welsh manor house with beautiful views of the Gwynant Valley and the Snowdon Range. It also introduced me to two very warm and hospitable proprietors, Norman and Peggy Wilson.

Norman is from Lancashire, and after all, anybody with the name Norman is bound to find a receptive audience in me. As we were touring the house, he explained that the word Sygun Fawr means high bog—literally, a high peat bog.

The rooms were very clean and comfortable with mountain views. Downstairs in a little back bar, which is used mostly by diners and friends, Peggy came out of the kitchen and we all had a cup of lovely morning tea.

"We found a wonderful new way of life up here," said Peggy. "We aren't Welsh, but the people of the village have taken us in most heartily. I've learned how to cook many of the traditional Welsh dishes, as well as those from England. We have visitors from all over the world, but I must say that in spite of all of our efforts, we simply can't get Americans to walk!"

We all had a good laugh at this and I hope this book encourages Americans to try, rather than hurrying through Britain and attempting to see Wales in three days, to settle down and find a place like Sygun Fawr and stay for three or four days to "get the feel" of the land.

As we stepped outside in the morning sunshine, I remarked to Peggy and Norman that this part of Wales reminded me a great deal of Norway, and they said that many other guests had also made that observation, although it was not the Norway of the fjords. "It's the mountains and the flowers, I think," said Norman. "You're headed toward Mount Snowdon now, and you'll see what I mean."

Yes, I, too, like the other Americans (not so much the Canadians), had to hurry on to get over the next hill and follow the river to the seaside and beyond. Someday, I'm going back to see Norman and Peggy and spend a week.

SYGUN FAWR COUNTRY HOUSE HOTEL, Beddgelert, Gwynedd, North Wales LL55 4NE. Tel: (076-686) Beddgelert 258. A 7-room (private baths) somewhat secluded country house hotel. Approx. 3 hrs. from Chester. Open all year. Dinner served to non-residents. Within an easy drive of all scenic points in north and mid-Wales. Located in the scenic Snowdon area. No credit cards. Norman and Peggy Wilson, Owners.

Directions: The A483 runs north and south along the imaginary boundary between Wales and England. There are several roads going west, including the A5 which can be followed west to Capel Curig, where 4086 goes southwest into the A498 at Pen-y-Gwryd. The Snowdon Area and Beddgelert are slightly to the south on A498. The hotel is just a few minutes from the center of Beddgelert over the brook on A498. Coming from farther south in England, after locating Beddgelert, using the above directions, work out your own way, it's really not difficult.

RHIWIAU RIDING CENTRE
Llanfairfechan, Gwynedd

Although I traveled throughout Britain and Ireland on a somewhat set schedule, I did allow time for an impulsive, unscheduled visit or so each day, and visiting the Rhiwiau Riding Centre came as a result of just such an impulse.

I was on the A55 about halfway between Conway and Bangor

when I saw the sign. I decided to follow the road and see what was at the other end. I found that the last one hundred yards was straight up and had to be done in first gear on a single-passage gravel road. I emerged at the top of a six-hundred-foot hill where I found the Rhiwiau Riding Centre and a marvelous view of the sea and a quite breathtaking panorama of several valleys and meadows of the North Welsh coast. Wild flowers bloomed in great profusion, as well as rhododendrons, oak, ash, sycamore, and fir trees.

I quickly learned that the main interest at Rhiwiau Riding Centre was, of course, horses and pony trekking. However, as Ruth Hill, who is a qualified member of the BHSAI (British Horse Society) and the proprietress, explained, "Our guests don't spend every waking hour on the back of a horse. We are situated most conveniently for exploring Snowdonia and the Isle of Anglesey, as well as Llandudno, Conway, and Colwyn Bay. In fact, there's a good number of guests who prefer our secluded, somewhat natural atmosphere and do a minimum of riding."

Other members of the Hill family involved in this endeavor are Ruth's younger sister Sarah and her father and mother.

The accommodations are somewhat similar to those of an American motel. They are nothing fancy, but most adequate. There are six rooms that will accommodate two people at a time and all have a shared shower; some have conventional beds and others have bunk beds. Incidentally, unaccompanied children are welcome and are "well cared for and supervised," according to Ruth Hill.

The food is under mother's watchful eye, and the menu includes chicken and mushroom pie, vegetables from the garden, and all home-cooked and prepared dishes that satisfy the outdoor appetite.

Since the emphasis is on riding, Ruth suggested that jeans or jodhpurs be packed as well as a warm jersey, riding boots, or sensible shoes. Riding hats are necessary, but can be borrowed from the centre if necessary.

It may well be that the Rhiwiau Riding Centre is not for all of the readers of this book, and I suggest that anyone who is intrigued by my remarks would do well to write to the centre for a more complete brochure. It is a totally natural, informal place where visitors can enjoy riding instruction, some really excellent supervised trail rides into the mountains, and are even permitted to participate in "practical stable work, if they so desire." (I think that last provision, which is mentioned in the brochure, is a euphemism for cleaning out the stables.)

I sincerely request any of my readers who visit here to please drop me a note and tell me of their experiences. Sometimes impulses turn up hidden treasures.

RHIWIAU RIDING CENTRE, Llanfairfechan, Gwynedd, North Wales LL330Eh. Tel: (0248) 680094. A 6-room (shared bath), somewhat informal guest ranch facility located about 5 mi. from Conway. Rates are available for both adults and children which include full board and riding. Bed and breakfast; or bed, breakfast, and evening meal available; as well as weekend and 7-day rates. Most suitable for children. Open every day in the year. Dinners to non-residents by reservation. No credit cards. Located on the northern coast of Wales, with horseback riding as the principal recreation. Hill walking, tennis, golf, fishing, mountaineering and rock climbing are nearby. Ruth Hill, Proprietress.

Directions: From London, take the M1 to Birmingham; M6 to Chester; A55 to Llanfairfechan. Turn left at the traffic lights and right at the top of the hill. After 1 mi. turn left and point upward (well signposted, if I remember correctly).

DERBYSHIRE

My interest in Derbyshire centered around the Peak District, comprising all of the North Derbyshire uplands. The Peak District National Park makes grand walking and touring country, easily explored from centers such as Buxton, Bakewell, Melbourne, and Ashbourne.

The region is characterized by many small villages with limestone houses and tiny greens. It is also the home of one of the great houses in England: Chatsworth, the home of the Dukes of Devonshire, which stands in the wide valley of the Derwent River. I think the best way really to enjoy the Peak District is to settle at one of the places I have suggested in the following text. The distances are not very far and the rewards are many. You might find it interesting to stay in one place for two nights or more and take lunch or dinner at the others.

There are three tours for Derbyshire in the AA Touring Guide to Britain.

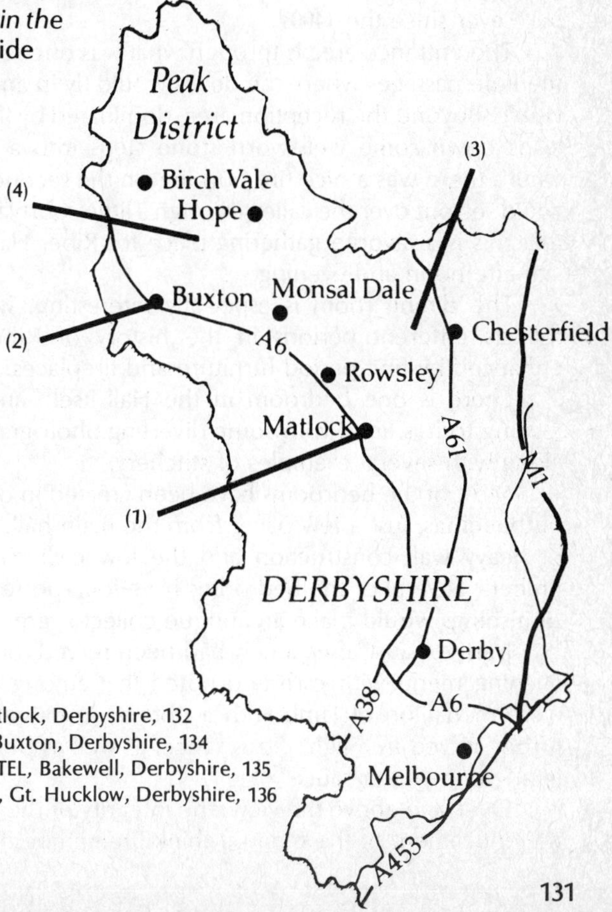

DERBYSHIRE

(1) RIBER HALL, Matlock, Derbyshire, 132
(2) THORN HEYES, Buxton, Derbyshire, 134
(3) CAVENDISH HOTEL, Bakewell, Derbyshire, 135
(4) ROWAN HOUSE, Gt. Hucklow, Derbyshire, 136

RIBER HALL
Matlock, Derbyshire

Riber Hall, on the borders of the Peak District, has many things to recommend it. Not necessarily in order of importance are the really auspicious views of the valleys and high, flat moors ending in dramatic cliffs, called "edges." There is also the house itself, dating to Elizabethan times, and so ancient that in 1668, seven generations of the same family had inhabited it. The latest addition (before 1970) was in 1661.

Certainly near the top of the list of its virtues is the wonderful walled garden, dominated by a great copper beech tree. In this garden I was allowing myself to be carried away with the entire Riber Hall atmosphere—being carried away was very easy with the wonderful English blue sky and fleecy clouds, the flittings of white-feathered birds, the green lawns, and beautiful flowers. The phlox and other spring blooms had made the garden their very own and I can well imagine that some most romantic scenes have been played here ever since the 1400s.

The entrance area is through what was once a dovecote, and the little passages where the doves would fly in and alight are still visible. Beyond the reception area, dominated by flowers, the way leads down some well-worn stone steps into a cozy bar area, where there was a nice fire burning on the second day of June. I could see out over the valley through a little courtyard. It is obvious that this is a favorite gathering place for Riber Hall guests in the late afternoon and evening.

The dining room is especially interesting, with decor that reflects different periods in the history of Riber Hall and is enhanced by fine period furniture and fireplaces.

There is one bedroom in the Hall itself, and the staircase leading to it is lined with some diverting photographs and prints, along with several examples of stitchery.

Most of the bedrooms have been created in one of the stone outbuildings, just a few paces from the main hall. The building is of heavy wall construction and the low ceilings have exposed timbers. Several of the bedrooms have four-poster beds, and the furnishings would make an antique collector green with envy.

I arrived just after lunch had been served, but I studied the evening menu with care and noted that among other offerings were medallion of lamb with a port and orange sauce, fillet of turbot served in a light citrus sauce, as well as pork fillets served in a lemon-butter sauce.

Over and above the view, the integrity of the old house, and the enticement of the menu, I think I remember Riber Hall most of all for that truly impressive walled garden. It has a wonderful tranquility and the opportunity for introspection so dear to the hearts of Britishers everywhere.

RIBER HALL, Matlock, Derbyshire, England DE4 5JU. Tel: (0629) 2795. A 12-bedroom (private baths) Elizabethan country house hotel on a high hill in the Peak District. Breakfast, lunch, afternoon

tea, and dinner. Open all year. Adjacent to Riber Castle. Conveniently located to enjoy all of the recreational, cultural, and scenic attractions in the Peak District. Alex Biggin, Proprietor.

Directions: Leave the M1 at Exit 28 and continue to A38 toward Matlock for 3 mi. Turn off on A615, signposted Matlock, for 7 mi., at the end of which you come down a very long hill into the village of Tansley. Continue to bottom of hill and about 20 yards on your left there is a UK filling station. The road to Riber runs on the near side of the filling station on your left-hand side. Continue on 1 mi. to the top of the hill.

THORN HEYES PRIVATE HOTEL
Buxton, Derbyshire

If, by some chance, you have not heard of the Peak District, much less visited it, I can assure you that in the process of traveling throughout the U.K. I have met many Britons who have yet to visit it.

I have explained the virtues of Derbyshire elsewhere, but a visit should be made to the spa town of Buxton, which was discovered by the Romans and nestles in a natural bowl in the high moors that surround it at a thousand feet above sea level.

The town has many interesting buildings, including the famous Crescent, the Old Hall, where Mary Queen of Scots stayed, and the newly restored Opera House, the focal point, with the Pavilion Gardens, for the annual festival, held during July and August each year.

Built in 1860 of local stone, Thorn Heyes was a gentleman's residence, and its architecture is quite in harmony with the Victorian elegance of the town.

It is a very quiet, rather conservative accommodation, where the traveler would be more likely to meet Britons than visitors from other countries. There are several other so-called private hotels in Buxton of the same size and demeanor, but I found the rather low-keyed atmosphere maintained by David and Pat Green quite appealing.

They offer bed, breakfast, and the evening meal on request. The dining room looks out over the very pleasant garden, as do many of the bedrooms.

The main dishes at the evening meal feature homecooked food and include soups, meat pies, roasts of beef, lamb, and pork. A vegetarian meal is also available. As Pat Green explains, "We try to be friendly, clean, and give good value at the table."

THORN HEYES HOTEL, 137 London Road, Buxton, Derbyshire, England SK17 9NW. Tel: (0298) 3539. A conservative 7-bedroom (some private baths) private hotel on the outskirts of Buxton. Open every day. Breakfast is included in the room rate. An optional evening meal is also served. Quite conveniently located to enjoy all of the many recreational, cultural, and scenic attractions of the Peak District. Pat and David Green, Resident Proprietors.

Directions: Locate Buxton on your map; note that it is about 45 min. from the M1, M6, and Ringway Airport (Manchester). Thorn Heyes is on A515 coming from Ashbourne.

CAVENDISH HOTEL
Baslow, Derbyshire

The British have a wonderful expression: "Good value for the money." I think that describes the many virtues of the Cavendish Hotel.

In the heart of the Peak District National Park, it is set in the Chatsworth Estate, owned by the Duke and Duchess of Devonshire. The Cavendish Hotel is actually within a very short walk of Chatsworth, one of England's most beautiful and best-loved "great houses" and one of the many reasons to visit the Peak District.

A very imposing, two-story stone building with extensive lawns, gardens, and terraces, the Cavendish is situated so that all of the public rooms, dining rooms, and bedrooms overlook the valley of the Derwent River.

The furnishings, some of which enjoyed an earlier career at Chatsworth House, are entirely in keeping with the subdued yet casual atmosphere, and great taste and care are evident throughout the hotel. There are open fires, oak beams, fresh flowers, lovely views, and a friendly staff.

It is my understanding that originally there was an inn called the Peacock here for so long it is uncertain when it was built. The Peacock was the property of the Duke of Rutland and served the turnpike between Chesterfield and the spa town of Buxton. It became the Duke of Devonshire's property about 1830, and in the early 1970s was rebuilt as the Cavendish, with decor and furnishings selected by the Duchess herself.

The hotel has all of the amenities the British are very fond of, including breakfast any time in the morning; lunch served either formally in the Paxton Room or in the bar or gardens or even as a picnic; dinner is served very late (until 10 p.m.).

The menu for both lunch and dinner is lavish, much larger

than I can cover here. For lunch I enjoyed "Pepper Water," an Indian soup of chicken, fruit, and rice and heavily seasoned with curry and garlic.

Golfers will enjoy the putting greens and a golf driving net, and fishermen will find the waters well stocked.

Like Buckland-Tout-Saints in South Devon, and other English mansions that have been turned into country house hotels, the Cavendish is a most unique experience—"Good value for the money."

CAVENDISH HOTEL, Baslow, Bakewell, Derbyshire, England DE4 1SP. Tel: (024 688) 2311. A 23-bedroom (private baths) country house hotel in the heart of the Peak District. Open every day of the year. Breakfast, lunch, dinner, and tea served. A few moments from Chatsworth, one of England's most beautiful stately homes, with private art collections, state apartments, gardens, cascades, and fountains (open Mar. 27 to Oct. 30). Cavendish is ideally situated to enjoy all of the recreational, cultural, and scenic attractions of the Peak District. The Duke and Duchess of Devonshire, Owners; Eric Marsh, Manager (and tenant).

Directions: From M1, use Exit 29 near Chesterfield; 2½ hrs. from London.

ROWAN HOUSE
Great Hucklow, Derbyshire

The village of Great Hucklow is high in the Peak District about twelve miles from the spa town of Buxton. Locating it and driving there is half the fun, although the directions I have included here should be adequate.

It is in many ways a typical, unpretentious, English B&B with two clean guest bedrooms, one with a wash basin, sharing a bathroom.

There is a small B&B sign at the front on a low stone wall, behind which is a very pleasant garden and some lawns.

As is the case with most B&Bs, the guests gather around the breakfast table. Here, Mrs. Susan Morgan serves a full English breakfast, and at the time of my visit there was lots of chatting about places we had all been, including the famous church at the nearby village of Eyam. There was also a comfortable lounge for guests and a good collection of literature, which would be useful in touring the Peak District.

ROWAN HOUSE, Gt. Hucklow (near Buxton), Derbyshire, England SK17 8QU. Tel: (0298) No. Tideswell 871715. A 2-bedroom (shared bath) village B&B in the beautiful Peak District of Derbyshire. Dinner served on request. Open year-round. Ideal center for a sightseeing holiday. Near Chatsworth House, Haddon Hall. Mrs. Susan Morgan, Proprietress.

Directions: From Buxton take A6 toward Bakewell; turn left on B6049 to Tideswell and through the crossroads at the Anchor Pub. After about 1 mi., turn right at the village of Windmill and follow signs to Great Hucklow and Gliding Club. In Gt. Hucklow look for B&B sign on the left opposite Unitarian Conference and Holiday Center.

THE WEST COUNTRY
Counties of Wiltshire, Avon, Dorset, Devon, Somerset, and Cornwall

Wiltshire has pleasant lofty downlands with rivers and meandering streams. It is a place of prehistoric monuments, the most famous of which is Stonehenge on the Salisbury Plain. Among its great buildings are the Salisbury Cathedral, the Malmesbury Abbey, and Lacock Abbey.

Dorset has uplands rising to 900 feet and a splendid coastline. This is the country embodied in many of Thomas Hardy's novels, and where examples of the thatcher's art can be seen in countless villages.

Avon is a new county in England, created on the first of April, 1974, and it includes part of Gloucestershire, North Somerset, and the city of Bristol.

Somerset is the home of cider and cheddar cheese. There are some fine beaches and open countryside. Christianity is said to have its earliest roots in Somerset. This is also the romantic land of Lorna Doone; where King Arthur held court at fabled Camelot, and Alfred sought refuge at Athelney.

Devon is one of Britain's leading holiday counties. It has sandy beaches, high-banked lanes, lush green valleys, rolling hills, and a mild climate. There are also wide open spaces like Dartmoor and Exmoor.

Cornwall is at the far southwest end of Britain and has a 300-mile coastline. The mild climate and semi-tropical foliage of the south coast has earned it the title of "Cornish Riviera." There are picturesque harbors crowded with fishing boats, many unusual villages and small towns with cobbled lanes. This is a photographer's and artist's paradise. Cornwall, as well as Devon, is famous for creamed teas.

The AA Touring Guide to Britain outlines seventeen tours among the West Country counties.

WEST COUNTRY

(1) THE LAMB, Hindon, Wiltshire, 140
(2) MANOR HOUSE HOTEL, Castle Combe, Wiltshire, 141
(3) HUNSTRETE HOUSE, Pensford, Avon, 143

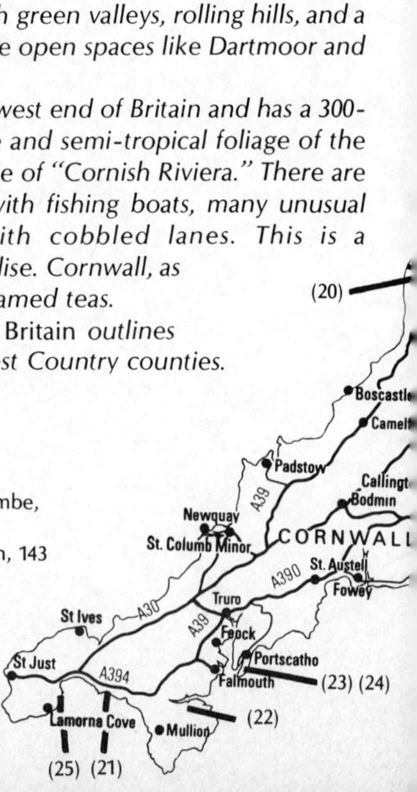

(4) DUNDAS LOCK COTTAGE, Monkton Combe, Bath, 145
(5) HOMEWOOD PARK HOTEL & RESTAURANT, Bath, Avon, 146
(6) THE PRIORY HOTEL, Bath, Avon, 147
(7) GEORGE & PILGRIM'S HOTEL, Glastonbury, Somerset, 149
(8) HOLBROOK HOUSE HOTEL, Wincanton, Somerset, 150
(9) OLD VICARAGE, Pilton, Somerset, 152
(10) OAK HOUSE HOTEL, Axbridge, Somerset, 153
(11) COMBE HOUSE HOTEL, Gittisham, Devon, 154
(12) WOODHAYES, Whimple, Devon, 156
(13) BICKLEIGH COTTAGE, Bickleigh, Devon, 157
(14) OXENHAM ARMS HOTEL, South Zeal, Devon, 159
(15) GIDLEIGH PARK, Chagford, Devon, 160
(16) SOUTH SANDS HOTEL, Salcombe, South Devon, 162
(17) BUCKLAND-TOUT-SAINTS, Goveton, Devon, 164
(18) OLD RECTORY, Barnstaple, North Devon, 166
(19) THE RISING SUN HOTEL, Lynmouth, Devon, 167
(20) WOODFORD BRIDGE HOTEL, Milton Damerel, Devon, 168
(21) LESCEAVE CLIFF HOTEL, Praa Sands, Cornwall, 169

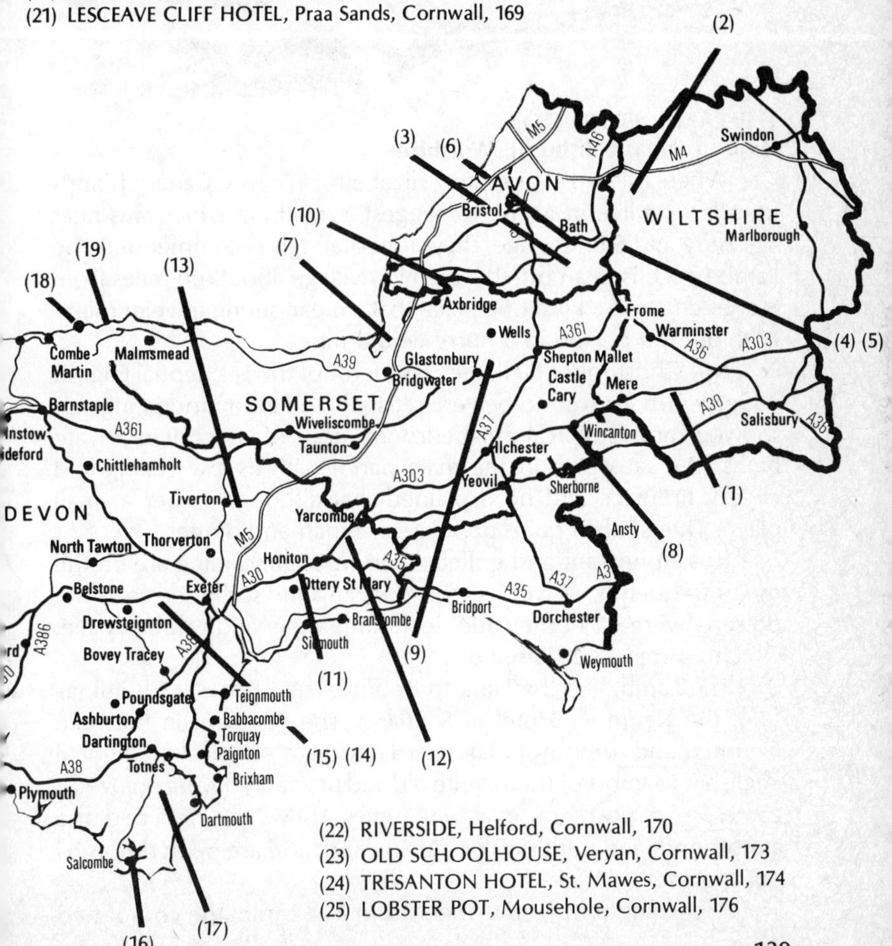

(22) RIVERSIDE, Helford, Cornwall, 170
(23) OLD SCHOOLHOUSE, Veryan, Cornwall, 173
(24) TRESANTON HOTEL, St. Mawes, Cornwall, 174
(25) LOBSTER POT, Mousehole, Cornwall, 176

THE LAMB AT HINDON
Hindon (Near Salisbury), Wiltshire

When I asked Walter and Elizabeth Lillie, my Canary Islands friends who live in Mere, to suggest a small inn which was near Salisbury and Stonehenge, they unhesitatingly recommended The Lamb which is in an off-the-highway village about ten miles from Stonehenge. The kind of a place that a meandering traveler might find, but the person in a hurry would miss.

Mr. Christopher Nell, the proprietor of this residential English country pub, proved to be very pleasant and accommodating and showed me his typical inn-bedrooms, four of which had private baths. We sat down in the main parlor with its low ceiling and cheery fireplace and he explained that although rather a small place, The Lamb is quite popular for lunch and dinner.

Roast pheasant and grilled Avon trout almondine are on the menu frequently, as well as roast duckling and scalloped veal. The desserts were all homemade, including apple and raspberry pie, which I sampled. Scrumptious.

The Lamb, like the Hark to Bounty, The Crown at Chiddingfold, the Kenmore Hotel in Scotland, The Pheasant in the Lake Country, and the Royal Oak near London, are typical, traditional English inns, most of them quite old and probably having enjoyed a career as a post house at one time. They have retained the atmosphere and traditions of old England, and are open throughout the year.

According to my tariff sheet from The Lamb, the cost of bed

and breakfast also includes dinner (see Addendum for rates and times of last orders for dinner).

THE LAMB, Hindon (Nr. Salisbury), Wiltshire, England SP3 6OP. Tel: (074 789) 225. A very pleasant 16-room (4 with baths) traditional village inn 16 mi. west of Salisbury. Open all year. Breakfast, lunch, dinner served to non-residents. Convenient for Salisbury, Stonehenge, Stourhead House and gardens. Riding, walking, fishing, and shooting available nearby. Breakfast and dinner included in lodging price. Christopher Nell, Director.

Directions: From London take M3 to A303. Continue until 10 mi. past Stonehenge, then look for turning to left, signposted "Hindon."

THE MANOR HOUSE HOTEL
Castle Combe, Wiltshire

Oliver Clegg, the owner of the Manor House Hotel in Bath, had given me directions to the village of Castle Combe which were perfect to the letter. I drove down through the glorious English countryside with beautiful old stone walls, really ancient farms, hedgerows, great oaks and yews, small hillside villages, meandering brooks, dark forests, and many cows and sheep standing in the meadows.

Driving through a little valley I proceeded over an old stone bridge and into the center of the village. At the Market Cross, which still survives after many centuries, the buildings are a beautiful Cotswold beige color. The reddish roof tiles, narrow streets, old signs, and the air of antiquity, all combine to make it one of the unusual travel experiences in the British Isles.

The Manor House Hotel is down at the end of a village lane which opens out into a great parkland with beautiful trees, a river, much open space and high hills.

Oliver Clegg was a most cordial gentleman. I had undoubtedly arrived at an inopportune moment for him, but he insisted that I would be most welcome at the midday meal with the other members of his family. "Then we will look the place over," he said.

Lunch was great fun for me, because it gave me the opportunity to meet more English people. They couldn't have been more gracious.

Oliver told me a few things about the building while I was enjoying a fine cut of roast beef.

"The manor of Castle Combe existed before the Conquest and the castle (now destroyed) was built about the middle of the 13th century. The manor house itself was not built until the late 14th

century, and during the 16th century fire destroyed much of it, but a little still remains. The present building is mostly 16th, 17th and 18th century, apart from our own additions in the 20th.

"We've done a lot of work here modernizing it to what might be called luxury standards, although we have tried to keep everything in the Manor House theme. That Italian frieze in the main lounge commemorates the Shakespearean character of Sir John Falstaff, and it may well be that Shakespeare got his inspiration from the lord of the Manor of that period, one Sir John Fastolf.

"While we were reconstructing some of the old cottages and the coach houses in the new garden wing, we found some most interesting things, such as open fireplaces, beamed ceilings, and even the remains of a circular staircase. We've now put them all together into an area that has 20 bedrooms with private baths."

After lunch Oliver and I took a leisurely tour of the Manor House and the really impressive adjacent gardens which have many sequestered walks, stone statues, secluded corners, and some unusual trees. There are many, many roses.

It was a beautiful Sunday afternoon and several luncheon guests now moved out onto the terrace and broad lawns to enjoy the sunshine.

Because so many guests bring their children, there are quite a few toys and other amusing things for young people. Particularly popular was a sizable hobby horse which was near the front entrance. However, I noticed there were as many adults riding it as children.

The lodging rooms have been thoroughly modernized with radio, television, intercom, baby listening, and telephone. Most of them have their own baths and WCs.

Since returning from England, I have learned that the village was used as a set for a Rex Harrison movie a few years ago. I am surprised it hasn't been used for many more, because the Manor House would be a perfect backdrop for a number of cinematic adventures.

MANOR HOUSE HOTEL, Castle Combe, Near Chippenham, Wiltshire, England SN14 7HR. Tel: (0249) 782206; telex: 44220 COMTEL G Manor House. A 34-room hotel within a historic manor house, 12 mi. from Bath. Breakfast, lunch, tea, dinner served to non-residents. Conveniently located to the Cotswolds, Salisbury Plain, the American Museum at Bath, and many famous country houses. Tennis, fishing on grounds. Golf available nearby. Oliver R. Clegg, Director.

Directions: From London leave M4 at Exit 17. Follow A489 towards Chippenham; 1 mi. short of it, turn right down hill to mini-roundabout on A420. Turn right and follow A420 2 mi. Take right fork on B4039 towards Yatton Keynell and Castle Combe. Follow signpost to Castle Combe. In center of village, double hard right around the Market Cross to Manor House Hotel.

HUNSTRETE HOUSE
Hunstrete, Near Bristol, Avon

I first saw Hunstrete House at a distance: a sedate, greyish-white stone Georgian house set against a glorious background of gracefully swaying green trees. It is completely surrounded by fields and parkland and has a truly remarkable garden and a most extraordinary croquet layout.

The occasion was a happy one for me, a reunion with John and Thea Dupays, who are the former owners of The Priory in nearby Bath. "We loved the Priory," declared Thea, "but when this marvelous property became available, John and I just couldn't resist turning it into a country house hotel. Do you know that we have ninety acres of land here? It seems way out in the country, but we're just eight miles from both Bath and Bristol. When John and I and our three daughters lived in Nigeria a few years ago, I'm sure that even in my fondest dreams I never imagined we would have a place like this."

There are nineteen most stylish lodging rooms at Hunstrete House, each named after birds that can be seen at various times of the year from the bedroom windows. Furnished in admirable taste, and individually decorated, each has its own bathroom, telephone, and television.

At the time of my arrival, John was on an errand in Bristol, and Thea was blackberrying. I set off in search of her, but was immediately diverted by the really incredible garden. The English are great lovers of gardens, and this is one of the most beautiful and well organized I have ever seen. I think of it in the same terms as the garden at Gravetye Manor in Sussex, and the one at Pittodrie House in Scotland.

We all caught up with each other at dinner where Thea announced that she was quite the better for her berry-picking excursion. "I love to get off in the forest every so often," she said. "It provides just the kind of quiet I need, and what's so wonderful is that it's just a few steps away."

Also on the grounds, just a few steps away, are the swimming pool and tennis court.

John oversees all of the activities in the culinary department which is most appropriate because he is an expert chef himself.

"Everything from the kitchen has to be just right to suit John," Thea said. "He's very particular."

"That's true" said John, "but I'm happy to say that we have an excellent chef."

The main courses were an indication that the Norman invasion of England left its mark permanently, because I found a number of tantalizing French dishes such as steak au poivre, guinea fowl roasted in cider, roast grouse, pheasant, turbot, and lobster. From a selection of eight desserts, I settled on chocolate St. Emilion, a delicious pudding with macaroons.

Thea tempted me to stay an extra night with the news that the Old Vic Bristol Company was playing *As You Like It.* "We have all the advantages of both Bristol and Bath. There's something interesting happening all the time—race meets, fairs, theater, and sports."

"Furthermore," declared John, "we're on one of the direct routes to Wales."

HUNSTRETE HOUSE, Hunstrete, Chelwood, Nr. Bristol, Avon, BS18 4NS, England. Tel: (07618) Compton Dando 578. A 19-room country house hotel approx. 8 mi. from both Bath and Bristol. Breakfast, lunch, tea, and dinner served daily. Closed first week Jan.; open Christmas. Tennis, swimming, croquet, deer park on grounds; riding nearby. Exquisite garden. No children under 9. John and Thea Dupays, Proprietors.

Directions: From Bath take A4, then A39 towards Wells. At Bences Garage in Marksbury, follow A368 toward Weston-super-Mare and Bristol Airport. Go 1½ mi. to first turn on right, signposted for Hunstrete; 200 yds. down that lane is the driveway to the hotel.

DUNDAS LOCK COTTAGE
Monkton Combe (Bath), Avon

The second of the two new additions in the Bath area is another extremely delightful, quite different place that I discovered only because I have a continuing curiosity.

The turning for Dundas is just down the A36 from the American Museum, and while I was getting a petrol refill at the Monkton Combe Garage, I noticed a sign that said "Dundas B&B." A small lane led down a dirt road through an archway of trees, and imagine my surprise at coming upon not just one waterway, but two! Actually, there is a canal and a river, and this is one of those wonderful places that only happen in England where the canal actually goes over the river on its own bridge and then continues down the valley. The canal locks here are called Dundas, hence the name of this little sandstone cottage.

Here, I found the cheerful and fresh-faced proprietress most accommodating and quite willing that I should see all of the bedrooms in the house, some of which overlook the river, the canal locks, and the very pleasant gardens.

There is a little bit more to this than meets the eye, because Wendy and her husband also are involved in arranging canal trips on the Kennet and Avon canals aboard the *John Rennie.* She explained that on Friday and Saturday nights they run a three-hour cruise that includes dinner on the boat. There seemed to be many more plans in the offing, and I would suggest that if this sounds interesting, readers should write ahead for advance information. Incidentally, I know these cruises are very popular, so advance reservations would be necessary.

The location of Dundas Lock makes it a very interesting and

rewarding center for enjoying the delights of this part of England, and in particular the delights of the city of Bath. It's really fun!

DUNDAS LOCK COTTAGE, Monkton Combe, Bath, Avon, England BA2 7BN. Tel: (022 122) Limpley Stoke 2292. A 2-bedroom (shared baths) canalside guest house near Bath with a few extra touches. Breakfast is the only meal served, but Friday and Saturday night canal cruise dinners are offered with advance arrangements. Write for brochure. Open from May 1 to Oct. 31. Near the American Museum and the city of Bath. No credit cards. Mr. and Mrs. T. Wheeldon, Proprietors.

Directions: From Bath take A36 through Claverton. About 1 mi. beyond, you will come to the Monkton Combe Garage (you have just overshot the entrance). Turn around, going north about 100 yards and look for Dundas B&B sign on right.

HOMEWOOD PARK
Hinton (Bath), Avon

Because the area in and around the city of Bath, in the county of Avon, is attractive to tourists, I have added two more accommodations.

If the reader will take a moment to look on the page with the map of the West Country, he or she will note that distances are very short, and it's possible, using Bath as the hub, to visit points in Somerset, Avon, and Wiltshire. I would suggest staying in one place for two or three nights; they are all excellent and somewhat varied in price.

The first of the two is the Homewood Park Hotel, a short drive from Bath, recommended by Richard and Annie Skipwith at the Old House Hotel in Wickham, a pleasant drive to the east in Hampshire.

The first thing I saw was a super croquet lawn bordered by extensive gardens. The main house is a very old building with the entrance through an attractive flower-bedecked patio.

The reception area and the other rooms on the first floor were bright and cheerful with a mixture of modern and traditional furnishings.

I had telephoned ahead and introduced myself as a friend of the Skipwiths', and I must say that Stephen and Penny Ross were most gracious, even though they were hosting a very large wedding party. I am sure I couldn't have chosen a more inopportune time; however, their good humor and excellent manners prevailed. As it turned out I was very glad to see this lovely family-run country house hotel at its brightest and most inviting, with the happy, celebrating guests all gathered around a fabulous buffet table.

There are ten bedrooms individually decorated, each with private bathrooms and lovely views.

Stephen, who is the chef, explained that the menu is a combination of French country cooking. "Mildly influenced," he explained, "by the new style. We would never admit to being cuisine nouveau, but our approach has the light touch."

Penny chimed in quickly, "I think we are running a country restaurant with comfortable bedrooms. Most people coming here have very high expectations, so we cannot relax in the kitchen when people are expecting to find the food interesting."

I could readily see that both of them had to attend to their guests and so I wandered about, both indoors and out, admiring the gardens and tennis court, and enjoying for a moment the idea of sharing in a real English country wedding party. It was delightful.

HOMEWOOD PARK, Hinton, Charterhouse, Bath, Avon, England BA3 6BB. Tel: (022122) Limpley Stoke 2643. A 10-bedroom (private baths) country house hotel near Bath. Breakfast, lunch, and dinner served daily. Closed Dec. 24 to Jan. 14. Located near the American Museum and all of the delights of the city of Bath. Good countryside walking and touring. Stephen and Penny Ross, Hoteliers.

Directions: Follow A36 south from Bath; look for sign that reads Freshford, then start looking on left for hotel sign.

THE PRIORY HOTEL
Bath, Avon

There were a few surprises awaiting me on my second trip to the Priory Hotel. The first was the new owner, John L. Donnithorne, late of Brown's and Grosvenor House in London. The previous owners, John and Thea Dupays, are now the owners of the Hunstrete House which is in the country to the west of Bath.

Bath, the city, is one of the most popular of travelers' objectives in Britain. There are many, many large hotels near the center of the city with its hustle and bustle.

It is this respite from the center of the town which attracts me to the Priory. Behind its high stone walls, the view from the dining room and drawing rooms is of the spacious lawn, cedars of Lebanon, numerous flower beds, and at the bottom of the garden, a swimming pool. The building is of greyish Bath stone in a combination of Georgian and Gothic styles.

There are fifteen individually decorated and furnished bed-

rooms all with private bathrooms and color television. Direct dial telephones are located on each floor.

John Donnithorne proved to be an apt conversationalist and, interestingly enough, was associated with a large hotel in Algeciras which I visited a few years ago. "That was early in the game," he said "and although Pat and I certainly enjoyed our long association with the London hotels, we are delighted to be here in The Priory. We have great plans for redecorating all of the fifteen rooms and we've been thinking about putting a fountain in front of the main entrance to give the place a lighter touch."

To refresh my memory, I made a short tour of the house starting at the top floor where there is an alcove bedroom with a bathroom in one corner. A bay window seat which was high in the treetops beckoned me to curl up for an afternoon with a good book. The Four-Poster Room overlooks the impressive back lawn and garden and has attractive brass beds.

Another room with a four-poster, which has accommodated one of the former First Ladies, was still as inviting and comfortable as ever.

The redecorating program includes the use of many bright and gay colors.

The restaurant draws a clientele from a wide area and to ensure a table, hotel guests are advised to reserve when making their room reservations.

The restaurant is in two separate rooms, the one an imposing Gothic room with Georgian furniture and period paintings; the other a terrace room overlooking a courtyard with an ornamented pond and fountain.

The culinary creations of chef Robert Harrison include lobster quenelles in a Nantua sauce; filet mignon of veal set off by chicken soufflé with basil, tomatoes, and madeira sauce; and a lemony blackberry and apple pie.

With its new owners at the helm, The Priory can look forward to many happy voyages.

THE PRIORY HOTEL, Weston Road, Bath, Avon, England BA1 2XT. Tel: (0225) 339122, Telex 44612. A 15-room hotel in a residential section of Bath, ½ mi. from the centre. Breakfast, lunch, tea, and dinner served daily to non-residents. Closed Christmas. Swimming pool on grounds. Convenient for pleasant drives in the west country and all of the attractions of Bath. J.L. Donnithorne, Owner.

Directions: From M4 use Exit 18. Follow A46 to Bath and take A4 towards Bristol (do not cross river). Turn right at Royal Victoria Park on Park Lane and left on Weston Rd. Bath also accessible by railway.

GEORGE AND PILGRIMS HOTEL
Glastonbury, Somerset

Although there is a lot of smiling and joking on the subject of ghosts at various castles and ruins in Britain, I got the feeling that the ghost at George and Pilgrims Hotel has been taken much more seriously than your average British ghost.

I think that even a ghost would feel easy at this truly ancient hostelry, because it's been providing comfort and hospitality to visitors for more than five hundred years. It was *rebuilt* in 1475, and pilgrims and visitors to Glastonbury have taken shelter here since before Columbus discovered America.

Major Jack Richardson and his wife Elzebie make certain that behind the ecclesiastical stone frontage and mullioned windows are found good food, modern service, and comfortable lodgings. In spite of the age of the building, bathrooms are plentiful and adjacent to bedrooms, if not actually private.

The entrance is through a flagstoned hallway with oak paneling and heavy furniture. Old timber beams adorned by carved angels and guarded by death masks of monks lend a very special character to the first-floor public rooms. There are many Cromwellian and Glastonbury chairs.

Many of the bedrooms have canopied beds and half-timbered walls. At one point during a major renovation in 1951, the original mud-and-wattle plaster was discovered, and a section has been preserved to show some heather and mud as a good example of the old construction methods.

The top floor has some of the most interesting lodging rooms, including the Abbot Whiting Room. He was hung, drawn, and quartered at the time of the Reformation. There is still another small bedroom which was once the confessional of the monastery.

Jack and Elzebie are two very lively and friendly people who are obviously having a wonderful time running the George and Pilgrims. I believe they see it as far more than just a wayside hotel. Jack put it this way:

"Glastonbury is the center of the Arthurian legends and we have the tomb of King Arthur and Queen Guinevere in the Abbey. Both Anglicans and Catholics are drawn here because it is the origin of Christianity in England. Joseph of Arimethea planted his staff on Wearyall Hill and this holy thorn still blooms at the time of the Nativity, when we cut a sprig for the royal Christmas table.

"We also have the Guy Fawkes Carnival every year. Miracle plays are staged in the Glastonbury Abbey ruins. The actors are our townspeople. Tor Fair has been held every September for the last eight hundred years."

The menu at the George and Pilgrims includes game soup made from local wild meats, homemade bread, poultry cooked in cider, delicious cheddar cheese, and a creamy trifle for dessert. During my noontime visit, there were some enthusiastic tour-bus patrons enjoying lunch in this atmosphere of antiquity.

Did you think I had forgotten about the ghost? The Richardsons assured me that he's been seen about three times in the last two years, and parties of ghost-hunters have visited the hotel. This apparition is apparently one of the monks who lived here before the shameful sacking of the Glastonbury Abbey by Henry VIII.

GEORGE & PILGRIMS HOTEL, Glastonbury, Somerset, England BA6 9BP. Tel: (0458) 31146. A 14-room village inn (7 with private bath) in one of England's most historic areas. Within walking distance of the famous Glastonbury Abbey. Breakfast, lunch, tea, and dinner served daily to non-residents year-round. Jack and Elzebie Richardson, Resident Proprietors.

Directions: Glastonbury is about 25 mi. from Bath and Bristol. Use Exit 23 from M5 to A39 and follow Glastonbury signs (13 mi.).

HOLBROOK HOUSE HOTEL
Wincanton, Somerset

The village of Wincanton is situated on a hill only a few miles from the East Somerset border. The surrounding country is well-wooded hill and vale with splendid views of the neighboring counties of Dorset and Wiltshire. All around are beautiful villages with historic churches, mellowed stone cottages, and gracious mansions, many of which, with their lovely gardens, are open to the public.

This is Camelot country, and nearby Cadbury Castle is one of the reputed sites of King Arthur's last battle. Within a thirty-mile radius lie Salisbury, Bath, Wells, Glastonbury, Dorchester, and the coasts of Dorset, and North Somerset.

The word that comes to my mind when I think of Holbrook House Hotel is "comfortable." It is situated in a rather large grove of cedar, beech, elm, ash, and rose trees, and I noted many familiar flowers as well.

Over half of the spacious rooms had their own bathrooms.

The menu has some typical Somerset dishes, including pork cooked with apples and cider; chicken garnished with a mead and honey sauce, and a number of dishes with cheddar cheese, whose origins are just a few miles away.

There are two unusual recreational features at Holbrook House. I found both grass and hard-surface tennis courts, and also squash courts—I didn't see many of those in Britain. There's also a heated outdoor swimming pool.

The word "Holbrook" is not a family name, but is derived from the Old English "holbroc," meaning a stream in a hollow. The property dates approximately to 1350, and some of the earlier owners lost their heads because of some injudicious political leanings. One family owned the property for nearly three hundred years.

It has been well preserved and the conversion to a hotel by its present owners has been planned with care, taste, and wisdom.

HOLBROOK HOUSE HOTEL, Castle Cary Rd., Wincanton, Somerset, England BA98BS. Tel: (0963) Wincanton 32377. A 20-room country house hotel (10 with private bath/shower) 2 mi. west of Wincanton. Open all year. Breakfast, lunch, tea, and dinner served to non-residents. Convenient to Stonehenge, Stourhead Gardens, and many famous houses in the Somerset countryside. Grass and hard tennis courts, squash court, croquet, and heated swimming pool on grounds. Golf and fishing nearby. G.E. Taylor, Owner.

Directions: From London, take M3 to Basingstoke, then A303 to Wincanton Bypass. Take exit signposted "Wincanton and Castle Cary." Follow signs to Castle Cary Rd.; 2 mi. beyond, on A371, is gate entrance.

THE OLD VICARAGE
Pilton, Near Shepton Mallet, Somerset

On the road from Shepton Mallet to Glastonbury I was humming a few bars of "Folks From Somerset," when I came upon Pilton. Had I not come to Pilton, I never would have seen the Old Vicarage or met the Stevenson family.

The Old Vicarage is a very ancient stone building set back from the highway in a small grove of trees. A small sign said, "B&B," so I turned into the car park and knocked on the old wooden door.

Colin and Nancy Stevenson and their children, Mark and Alexandra, offer a cheerful atmosphere for families, with bedrooms with double and single, as well as bunk, beds. There are five bedrooms in all, two of which are single rooms. These share a bathroom with bath, shower, and w.c.

The view from some of the old stone mullioned windows looks across the rolling hills and meadows toward the famous Glastonbury Tor (tower) five miles away. This is where King Arthur reigned over Camelot. Not far are such interesting historic sites as Stonehenge and Wells.

Nancy Stevenson, being a potter, has a busy pottery and showroom on the premises and she is always ready to give a demonstration to those who are interested. Colin tells me they are planning to offer a two- or three-day holiday with pottery lessons for those who wish to try their hand at something different.

The evening meal, available at a very reasonable price, is comprised of soup, a main course, fresh vegetables, and a sweet, with a choice of tea or coffee. A full breakfast is included in the room rate.

THE OLD VICARAGE, Park Hill, Pilton (Nr. Shepton Mallet), Somerset, England, BA4 4AY. Tel: (074989) Pilton 573. A 5-room guest house midway between Wells and Glastonbury. Open all year, serving breakfast and dinner to residents only. Convenient to all of the historic attractions of Glastonbury and the Mendip Hills. Golf, country walking, fly trout fishing, and horse riding nearby. No credit cards. The Stevenson Family, Resident Owners.

Directions: The Old Vicarage is on A361 'twixt Shepton Mallet and Glastonbury.

THE OAK HOUSE
Axbridge, Somerset

Let's have some fun. Let's see what goes on at this West Country British hotel during the Christmas season. Actually, it would be hard to choose a better example of really British Christmas spirit, because the Oak House has a history and continued associations dating back several hundred years. The present building was built in 1928 by an Australian shipping magnate. I understand there was an old manor house here from the 16th century that didn't please the man from "down under" and he tore it down. The new one didn't work either, so he built another house, which he didn't like; he tore that one down and built the present structure. For the most part, it's modeled after Tudor architecture.

Some of the bedrooms have a real old-world feeling to them, but they have modern bathrooms, color television, radio alarms, and beverage-making facilities.

There are two restaurants in the hotel. The main restaurant offers a wide selection of such dishes as home-smoked ham, local game, Blagdon trout, and Wye valley salmon. The other restaurant, the Somerset Room, is more informal and offers an inexpensive but enticing menu of appetizing dishes.

A series of pre-Christmas lunch parties and dinner parties take place several days before the actual holiday, culminating in the Christmas Eve dinner that features pot-roasted pheasant cooked in red wine, or steak in pastry with a sherry sauce, or escalope of pork with Stilton sauce—Stilton being one of the distinguished cheeses of England. On Christmas Eve everyone goes to the beautiful church in Axbridge for Midnight Mass and returns afterward to toast the occasion.

On Christmas day there are gifts for everyone and entertainment for children with jamboree bags and gifts, free squash, hats, novelties, and decorations, plus a meal that almost defies description. In this case, the choice includes roast turkey with chestnut stuffing. I might add that there is an abundance of mince pies, as well.

Wouldn't it be fun if we could all go to Axbridge and enjoy the Christmas season at the Oak House Hotel?

THE OAK HOUSE RESTAURANT AND HOTEL, The Square, Axbridge, Somerset, England BS26 2AP. Tel: (0934) Axbridge 732444. Telex: 449748. A 12-room hotel set in a medieval market square in an old town with history dating back to Saxon times; 18 mi. from Bristol, and 9 mi. from the sea at Weston-super-Mare. Breakfast, lunch, and dinner served daily. Open every day in the year. Henry Love, Proprietor.

Directions: Leave the M5 at Exit 21 and take A371 in the direction of Cheddar and Wells.

COMBE HOUSE HOTEL
Gittisham (Near Honiton), Devon

Dusk had fallen on the A30. A scant twenty minutes earlier I had left Exeter and was now anxiously looking for the signpost for Gittisham. Ah, there it was. I turned into a truly ancient village with cob and thatched cottages and a babbling brook. There was a parish church which enshrined 500 years of the community's history.

A gate at the end of the village led to a narrow road that wound its way through the meadows of an extensive country estate. I parked in front of a large three-story stone building with many towers and windows, surrounded by beautiful hedges and flowers.

In the impressive main hall I found no reception desk or porters in white jackets, but rather a large, imposing man, his face wreathed in smiles, who said, "Welcome, Mr. Simpson, to the Combe House Hotel."

This was my introduction to John Boswell, who, with his wife Thérèse, is the proprietor of this remarkably well-preserved Elizabethan mansion house which possibly dates as far back as the

13th century. Standing at the head of a secluded valley, it commands extensive views over the hills where there are beautiful walks and a sublime serenity.

The Boswells came to Combe a number of years ago and found this old country house in a very dilapidated condition. John, whose early Scottish ancestors included the famous James Boswell, author of *The Life of Samuel Johnson,* had previously worked for a shipping organization in the Far East. Thérèse attended the Cordon Bleu School at Winkfield, and lived in France for some time.

"The improvements we made are not of the obvious sort," John commented. "We've re-electrified the house, got the water works right, and have done a lot to the inside, including adding more bathrooms and shower rooms and other such essential things.

"The gardens were in an almost hopeless condition, and it pleases us when people enjoy all the flowers. In addition to our kitchen garden, where we grow our own peas, tomatoes, lettuce, french beans, radishes, Brussels sprouts, corn, chinese lettuce, artichokes, and broccoli, there are several farms on the place. We are really self-contained, right down to our fresh eggs."

There are thirteen spacious, rather elegant bedrooms, seven with their own bathrooms.

The passage of time has left many noteworthy relics of Combe's illustrious owners. Antique lovers will enjoy the fine architecture, furniture, and decor which echo their tastes throughout the centuries. John and Thérèse have added considerably to the atmosphere with their own cherished furniture, books and pictures from Auchinleck House in Scotland, the ancestral home of James Boswell.

Dinner that evening in the sedate candle-lit dining room, included Dover Sole Mere Recamier which Thérèse explained later was deep-fried with the backbone removed and filled with shrimps, prawns, and cream. Other specialties include Veal Escalope Vallee d'Auge and fresh local lobster which is cooked in a special cream sauce.

I spent the remainder of the evening talking with John, who is a superb conversationalist, learning about the history of Combe House and being shown the many oil portraits of its famous and infamous past owners.

I was delighted on my return visit to Gittisham to discover that nothing had really changed since my first visit. But, after all, nothing has changed in Gittisham village for upward of 500 years, so that really wasn't so surprising.

COMBE HOUSE HOTEL, Gittisham (nr. Honiton), Devon, England EX 14 OAD. Tel: (0404) Honiton 2756. U.S. reservations: 800-323-3602. A 12-room country house hotel dating to Norman times. Breakfast, lunch, tea, and dinner served daily. Fishing and croquet on grounds; riding, swimming, squash, tennis nearby. Located a short distance from theatres and museums in Exeter, and many houses and gardens of historical interest, including Forde Abbey, Powderham Castle, and the Roman baths and Georgian architecture in Bath. Member: Pride of Britain. John and Thérèse Boswell, Resident Proprietors.

Directions: From Honiton take the A30 (Exeter road) after approx. 1 mi., turn left at the signpost for Gittisham. This road leads to Combe House.

WOODHAYES
Whimple (near Exeter), Devon

For at least six months before my arrival I had been looking forward to visiting Woodhayes. For one thing, I had met John Allan, the proprietor, when he was with an excellent country house hotel in Scotland. Then on two separate occasions he had journeyed to America to take part in innkeepers' conferences. So, besides being a first-time visitor to a highly recommended small country house hotel, I had the opportunity to see John once again.

We all would like our friends to be happy and successful, and as soon as I pulled up to the front of the house and walked through the entrance, I knew that both happiness and success were John's. He looked exactly the same, a very cordial, smiling, English face, as soft-spoken and considerate as ever. He beamed with pleasure as I commented on how handsome the house looked and how pleasantly it was situated.

"Thank you very much," he replied. "I've tried to preserve the original Georgian architecture and at the same time provide accommodations that would be exactly what I would like to find."

This is a simple Georgian house (as opposed to an opulent Georgian manor). The exterior could be described as plain, but the interior has an understated elegance. There are two drawing rooms on the first floor, one with a fireplace. The six bedrooms are all centrally heated and have very comfortable and appropriate furnishings. As John pointed out, they aren't really authentic Georgian pieces because Georgian isn't that comfortable.

Over dinner that evening he explained that the house was probably built for a squire; perhaps built by the lord of the manor for one of his sons. "We made some changes to accommodate bathrooms and, in fact, when we came here, some of the rooms had been considerably altered from the original, so we put it back to rights again."

Food is given prime attention in the hotel, and John went to some trouble to explain that the local food in Devon is quite as good as one can get anywhere. Lamb and beef are from the region, as well as the fish, with both the north and south Devon coasts just a short distance away. Preparation and presentation have also been given much thought. "We try not to overwhelm our dining room guests," John said with a faint smile, "but to provide them with just enough to make them feel comfortable."

After dinner, over coffee in front of the low fire, we discussed the fact that it really was an excellent first- or last-night stop for anyone using Heathrow airport. It's about three-and-a-half hours on the Motorway via the M4.

It was really a pleasure to see John Allan and what he has done with Woodhayes. Since my visit, his letters indicate that his happiness and success are even more assured.

WOODHAYES, Whimple (nr. Exeter), Devon, England EX5 2TD. Tel: (0404) Whimple 822237. A 6-bedroom (private baths) elegant Georgian country house just a few miles from Exeter. Open every day; closed January. Dinner served to resident and non-resident guests. Most conveniently situated to enjoy Devon countryside and the north and south coasts. John Allan, Proprietor.

Directions: Whimple is a small village located to the north of A30. Look for signpost for Whimple a few miles west of Honiton.

BICKLEIGH COTTAGE GUEST HOUSE
Bickleigh (Near Tiverton), Devon

Stuart and Pauline Cochrane and I were strolling on the banks of the River Exe in the grassy garden in front of the Bickleigh Cottage Guest House. We were talking about what for me was a new discovery: Devonshire cream.

"For one thing, it is a very thick cream," explained Pauline. "It is not runny, it is thick and solid. The cream here is different from that which is served farther west, and one of the things that determines the quality of the cream is the type of cow.

"Our cream is scalded and left to settle. Then, it is skimmed off leaving the thin milk underneath. This 'skimming off' in large pans occurs several times." I soon learned there is nothing quite like thick, buttery Devonshire cream served on scones with fresh fruit jam.

At thatch-roofed Bickleigh Cottage, Stuart and Pauline are carrying on a family tradition that started almost fifty years ago. "The cottage dates back to 1640," explained Stuart. "It was originally two cottages used by the Bailiff of Bickleigh Castle. In recent years, we have made some improvements and additions, and now have a total of eleven rooms, two of which have private baths. The other rooms all share three bathrooms."

Incidentally, the painting on the cover of this edition is of Bickleigh Cottage.

As we paused to look up the river toward the historic bridges which are reputed to be haunted on Midsummer's Eve, I caught the quick flash of a kingfisher diving in the water.

Pauline laughed and said, "That's one of Stuart's principal competitors. You see, he catches the salmon we use for dinner right here in the river. We also specialize in roast meats, including lamb, beef, steak and kidney pie, and other traditional dishes. Our set menu at night includes home grown fruit and vegetables. We have our own vegetable garden. We always have pies and crumbles which our guests seem to enjoy very much." They offer a full English breakfast with cereals, fruit juice, bacon and eggs and sausages.

We stepped inside one of the two dining rooms whose windows overlook the pastoral scene of the river and the meadows beyond with the ever-present sheep. There was a little fireplace in

the low-ceilinged room, and lots of brass, copper, and pewter, with a rush matting on the floor. Its comfortable and homey aspect certainly would invite a visitor to stay on indefinitely.

BICKLEIGH COTTAGE GUEST HOUSE, Bickleigh (Nr. Tiverton), Devon. England EX16 8RJ. Tel: (08845) Bickleigh 230. An 11-room riverside country cottage. Most rooms have shared baths. Located between Tiverton and Exeter. Bed and breakfast offered from April 1 to Oct. 15; dinner served from May to Sept. Fishing, golf, riding, nearby. Many museums, castles, theatre, cinema, and other natural attractions within a short drive. Open April 1 to approx. Oct. 15. Mr. and Mrs. Stuart Cochrane, Proprietors.

Directions: Use Exit 27 from M5, follow A373 to Tiverton. At Tiverton, follow A396 (signposted: Exeter) for 4 mi. Bickleigh Cottage Guest House is on the left, adjoining the Trout Inn Car Park.

THE OXENHAM ARMS
South Zeal, Near Okehampton, Devon

The Oxenham Arms dates back to 1477, although the inn is believed to have been built in the latter part of the 12th century by lay monks. After the Dissolution of the monasteries by Henry VIII, it became the Dower House of the Burgoynes (a name familiar to American history buffs), whose heiress carried it to the Oxenham family, after whom the inn is named.

Oddly enough, this ancient and distinguished traditional inn has been owned for the past eight years by Pat and Jim Henry, who were formerly farmers in Louisiana! "It's been a wonderful experience for us," declared Pat. "We've had much fun being American innkeepers in Britain."

"Although a great many of our guests stop here for just one night on the way from London to Cornwall," said Jim, "many of them return for a longer stay on the trip back. We provide the home base from which our guests take advantage of the many attractions of this part of England's West Country. We're open the year around, and in winter guests come to relax, enjoy our food, and warm their feet in front of the log fires."

There are eleven bedrooms, seven having private baths. The white walls with half-timbers, heavy posts, and slanty floors reminded me of the Mermaid Inn in Rye. While looking in Room 9, which had been recently vacated, I happened to notice a copy of the European edition of *Country Inns and Back Roads.* Pat commented that the lady must have forgotten it. I autographed it and then left it there, in case she came back.

A very interesting part of the inn is the small lounge behind the bar where a monolith is set in the wall. The theory of archaeologists is that the lay monks built their house around this prehistoric stone, shaped by man five thousand years ago. "We've dug down quite deep, but have never reached its foundations," said Jim.

A large granite fireplace of great beauty dominating the main lounge, and a granite pillar supporting the beam in the dining room are two objects of great interest.

"We find that in this country, we have to be careful not to let our menu appear too sophisticated," said Jim. "We avoid French names, because people don't expect it when they come here; they're looking for simple dishes. Our specialties are Devon porkers—chops cooked in local farm cider; fresh local salmon and trout; roast Devon beef and lamb; and pheasant in season. We also added some New Orleans creole cooking which is an oddity here in Devon, but even the 'locals' enjoy it."

As Paul Henderson of the Gidleigh Park Hotel said when he recommended that I stop to see the Henrys at the Oxenham Arms, "It's not just because they are fellow-Americans, but because I think the Oxenham Arms is one of the most authentic, traditional, old-fashioned village inns I've ever visited."

THE OXENHAM ARMS, South Zeal, Nr. Okehampton, Devon, England EX20 2JT. Tel: (083-784) Sticklepath 244. An 11-room inn in a quiet Devon farm town 19 miles west of Exeter. Many cultural attractions nearby, including Roman ruins in Exeter, theatres, museums, and many castles and great houses. Breakfast, lunch, tea, and dinner served daily year-round. No recreational facilities on grounds, but almost everything else located within a short drive. Pat and Jim Henry, Proprietors.

Directions: Follow the A30 west to Okehampton. Two mi. past Whiddendown watch for signpost on right to South Zeal, A382.

GIDLEIGH PARK
Chagford, Devon

It was morning coffeetime on the terrace of the Gidleigh Park. The sun in addition to burning off the morning fog, was also warming up the temperature on this rather brisk autumn morning. Earlier, moving across the terraced lawns, replete with rosebeds, I had strolled down to the banks of the North Teign River where

some adventurous birds sallied forth from the beech forest into the magnificent fifteen-foot-tall rhodendrons.

Now, two guests from Buffalo, New York, joined me over coffee for a moment or two, and we talked about the joys of traveling in England and the prospects of playing tennis on a real grass court for the first time.

"We drove out from Heathrow Airport two days ago," one said. "I think it's so exciting to be in a place like this. It's our first stay in England. The country roads in Devon are such a contrast from the motorways and principal highway. I can hardly wait to take a walk on Dartmoor."

Anxious to get started on their day they gulped the last of their coffee, and I bade them farewell promising to see them at dinner in the evening. Meanwhile, Paul Henderson, the proprietor joined me.

"It's going to be a bully day," he said, with a twinkle in his eye. Paul and his wife, Kay, met at Purdue University in Indiana, and have lived in Europe for the past thirteen years. I knew that he was pulling my leg because with that remark about it being a "bully" day, he was playing the British innkeeper.

"We love it," he said, "it's an opportunity to put together all of the ideas that Kay and I have developed as a result of traveling so much.

"What we're aiming for here is to be one of the best five or ten country house hotels in England. We try to treat our guests as if they are in our own home. Kay supervises the cooking and occasionally prepares some of the main dishes herself. She is the first American woman to get a 'star' from Michelin." (There are only 35 Michelin-starred restaurants in Britain.)

The house is Tudor style and is set in thirty acres of gardens and forests in Dartmoor National Park. There are twelve bedrooms, each with its own bath.

In reply to my question about guest activities, Paul replied, "The walking around here is magnificent. There are literally hundreds of footpaths. You can walk off onto the moor which is wild and open country, or down through the valley along the riverside, or perhaps up to the pastures. There's really great exploring.

"The north and south Devon coasts are within an hour's drive, but Dartmoor is the real attraction. Within five miles of the hotel you can discover prehistoric megaliths that are similar—although smaller—to those at Stonehenge and Avebury. There are even Stone Age hut circles and villages, and several delightful 15th-century churches.

"As you might expect, there's good fishing and golf nearby, and also horseback riding or pony trekking on the moors."

Chagford, Devon, is a long way from Lafayette, Indiana, but it's very obvious that Kay and Paul Henderson have found in this extremely sequestered, almost idyllic corner of England, one of the best of all possible worlds.

GIDLEIGH PARK, Chagford, Devon, England PQ13844. Tel: (06473) Chagford 2367; 2225. A 12-room country house hotel on the edge of Dartmoor. About 4 hrs. west of London; ½ hr. from Exeter; and 1 hr. from Plymouth. Breakfast, tea, and dinner served daily year-round. Not particularly suitable for children. Tennis, fishing, riding, and golf available. Paul and Kay Henderson, Proprietors.

Directions: From the M5 take the A30 toward Okehampton. At Whiddon Down take A382 towards Chagford and follow signs to Chagford Square. Turn right on Mill St. at Lloyds Bank. After 200 yds., take right-hand fork. Follow lane downhill to the crossroads. Straight across, then 1½ mi. up to the end of the lane. (Is this the longest 1½ mi. in the world?)

SOUTH SANDS HOTEL
Salcombe, South Devon

Peter Hey raised his champagne glass high in the air, his action duplicated by the many guests of South Sands Hotel: "I give you the Prince and Princess of Wales and a new heir to the throne of England."

I daresay this scene was being repeated throughout Britain and the Commonwealth Countries many times on this particular evening, for it was the day that Princess Diana gave birth, and Peter and Elizabeth Hey, the innkeepers at the South Sands Hotel, like all of us, were caught up in the marvelous celebration.

This was my second visit with the Heys—the first being a few years ago at a small country hotel in Lancashire. We had a most entertaining evening at that time, and since then, they discovered the South Sands Hotel and have moved here lock, stock, and barrel, with a great many of their staff members as well.

"Oh, we will always love Lancashire" exclaimed Elizabeth. "However, as soon as Peter and I saw this hotel a couple of years ago we knew we just couldn't resist. I've always wanted to live on the water in this section of South Devon. It's beautiful, and there are no coaches and day-trippers with funny hats and electronic game centers and things like that. What we *do* have is a beautiful, safe, sandy beach, sailing, boating, wind-surfing, and a lovely, mild climate. Do you know that Indian summer is enjoyed through November here?"

The evening went on with much celebrating and music by three musicians, one of whom played the spoons and another who put on some of the bells worn by Morris dancers. Peter led the applause.

The next morning I wandered into the spotless kitchen where Peter was cooking breakfast and members of the staff were bustling around getting ready for the chores of the day. He served up scrambled eggs, hot smoked mackerel, and Lancashire pork sausage.

"Actually," he said, as we had a second cup of coffee in the dining room overlooking the harbor, "Salcombe is one of the few places where it is still possible to get away from it all. I guess we are a bit difficult to find, but when you get here it's worth it. We're a haven for yachtsmen, fishermen, families with children, and just sun-worshipers. In the spring the wildflowers must be seen to be believed. Yet, we're within easy reach of the shops and entertainment in Plymouth or Torbay. Dartmoor is only a short journey, and you can walk on the moors or have a day's pony-trekking."

It was wonderful to see Peter and Elizabeth Hey once again, and I was happy for them and the good life they are enjoying at the South Sands Hotel. Peter has told me in a subsequent letter that plans are afoot for an indoor swimming pool, which, of course, will make this lovely part of South Devon even more desirable during all seasons of the year.

SOUTH SANDS HOTEL, Salcombe, South Devon, England TQ8 8LL. Tel: (054-884) 2791. A 23-room (private baths) waterside hotel on the picturesque and inviting South Devon coast. Breakfast, lunch, and dinner served daily. Open all year. Most conveniently located to enjoy all of the year-round natural, cultural, and scenic attractions nearby. Exceptional beach. Children most welcome. Deep water moorings available with prior reservations. Peter and Elizabeth Hey, Hoteliers.

Directions: A38 is the road from Exeter to Cornwall. After Exeter, look for A381 and continue through Newton Abbot, Totnes, and Kingsbridge. Look for a sign out in the country for Salcombe. The river estuary will be on the left; continue straight on with a lot of multi-colored row houses on your left. You will come to a three-way junction, signposted Town Center, Bennett Road, and Sand Hills Road. Take the latter, which is the extreme right fork, and you'll drop down into the harbor. Continue through North Sands to South Sands with hotel on your left.

BUCKLAND-TOUT-SAINTS
Goveton, Devon

Take a moment to look at the map of western England and you will note that at Exeter the main roads to Cornwall split, going around Dartmoor National Park to the north and south. There are roads through Dartmoor, principally B3212; however, the average visitors to Britain want to get to Cornwall as quickly as possible, so they usually opt for A30 to Okehampton or A38 going south toward Plymouth. It is to this second road that I would like to call your attention.

This peninsula, extending down into the sea and including Dartmouth, Salcombe, and Kingsbridge, is known as South Hams, so-called for the excellent quality of the native porkers. It is one of the holiday areas of the well-informed Briton.

Kingsbridge is a key turn-off for the village of Goveton, which I'm sure is only on the most specific of maps. I have been very specific about directions, but I'm certain that before you reach Buckland-Tout-Saints, just outside of Goveton, you will be convinced that you are totally lost. The sunken lanes are so deep and the hedges on top are so high that they are almost double the height of the car.

Regardless of whatever problems you may encounter, this exceptional Queen Anne mansion, part of which dates back to the 12th century, will be worth any motoring anxieties.

The hotel derives its name from the French Norman family of Toutsants, who held this manor after the Norman conquest of

1066. Today, it is a country house hotel of great dignity and grace in a delightful and remote park.

Ashburton marble fireplaces, 17th- and 18th-century molded plaster ceilings, intricate oak foliage scrollwork and mahogany-and-gilt doors are just some of its characteristics. The main bedrooms are lofty and luxurious with tasteful furnishings and very choice views of the surrounding countryside. It has an excellent reputation for food.

The gardens are exceptional and feature, among other things, a species of New Zealand fern that demands subtropical conditions, shelter from the winds, and constant attention.

This particular part of South Devon is known to many servicemen from WW II, because it was used as a training area previous to the Normandy landings. Many have returned just to revisit the countryside.

Buckland-Tout-Saints was a complete surprise and a delight to me, and I think it provides, along with the South Sands Hotel in Salcombe, an excellent reason to stop off on the South Devon coast.

BUCKLAND-TOUT-SAINTS, Goveton, Kingsbridge, Devon, England TQ7 2DS. Tel: (0548) Kingsbridge 3055. Reservations in U.S.A.: 1-800-528-1234. A palatial 13-bedroom country house hotel (private baths) near the South Devon coast. Breakfast, lunch, and dinner served every day. Open all year except January. Most conveniently located to enjoy all of the recreational advantages of the south coast. Golf courses, swimming, water skiing, fishing, tennis, squash nearby. Owned and run the the Shephard Family.

Directions: From London take the M4 and M5 to Exeter; the A38 to Buckfastleigh. From there take A384 to Totnes, then A381 for Kingsbridge and look for hotel signs beyond Halwell. It is reached by a single passage road through the fields.

THE OLD RECTORY
Martinhoe, Parracombe, Barnstaple, North Devon

Tony Pring, the proprietor of the Old Rectory, and I were talking about the North Devon coast. "It's a most interesting area," he observed, "one that is quite neglected by American travelers. It is possible to wander around by car on the country roads and better still, to enjoy excursions on the footpaths. The vistas are magnificent, with great farmlands and occasional views of Bristol Bay."

Tony and I were sitting in the conservatory of the Old Rectory, a trim little Georgian house built in the early 1880s, adjacent to an 11th-century church. It is surrounded by well-maintained gardens and a small stream that crosses the garden in a series of waterfalls.

All of the bedrooms are rather elegantly furnished, and there are various combinations of twins and doubles, mostly with private bathrooms. The atmosphere is pleasant and relaxing with nice views of the countryside.

The dining room has some lovely antiques, and Tony assures me that local fresh vegetables, meat, fish, eggs, and cream help to provide dishes such as stuffed and baked rainbow trout, kidneys in sherry sauce, roast lamb with rosemary stuffing, and fresh fruit pies. Picnic lunches are available, if requested the previous evening.

Although rates in the Index are for bed and breakfast, Tony assures me that most of the guests also take the evening meal.

THE OLD RECTORY, Martinhoe, Parracombe, Barnstaple, North Devon, England. Tel: (059 83) Parracombe 368. An 11-bedroom (7 with private baths) hotel on the attractive North Devon coast. Breakfast included in tariff; dinner available. Open from April until the end of October. Conveniently situated to enjoy all of the Devon cultural, scenic, and recreational attractions nearby, including Exmoor National Park. Tony and Elizabeth Pring, Proprietors.

Directions: Turn north off A39 at Martinhoe Cross (look for the hotel signpost); go across Martinhoe Common for about 1½ mi. to the village sign. The entrance to The Old Rectory is immediately on your right.

THE RISING SUN HOTEL
Lynmouth, North Devon *(See illustration on Page 8)*

On my arrival at Lynmouth and the Rising Sun, I immediately sensed a feeling of *deja vu.* Where had I seen the thatched roof, climbing roses, whitewashed walls, and the ascending path that leads upward from the quay?

The Sunday afternoon journey from Glastonbury eventually had found me on the A39 through Minehead, then Porlock, where I had a choice of roads to Lynmouth. One is a toll road and, remembering some earlier advice, I elected to pay the few pence and was glad I had, because it afforded a panoramic view of the Bristol Channel with Wales on the other side. This road rejoins the A39 at the top of the cliffs, and it's only a few more miles to Lynmouth.

The many buildings of the Rising Sun—one of which, by the way, Shelley is supposed to have stayed in—enjoy a splendid view of the ever-changing harbor. At the time of my arrival the tide was out and the sailboats and working boats were on their sides on the mud flats.

Upon checking in I was immediately shown around by one of the proprietors, a very personable gentleman named Mr. Wade. Because the building is quite ancient, the hallways and staircases are rather narrow and twisty, and some of the rooms might be described as "snug." Most have views of the harbor.

One of the surprises is a very pleasant, protected garden, carefully designed and manicured, with many types of blooms and a view of the Bristol Channel. During this tour I learned that the novel *Lorna Doone* was somewhat inspired by this inn.

That evening in the low-ceilinged dining room I, appropriately enough, had excellent lamb chops, Devon being well known throughout England for its lamb. The room had a most congenial atmosphere, and I struck up a conversation with a couple from Tampa, Florida, who were enjoying their stay very much.

In the morning, the little harbor was again filled up with water almost to the top of the wall, and the boats were bobbing merrily on the waves. The Devon cliffs and the town itself (which reminds me of Portofino, Italy) is very, very pleasant and the prospect of walking on the tops of the cliffs was most inviting. I learned that it is quite crowded in July, August, and September, so plan to visit during other months.

It was only as I was leaving that I remembered where I had previously seen the view of the Rising Sun. Jan Lindstrom had painted this scene from her mind's eye as a cover for a book I had written about eight years ago. Later on when I showed her the postcards with the view of the hotel, we both marveled, perhaps it was *deja vu* for her as well!

THE RISING SUN HOTEL, Lynmouth, Devon, England EX35 6EQ. Tel: (05985) Lynton 3223. A 16-bedroom (shared baths) traditional inn overlooking the Lynmouth Harbor in North Devon. Breakfast, lunch, and dinner served daily. Open all year. Most conveniently situated to explore and enjoy the wonderful walks, the Exmoor National Park, and the "Lorna Doone" country. Sailing, fishing, horseriding, and golf nearby. D.H. Wade and H.F. Jeune, Joint Proprietors.

Directions: A39 is the main road traversing North Devon, occasionally providing wonderful glimpses of the Bristol Channel and Wales. Outside of Porlock, take the Toll Road, which rejoins A39 and continues on to Lynmouth and Lynton. Hotel is on the harbor.

THE WOODFORD BRIDGE HOTEL
Milton Damerel, Devon

The North American visitor to Britain should always bear in mind the fact that distances in the United Kingdon are much less than they are in many other parts of the world. A case in point is the location of the Woodford Bridge Hotel on one of the roads to Cornwall in North Devon, which not only is less than a day's drive from London, but also has the advantage of being within a short distance of both Dartmoor and Exmoor. For those who like the seaside, there are excellent surfing and bathing beaches nearby, as well as secluded rocky coves where one can explore rock pools left by the retreating tide.

The hotel is an interesting mix of the old and new, the contemporary and the classic. The main building is a beautiful, thatched, whitewashed, 15th-century building where several of the rooms have brass bedsteads and antique furniture. The country atmosphere is enhanced with many nature and bird prints and paintings, and every bedroom has arrangements of fresh flowers, most of which are gathered in the hotel garden.

In addition to conventional accommodations, the hotel also

has luxury cottage suites on a south-facing hillside running down to a lake.

As if this wasn't enough, also on the grounds there is an indoor heated swimming pool, a sauna and solarium, two squash courts, a skittle alley, and an all-weather tennis court. So even if the weather should be inclement, recreation abounds. There is also good fishing on the River Torridge, which flows through the hotel grounds, where many quiet walks may be enjoyed.

Very close to the hotel are the remains of a large Roman fort and an ancient Roman vineyard. Proprietor Roger Vincent states, "There has most probably been an inn on the present site of the hotel ever since men required shelter and sustenance between the small market town of Holsworthy and the port of Bideford. There is a tradition of innkeeping here."

I'll add that if the size and character of the menu is any indication, there'll be a hotel here for many years to come.

WOODFORD BRIDGE HOTEL, Milton Damerel, Devon, England EX22 7LL. Tel: (040 926) 481. A 16-bedroom (some shared baths) luxurious country house hotel near the Devon-Cornwall border, a few miles south of the North Devon coast. Also holiday cottages. Breakfast, lunch, and dinner served daily. Open all year. Fishing, bird watching, beachcombing, enclosed swimming pool, sauna, all-weather tennis courts, and squash court. Well located to enjoy both of the Devon coasts, as well as excursions into Cornwall. Member Romantik Hotels. Roger and Diana Vincent, Proprietors/ Managers.

Directions: Woodford Bridge is on the A388 between Bideford and Holsworthy.

LESCEAVE CLIFF HOTEL
Praa Sands, Near Penzance, Cornwall

The mid-October sun on the south Cornish coast had an almost July quality as I drove along the A394 between Helston and Penzance, where there are occasional glimpses of the sea to the south. A sign for the Lesceave Cliff Hotel pointed down a narrow dirt road which obviously led to the sea. Hoping for a more panoramic view, I swung into it and within a very short time found myself high on a cliff with a breathtaking view of the coastline and the sea.

Continuing on, about halfway farther up the rather steep hill above the beach was a modern white building with green trim and terraced gardens—this was the Lesceave Cliff Hotel. Walking up the steps through the front door, I rang the bell at the front desk and a very pleasant woman answered my call.

When I remarked that it was unusual for such a large area of sea, cliff, and sand to remain unspoiled, she told me that the founders of the hotel purchased the surrounding cliffs and approaches, and eventually bequeathed them to the National Trust.

My informant, warming to her task, explained that the location was ideal for a holiday in Cornwall, and she made a special point of saying that the rates were rather attractive during the low season, as is the case with most British country hotels.

Immediately below the hotel is a very inviting sandy beach, "ideal for children," because, as she explained, a wide strip of sand remains uncovered even at high tide. There is also a swimming pool.

Most of the bedrooms, as well as the lounge and dining room, face due south and enjoy a view of Mount's Bay, extending from the Lizard Peninsula in the east, to Mousehole in the west.

This hotel is not Olde England with chintz curtains and photographs of the Queen Mother; the design, decor, and colors are all lively and contemporary. For someone who enjoys long uninterrupted summertime walks on sandy beaches, or following the paths that lead up over the cliffs into the rolling fields, this looks like fun. I imagine it's a pretty lively place in high season, and extremely quiet the rest of the year.

LESCEAVE CLIFF HOTEL, Praa Sands (Nr. Penzance), Cornwall, England TR 20 9TX. Tel: (073 676) Germoe 2325. A 26-room seaside hotel with a spectacular view of the South Cornwall coast (13 rooms with private baths/showers). Breakfast, bar snacks, tea, and dinner served to non-residents. Open year-round. Beautiful sandy beach. Outdoor recreation and excursions in abundance nearby.

Directions: Take M5 to Exeter; A30 to Penzance; A394 to Ashton Village and turn left at Hendra Lane at hotel sign.

RIVERSIDE GUEST HOUSE
Helford, Helston, Cornwall

As much as I hate to mix metaphors, I must say that the hamlet (it isn't even a village) of Helford has a definite *Brigadoon* quality. Even after visiting Riverside, meeting Heather Crosbie, and partaking of one of George Perry-Smith's superlative dinners, I wondered if it all really happened or was I under the enchanting spell of Cornwall.

At the outset, let me explain that Helford is not all that easy to find. I'm afraid that my directions somewhat over-simplify the situation. Helford is at the top part of the Lizard Peninsula, which has become famous for its outstanding natural beauty. Helford is on the south side of the Helford River over which I found no bridges. Look on the map and you'll see what I mean. Autos are not allowed within the village in high season.

Whatever confusion may arise as a result of a search for Riverside, I can assure the hesitant traveler it is well worth the trouble. It sits on a very narrow lane bordering the river and is partially hidden behind a green hedge. The view is of a very small harbor.

There are five lodging rooms, each with its own bath. There are fresh flowers, lots of books, and a residents' sitting room which allows houseguests to get acquainted.

The five lodging rooms are usually fully booked during the high season (June-September). Thus, it is for the evening meal that most travelers drive some distance out of their way.

The daily menu, which is handwritten and changes every day is for a table d'hote dinner with a starter, a main course, and dessert. Among the main dishes are chicken roasted with tarragon and finished with cream and brandy; shoulder of lamb cooked slowly with wine, herbs, and vegetables; and turbot à l'espagnole and moussaka add an international touch. The ice creams are home-

made, and the Danish apple cake that I tasted was dreamy, as was the lemon cheesecake.

Everywhere I traveled in Britain, I heard compliments from other hoteliers and chefs about George Perry-Smith's cuisine. He's a very modest, private individual who left a thriving restaurant of his own in Bath to come to the Cornish countryside. He enjoys the satisfactions of cooking for fewer people and leading a more quiet life.

A word of caution: As I have hinted above, Riverside is fully booked during the summer and early fall. Dinner reservations are imperative.

Through the courtesy of the publishers of *This England,* I am enclosing a short poem by Dudley F. Walker. I think it catches the spirit of Helford and Riverside quite admirably.

HELFORD CREEK

If it is peace you seek
In England at its best,
Come you to Helford Creek
In Cornwall's furthest west.

Here when the tide flows in
From Helford's river wide,
White swans that glide serene
Come to us on the tide.

The twisting narrow lanes
That gently lead you here,
Ensure the peace one gains
For those who hold peace dear.

Stand you atop the creek,
The wooden bridge has spanned
And you will find the quiet
You seek in England's land.

RIVERSIDE, Helford, Helston, Cornwall, England. Tel: (03263) Manaccan 443. A restaurant with 5 lodging rooms located in a hidden village on the Lizard Peninsula in Cornwall. Dinner served to travelers. Closed mid-Nov. to early Mar. No credit cards. George Perry-Smith and Heather Crosbie, Partners.

Directions: From Plymouth follow the A38 to Liskeard, St. Austell, and Truro. From Truro follow A3083 to Helston. Turn left for St. Keverne on 3293 about 4½ miles. Turn left for Helford. Riverside is on the left just beyond the public car park on the right. Good luck and don't be afraid to ask directions. The natives are very friendly.

The West Country could well be called a "Kingdom of Legends." Not only does it hold many of the great national legends of Britain that are a part of any national heritage—the Arthurian Legends, the search for the Holy Grail, and the Glastonbury stories, but it is full of stories of giants and saints, supernatural happenings, ghostly ships, holy places, wreckers and smugglers, pixies and witches, in such a profusion as to give the whole of the area a touch of magic.

THE OLD SCHOOLHOUSE
Veryan, Near Truro, Cornwall

Let's begin this story by explaining that the Old Schoolhouse, which is owned by Mr. and Mrs. J.W. Baseley, is a private house which has a twin-bedded apartment with a full kitchen for rent on a weekly basis. I've included the telephone number, but please arrange for accommodations in advance by letter.

Now, for the story.

I had discovered, with some chagrin, that my portable radio was broken. St. Mawes was behind me, and when I saw the sign for the village of Veryan, I turned off the main road hoping to find a repair shop. Veryan proved to be a tiny hamlet with a few snug homes tucked behind their gardens. Coming toward me was a hearty-looking man wearing a brown corduroy coat, smoking a pipe, and accompanying a dog on a brisk mid-morning walk. When I stopped to inquire about an electronics shop, he smiled and said, "Well, we have no such thing here, but let me take a look at it."

It took him about five seconds to decide, "I can do that in my little workshop. Just drive around the corner to my garage and we'll see what we can do."

While he worked on my radio, I learned that he was John Baseley, formerly a Midlands businessman, who had, with his wife, moved out to Cornwall a few years ago to open up a tea shop.

Well, one thing led to another, and after deftly connecting the radio's errant wires, he invited me inside to meet his wife Katie, and to have a cup of tea. Before I knew it, I was seated in a very comfortable little parlor talking about Cornwall creamed teas and the joys of Cornwall in general, I soon discovered that John and Katie had some limited accommodations available at The Old Schoolhouse.

"Even though we're not listed, we have people who come to us every year," said Katie, handing me another cup of tea. "This is one of the most beautiful parts of Britain. We're just a mile from the water in two directions. Our little village with its thatched roofs and stone houses and public footpaths is just perfect for a quiet holiday."

They assured me that if any of our readers gave them a ring and they were booked, they would try to refer them to other similar places in the area. "We would prefer to have people contact us by mail, well before the start of the season," said John.

The village of Veryan is distinguished by having four ancient, completely round buildings, two of them at each end of the village. In olden times, these were supposed to protect the villagers from evil spirits who could not live in a round house because there are no corners where they could hide. A cross on the top of each building was supposed to keep them away from the village altogether.

If any of our readers stop at the Old Schoolhouse, I would be most grateful if they would extend my warmest greeting to Mr. and Mrs. Baseley.

THE OLD SCHOOLHOUSE, Veryan, Nr. Truro, Cornwall, England. Tel: (087-250) 1440. A vintage Cornish thatched private house, having for let a twin-bedded apartment annex with a full kitchen. Located in the Roseland peninsula just a few miles from St. Mawes. Please arrange for accommodations in advance by letter. Mr. and Mrs. J.W. Baseley, Proprietors.

Directions: A few miles east of A3078, Veryan is on the St. Mawes-Tregory road.

HOTEL TRESANTON
St. Mawes, Cornwall

I'm indebted to a fellow-North American from the University of Minnesota for at least a part of my warm feeling towards the town of St. Mawes.

We met on the terrace of the Hotel Tresanton, after the professor had been out for his morning jog, and I had taken a pleasant stroll through the gardens of the hotel and down into the still-sleeping village.

"I've taken vacations and sabbaticals in Britain for many years," he said, "and St. Mawes is my favorite." I noticed that he pronounced the name of the village in the traditional British manner: "Sint Mawz."

We sat down for a moment to quietly enjoy the sight of a group of sailboats playing tag in the harbor. He put his finger to his lips as a seagull landed on a rock a few yards away and studied us contemplatively. The fields and hills across the harbor reminded me very much of the view over Lake Bras d' Or in Baddeck, Nova Scotia.

"October and April are good months to be here," he pointed out. "That's because this is really amost a subtropical climate. I suppose you've noticed some of the more exotic flowers and bushes. This section of Cornwall is sometimes called 'Britain's Riviera.'

"Have you had a chance to visit the castle yet? It was originally built in 1540 to protect the entrance to Falmouth Harbor. In those days they were subject to raids by the French.

"Perhaps you saw the British television series 'Poldark'?" I responded enthusiastically that I had enjoyed it very much. "Well, the scenes where Poldark is supposed to have been imprisoned in France were filmed in the little castle. It's open on Sundays and is well worth the visit if you've got time.

"Another reason that I like it here is because of this hotel," he said. "It's rather luxurious, but at the same time the atmosphere and staff are very friendly. It has been cleverly designed so that all of the bedrooms have a view of the harbor and gardens." My bedroom had a very stylish air about it, as did the dining rooms, lounges, and drawing rooms at the Hotel Tresanton.

Except for my new friend, the other guests were all Britons, and I had a pleasant encounter with four who were a mixture of Scottish and English. They were on a long weekend holiday and after staying up talking quite late at night, we met for breakfast the next day. Being Britons, they were all entranced by the great number and variety of flowers that graced the terraces and walks of the hotel.

The Hotel Tresanton is in the luxury class. There are many additional services provided, including car parking. The atmosphere is most pleasant and the menu is in both French and English.

HOTEL TRESANTON, St. Mawes, Cornwall, England TR2 5DR. Tel: (03266) St. Mawes 544. USA: 1-800-323-3602.

[Since the first printing of this edition of this book, the above inn has had a change in ownership (one of the built-in dangers of guidebook writing). In all but the most exceptional circumstances, it is my policy not to continue to list an accommodation that has changed hands unless I have had the opportunity to meet the owners/managers personally and to ascertain the prevailing conditions and policies.

Therefore, I am unable to recommend this hotel at this time; however, should you decide to give it a try, I would appreciate any comments you might have about your stay.]

THE LOBSTER POT
Mousehole, Cornwall

The very first time I stopped to ask for directions to Mousehole, a good-natured Cornishman set me straight as to the correct pronunciation: "It is not Mouse-hole," he said, repeating my original pronunciation, "it is Mao-zil." I practiced saying "Mao-zil" assiduously for several miles as I passed through the town of Penzance on Route 3315. Penzance, by the way, is the very one featured by Gilbert and Sullivan, and it is a most pleasant town located on a broad bay with a good view of St. Michael's Mount, a castle on an island in the bay.

Mousehole is somewhat similar to Camden, Maine, having much the same aspect with all types of watercraft in the harbor and also behind the quay. Signs have many references to smuggling and pirates, and several restaurants and pubs derive their names from these Cornish traditions.

The Lobster Pot is a very attractive inn overlooking the quay and sheltered by the sea wall. Major John Kelly has been its proprietor for over thirty-five years and has built the place up from almost nothing. The guest lounges, restaurant, and tiny little bar all have completely enchanting views of the harbor. I noticed many, many books on the shelves, and some loose-leaf folders with quite a number of brochures for other hotels in Great Britain. There were also several water colors of St. Michael's Mount just up the coast, three miles off Penzance. In both the public and lodging rooms, there were a great many flowers.

The bedrooms all appeared to be quite comfortable, and most have their own private bath. Prices vary considerably, depending upon the location of the rooms.

Among the culinary treats at the Lobster Pot are shellfish, particularly lobster and crawfish. They also have the famous Helford oysters which are available all year-round.

Dylan Thomas has an interesting association with the Lobster Pot and Major Kelly was kind enough to send me a copy of a letter written by Thomas in July, 1937 which, among other things, mentions that he had been married just a few days earlier in the Penzance registry office. Evidently, The Lobster Pot was a honeymoon haven for this well-known poet.

As I was leaving, I saw the attendant for the town car-park leaning on the windowsill of his little booth watching the youngsters in kyaks skimming about in the harbor. "Ever been in one of those?" I asked. He replied, "No, and I ain't bloody likely to be in one either."

THE LOBSTER POT, Mousehole, Cornwall, England. Tel: (073 673) Mousehole 251. A 24-room waterside inn (21 with private bath) in one of Cornwall's most fetching small villages about 3 mi. from Penzance. Just short drives to Land's End, the Minack Theatre, and all of the other attractions on both the south and north Cornish coasts. Shark and sea fishing available. Golf about ten miles away, as well as tennis, squash, and horseback riding. Breakfast, lunch, tea, and dinner served daily. Open from mid-March to the end of Dec. No credit cards. Major John Kelly, Proprietor.

Directions: Mousehole (Mao-zil) is about 5 hrs. driving time from London. Use either the M4 or the M5, and then either A38 via Plymouth or A30 via Bodwin. Follow Rte. 3315 from Penzance.

LANCASHIRE
County of Lancashire

Lancashire is one of the most diversified areas in England. Along the coast are invigorating holiday resorts, such as Blackpool and Morecambe. It is a region of vast and beautiful estuaries, old-world villages, and wide recreational areas.

A great deal of my interest was centered in the fell country to the northeast of Preston, near the town of Clitheroe.

This area is well outlined in the Tour Number 83 in the AA Touring Guide To Britain.

(1) HARROP FOLD FARM, Clitheroe, Lancashire, 179
(2) PARROCK HEAD FARM, Slaidburn, Lancashire, 180
(3) INN AT WHITEWELL, Clitheroe, Lancashire, 183
(4) RIVER HOUSE, Skippool Creek, Lancashire, 184

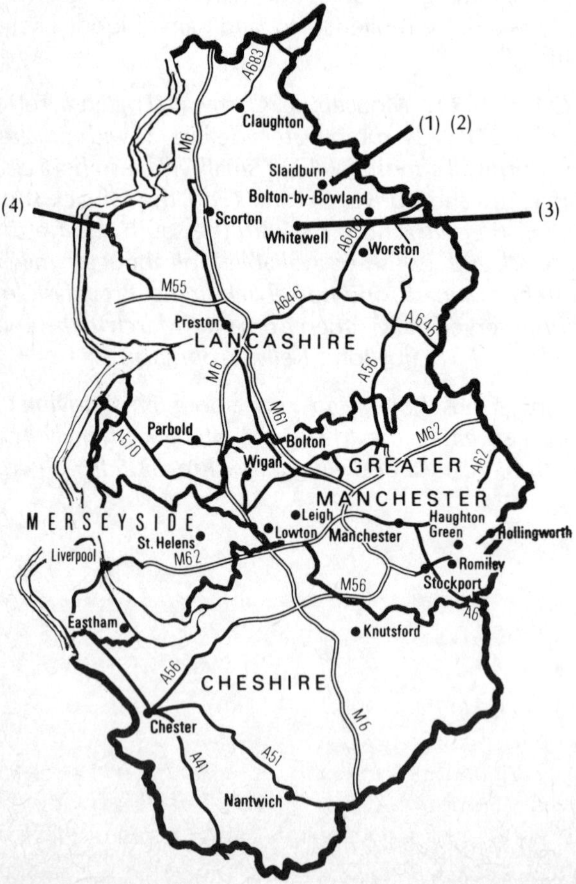

HARROP FOLD FARM GUEST HOUSE
Bolton-by-Bowland, Clitheroe, Lancashire

Let me share a portion of a letter I recently received from Victoria Wood, who, with her husband Peter and their two sons, is the proprietor of Harrop Fold Guest House.

"Harrop looks really lovely now—everything is at its best. The hawthorne blossoms are magnificent, weighing the branches down on the trees. Swallows and swifts are darting to and fro catching flies for their young. The hedgerows and fields are full of wild flowers, their growth has been encouraged by the wet spring, and now the warmth. Farming-wise we are waiting for the grass to thicken in leaf and in about another ten days Daniel will be ready to reap. Before then he will start to clip the sheep—all 200 of them! We have had a good lambing time in spite of the weather, due largely to Daniel's expert shepherding—what a difference it has made to Peter to have him at home.

"The garden is looking super too—Andrew's patient care is paying dividends. His attentions have extended to keeping the common well under control (at great expense, I may add). Harrop has become home for a second-hand Montfield tractor that makes light work of grass cutting. It's a good thing he has cut time on one job as he now bakes all of our bread, which is quite a mammoth task and it is so good. He has finally settled on a granary recipe and is swapping bread-rising stories with all the whole-food enthusiasts."

Harrop Fold Farm is not only a guest house, but obviously a working farm, and Daniel Wood, who is also a Cordon Bleu chef, divides his time between the fields and the kitchen.

The farmhouse accommodations are rustic-elegant. They all have private bathrooms, very comfortable, firm mattresses, and such fetching names as Meadow Suite, Forget-me-not, and Poppy Field.

The old farmhouse lounge is comfortable and easy to relax in with the original oak beams and meat hooks and a mellow pine cupboard with brasses and interesting pieces. A log fire burns merrily in the evenings in the stone fireplace.

If all this sounds rather intriguing, may I suggest you write to Victoria Wood for a brochure about the farm. I'm certain you'll find it a most interesting and instructive literary experience.

HARROP FOLD FARM GUEST HOUSE, Bolton-by-Bowland, Clitheroe, Lancashire, England, BB7 4PJ. Tel: (02007) 600. A 5-bedroom (all have private baths) guest house in the lovely farming country of Lancashire. Open all year. Breakfast and evening meal (on request) served. Conveniently located to enjoy excursions into the Lancashire and Yorkshire Dales. Private trout and salmon fishing on the Hadden and Ribble rivers. Peter and Victoria Wood, Proprietors.

Directions: Clitheroe, which is reached by taking Exit 31 from the M6 and continuing on A59, is the key to locating Harrop Fold. When you get to Clitheroe, telephone the farm for directions into the rural countryside.

PARROCK HEAD FARM
Slaidburn, Clitheroe, Lancashire

The coffee was hot and the cream was thick. Pat and Richard Holt, the proprietors of this guest house, and I were enjoying the marvelous euphoria that follows a satisfying dinner. It was quite natural for the conversation to turn to regional British cooking. Richard was unstinting in his praise of Pat's cooking, "She makes the best roast beef and Yorkshire pudding I've ever had, and I'll put her Lancashire hot pot up against anybody's! Here on the farm we serve lots of local roast lamb with mint sauce, and also cheese and onion pie."

They were full of enthusiasm over what fun it is to keep a guest house and how they meet people from all over the world. "We try to keep our farm as natural as possible," explained Pat, passing me another helping of a tasty tart. "My son runs this as a farm, and almost everything we have on the table is raised right here on the property. I love to cook and this makes it all the more fun. We keep our kitchen door open to the guests and many of them come out to

visit with me while I'm mashing the potatoes or basting the lamb."

Parrock Head Farm is a guest house offering dinner as well as bed and breakfast. The guest lounge has a whole wall of books, a table with many maps and suggestions about all the things to be enjoyed in this part of Lancashire and nearby Yorkshire.

There are several combinations of suites and bedrooms all with private baths.

Even as we talked, the sun went down behind the fells and the wonderful countryside was bathed in a golden light.

During the recent Christmas season I was delighted to receive a beautiful full-color Lancashire Life Calendar from Pat and Richard. Among the photographs of the Lancashire Fells area there was one of a farm in the Trough of Bowland, which is not far from Parrock Head. Others brought back memories of the happy hours I spent getting acquainted with Pat and Richard, and the good time that every guest can expect at this snug guest house.

PARROCK HEAD FARM, Slaidburn (Nr. Clitheroe), Lancashire, England BB7 3AH. Tel: (02006) Slaidburn 614. A 7-room guest house 8 mi. from Clitheroe and about 1 mi. from Slaidburn, located in the Bowland Fells area. Breakfast, lunch, and dinner served to house-guests. Open all year except Christmas. Conveniently situated for walking and driving trips in the Lancashire countryside. Located just 30 mi. from the coastline, 35 mi. from the Lake District, and 35 mi. from the Yorkshire Dales. Credit cards not accepted. Patricia Holt, Proprietress.

Directions: Leave motorway M6 at Junction 31. Follow A59 to Clitheroe, 15 mi. Turn left at Clitheroe roundabout to B6478. Continue to Waddington, Newton, and Slaidburn. Turn left at Slaidburn and after 1 mi., Parrock Head Farm is on the left-hand side and plainly marked.

A LANCASHIRE IDYLL

Some people take their dogs for a walk; I take my tape recorder. Such was the case in late May when I rose early and went for a walk in the Lancashire countryside. Here are a few of my impressions as I dictated them into my recorder:

"Beautiful stone walls on each side of the road leading past ancient farmhouses . . . Rippling waters of the brook mingling with the sound of early morning crows and the animals at the watering troughs . . . Milk already out on the platform waiting for

the pickup . . . Trees getting well armed for their full leaf . . . The sheep ever placid, ever grazing, to be seen in all directions, and always turning to watch me as I pass by. I think they can hear me talking to the tape recorder. Here's a public footpath . . . continuing down into the meadow and over the rise into the forest . . . More black-faced sheep with lambs still at the nursing stage, and as the mothers move away from me their young charges plainly show their annoyance.

In front of me a rabbit disappears into the underbrush . . . down in the meadow, white birds dot the lush green grass . . . Now, near the crest of the hill, a bench with a small medallion that says simply: "Elizabeth, 1953." This is the simple country way of recognizing the Queen's coronation . . . A wooden bench has been placed on a concrete slab and is ideal for sitting and looking over the fells and the peaceful countryside, down into the village of Slaidburn.

. . . Now along the side of the road, a huge oak whose center section has been torn away by the elements—its two side branches still remain, looking for all the world like some gigantic figure with its arms raised imploringly to heaven . . .

Here, a herd of cows moving toward the barn . . . overhead, two birds shrilly signal to each other . . . in the middle distance, a sheepdog running through the fields . . .

Reluctantly turning back to the village . . . my presence is being announced by feathery watchers calling back and forth . . .

different calls and different greetings to the morning . . .

Two or three errant sheep on the road finding grass on the outside of the fence sweeter than on the inside . . . there are always a few who seem to find their way out of the enclosures. Across the valley, a man walking in the field approaching a herd of sheep . . . he seems to be searching for something, I know not what.

Most of all, it is a refreshingly complete natural quietness, with the pastoral accompaniment of the sounds of nature wafting up from the valley—the occasional baa-ing of the sheep and the moo of the cattle. These are the sounds that inspired the poets of the English countryside . . .

Returning to town on the quiet road . . . the small garden area overlooking the Ribble River . . . a wonderful view of its three arches. On one of the benches, a small plaque saying, "Presented by the Ribble Valley Borough Counsel To Slaidburn, the Best Decorated Village in the Queen's Silver Jubilee Year, 1977."

THE INN AT WHITEWELL
Forest of Bowland, Clitheroe, Lancashire

"Typically English"—how blithely we Americans use that term, and yet as I went back over my notes on the visit to the Inn at Whitewell those two words kept coming to the front of my mind. It is a real country-cum-village hotel in a section of England that really has not yet been discovered by the North American traveler. I think this inn is difficult to find, and if it were not for the good offices of Pat and Richard Holt at Parrock Head Farm in nearby Slaidburn, I never would have discovered it at all.

As soon as I saw the Inn at Whitewell one beautiful Saturday morning, I knew it would be a special place. It was indeed a rather bustling hotel, as evidenced by the numbers of English couples who were making use of the reception room and lounge on a weekend holiday. Meanwhile, more guests were coming in for that great English tradition, morning coffee, which has become almost as important as afternoon tea.

I was given a very courteous tour of all of the bedrooms, many of which look out over the Hodder river. The view is of the valley with the fells on each side. The large dining room has a big bow window that also overlooks the river. I was amused to see some interesting and colorful prints by Thomas Rowlandson.

The evening meal has four courses, including duckling, lamb, pork, and halibut as the main dishes.

Mention should be made of the parish church of Saint

Michael, immediately adjacent, with a history dating back many centuries. Walking through the graveyard and into the church itself reminded me that my good friend, Rev. Robert Whitman in Lenox, Massachusetts, a fellow Anglophile, would indeed find it interesting and worthwhile. At the back of the church there was a reproduction of the list of disbursements made for the repair of the chapel in the year 1666, which came to 37 pounds 2 pence. I dropped a donation in the milk churn, which had been placed at the gate of the church; the coins bounced around on the bottom with a hollow, tinny sound.

Visit Whitewell and stay overnight at the inn, or at least enjoy a bar lunch or dinner. I promise you'll never forget it.

THE INN AT WHITEWELL, Forest of Bowland, Clitheroe, Lancashire, England BB7 3AT. Tel: (02008) Dunsop Bridge 222. A 10-bedroom (6 have private baths) traditional country inn situated in a most pleasant hamlet in the valley of the Hodder River in rural Lancashire. Breakfast, lunch, and dinner served. Open all year. Most conveniently located for pleasant walks or drives into the Lancashire and nearby Yorkshire countryside. Richard Bowman, Innkeeper.

Directions: The key once again is the town of Clitheroe, which is on A59 between Preston and Skipton. Once in Clitheroe, telephone the inn for further directions.

THE RIVER HOUSE
Skippool Creek, Thornton-le-Fylde, Lancashire

There is so much to write about concerning the River House, that I wonder just where to begin. It's situated on the banks of the River Wyre estuary, which is most attractive. The furnishings and decorations in the house deserve more than a passing mention. The same is certainly true for the unusual menu. Furthermore, there are a few pieces of very small adult furniture actually used by General Tom Thumb, who was one of P.T. Barnum's prime attractions during the 19th century.

Proprietor Bill Scott, who is also a man of opinions and ideas, speaks of the River House food as being the principal reason for guests to make a visit. "We have been included in many of the U.K. country house hotel guides, as well as the Master Chef's Guide. Both Carole and I are very proud of our growing reputation."

Whilst I was enjoying an extremely gratifying bar lunch at this

Victorian house, built in 1830 as a gentleman farmer's residence, Bill explained some of his philosophy of cuisine:

"We cook each meal individually and all food is freshly cooked from top-quality produce. Incidentally, all of our meals must be booked in advance.

"Our à la carte menu includes trout cooked with port wine, almonds, and cream, Dover sole, and other local seafood. We also serve suckling pig, roast breast of chicken, duckling in orange sauce, guinea fowl with apricots and almonds, veal schnitzel, partridge, grouse, pheasant, and venison.

"We also have a few oriental dishes, including fish Mikado and salmon Angelique. Both of these are cooked in a little pot. The Mikado is monk fish with cream, herbs, and saki. We may well be the only non-Japanese restaurant in the country serving Japanese food."

The bedrooms are very comfortable in a natural, relaxed way. I mentioned this to Bill during our little tour, and he responded, "We were once described in *Cosmopolitan* as being "shabbily comfortable. I took that as a compliment."

The dining room has a most attractive view of the River Wyre. The view is out over the lawn and the rose garden to the boats moored at the quaint little wooden jetties that go out from the road over the salt marsh to the mud bank. This is a tidal scene that changes almost every fifteen minutes.

There is much more to say about the River House, but Bill was particularly adamant about my being certain to feature their food as the real attraction. I just don't have space to explain the General Tom Thumb furniture, do I?

THE RIVER HOUSE, Skippool Creek, Thornton-le-Fylde, Lancashire, England FY5 5LF: Tel: (0253) Poulton-le-Fylde 883497. A 4-bedroom waterside hotel just off the M6, south of Lancaster and east of Blackpool. Breakfast, lunch, and dinner served daily except for two-week staff holiday (please inquire). Pleasant amenities, including television, room telephones, and electric blankets. Fishing, golf, and boat hire nearby. Bill and Carole Scott, Proprietors.

Directions: From M6 follow M55 to Exit 3; go north on A585, following signs for Fleetwood through three traffic lights to big roundabout, following sign to Little Thornton. On leaving roundabout, immediately follow sign to Skippool Creek (this is a very small road to the right, immediately before the Buccaneer Pub). This leads down to the River Wyre estuary. Look for a small sign pointing to the River House.

CUMBRIA
The County of Cumbria

Cumbria, which includes all of the English Lake District, is one of the most sought-after tourist objectives in the U.K. The three tours outlined in the AA Touring Guide To Britain gently direct the on-the-scene motorist or the armchair traveler through the fells and passes, although some of the roads are narrow and quite steep. The extensive description of each community and the handsome full-color photography is almost the next best thing to being there. There are switch-back roads and tranquil lakes interspersed with majestic mountains and sweeping views.

Nearly every town or village in Cumbria has a literary association. The great Lake Country poet, William Wordsworth, was born at Cockermouth, went to school in Hawkshead, lived in Grasmere at Dove Cottage which is now the Wordsworth museum, and then moved to Rydal Mount. He is buried in the churchyard in Grasmere. Matthew Arnold lived for a time in Ambleside, and Charlotte Brontë stayed there for a week visiting the Arnold family. Coleridge found a house in Keswick with a magnificent view and was in frequent contact with Wordsworth. Charles Lamb and Robert Southey also visited Coleridge. Coniston contains the Charles Ruskin Museum with a collection of drawings and letters. Nab Farm, on the shores of Rydal Water, provided a setting for a series of rather bizarre relationships involving Thomas DeQuincey (Confessions of an English Opium Eater) *and the Wordsworth family. It's worth investigating.*

I'm indebted to Bronwen Nixon, the proprietress of Rothay Manor, for an unusual overview of all the activities in the English Lake District. There are national parks, museums, forests, market days in various villages (usually Wednesdays and Saturdays), castles, gardens, festivals, sheep dog trials, boating, cycling, pony trekking, 23 different golf courses, craft workshops, and all manner of Wordsworth memorabilia. There is summer theater, a wildlife center, and of course, that great Lake Country diversion, fell walking.

June, October, and November, are excellent months to visit, but please make reservations well in advance.

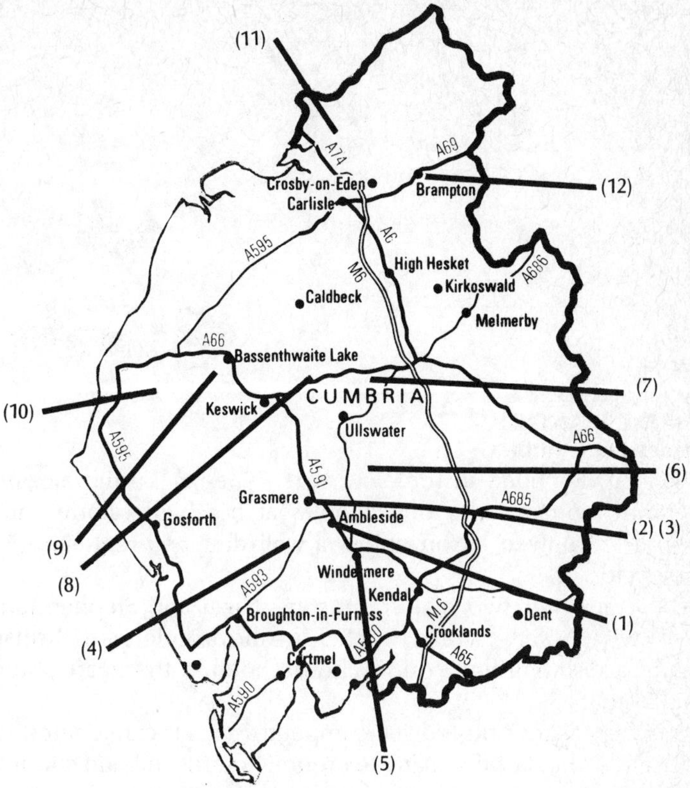
(11)
A74
A69
Crosby-on-Eden
Brampton
(12)
Carlisle
A6
A595
M6
High Hesket
Kirkoswald
A686
Caldbeck
Melmerby
A66
Bassenthwaite Lake
CUMBRIA
(7)
(10)
Keswick
Ullswater
A66
A595
A591
(6)
Grasmere
A685
Ambleside
(2) (3)
Gosforth
(9)
(8)
Windermere
A593
Kendal
M6
Dent
(1)
Broughton-in-Furness
Crooklands
(4)
A590
A65
Cartmel
A590
(5)

CUMBRIA

ROTHAY MANOR
Ambleside, Cumbria

Once described in the *New York Times* as "a thin elegant Yorkshire woman, who only nibbles at her high-calorie confections," Bronwen Nixon enjoys a well-deserved reputation in many fields.

She and her two handsome sons, Nigel and Stephen, and Nigel's wife, Colette, who is the chef, are the proprietors of Rothay Manor, a distinguished country house hotel in the heart of the Lake District.

Rothay Manor bested 100 competitors in a recent contest to determine which of the many tea room, hotels, inns, and country house hotels in England served the best afternoon tea.

"Tea, of course," smiled Bronwen, "is not having a cup of tea, but includes all kinds of buttered breads, homemade preserves, scones, cookies, and an assortment of cakes and tarts.

"It was lovely to receive the award, but all of us feel dedicated to caring for our guests under all circumstances. We want them to feel at home, enjoy gourmet food, and appreciate the extra things that we do. We've had Rothay Manor for more than fifteen years, and I myself spent many years supervising and cooking in the kitchen. Fortunately, Colette and my two sons are now able to take a great deal of that responsibility from me and I enjoy being in the dining room and lounges greeting my guests. All of us work together to make our guests feel relaxed and we try to offer as many kindnesses as possible. We are really delighted to look after them."

"Looking after" includes quite a number of additional conveniences in each of the guest rooms. For example, there are separate dimmer switches on the good reading lamps, bedside control of all the other lamps in the room, a bedside telephone, a hair dryer, a handsome wash basin set into a dressing table with plenty of space for cosmetics, shaving kits, and the like, a bowl of fruit with a sharp knife for assuaging hunger before bedtime, an excellent bathroom, with towel warmers and—wonder of wonders—a rack folding out from the wall over the bathtub to provide a quick, ready method of drying those small items that may have to be washed.

Decorated in shades of brown with beige accents and with candles on each table, the dining room at Rothay Manor has a wonderful feeling of relaxed elegance. The menu includes an interesting combination of British and Continental cuisine. In addition to serving roast mallard, pheasant, venison, lamb and pork, Bronwen conducts occasional special gourmet dinners in the winter, each of which has a special theme, including cuisine from various regions of France.

Just before the revised edition of this book went to press, I paid a visit to Rothay Manor and shared the Nixon family pleasure in the completion of new bedrooms, a new cottage of Lakeland design, and additional dining room facilities.

Incidentally, many country innkeepers from North America have visited Rothay Manor in the past few years and have conveyed to me enthusiastic praise for their experience. "We were really 'looked after,'" said Cliff Rudisill of the Village Inn in Lenox, Massachusetts.

ROTHAY MANOR, Ambleside, Cumbria, England LA22 OEH. Tel: (09663) Ambleside 3605. An 18-room country house hotel in the heart of English Lake District, 46 mi. from Carlisle. Open March 1 to Jan. 4. Lunch, afternoon tea, dinner served to non-residents. Ambleside is in the center of the national park famous for its mountains, lakes, and rivers. The sea is 20 mi. away. Carlisle and Hadrian's Roman Wall, 45 mi. Wordsworth's Dove Cottage and museum, 4 mi. Rydal Mount, 2 mi. The Lake Country abounds in theater, museums, and galleries. Croquet on grounds, mountain and fell walking, pony trekking, sailing, boating, fishing, and golf nearby. U.S. reservations: 800-323-5463. The Nixon Family, Proprietors.

Directions: From London leave M6 to Exit 36. Follow A591, 16 mi. Fork left on A593, signposted "Coniston and Langdales"; ½ mi. beyond, there's a black and white Georgian house on the right.

RAISE VIEW BED-AND-BREAKFAST
Whitebridge, Grasmere

Things have changed a bit since my last visit with Mrs. Brenda Roberts at the Raise View in Grasmere. Her young son, whom I saw on my first visit, is now a grown man and is no longer involved in the running of this guest house.

There has also been much redecorating and refurbishing, which is all to the guests' advantage.

Each of the bedrooms offers a lovely view of the surrounding fells, and Mrs. Roberts prepares a good English breakfast, which, as she says, "Will set you up nicely for a day of exploring the Lake District beauty spots." A light supper is also available.

The Raise View is very popular during the high season and Mrs. Roberts has joined with a small group of other B&Bs and guest houses in the area to try to accommodate guests who telephone, particularly from overseas.

THE RAISE VIEW (also known as The Dairy), Grasmere, Cumbria, England. Tel: (096-65) Grasmere 215. A 6-room very tidy bed-and-breakfast accommodation (sharing 3 bathrooms, 1 shower) in the village of Grasmere, open from April to Nov. 1.

Directions: Coming from Windermere and Ambleside on A591, ignore first sign posted "Grasmere Village" and turn left at second sign which is opposite the Swan Hotel. Turn right at first corner and the sign is visible.

THE WHITE MOSS HOUSE
Grasmere, Cumbria

It was a wonderfully sunny day in May, and the English Lake District was never more beautiful, Wordsworth or no. For almost three years I had been looking forward to returning to Grasmere and having a cup of tea and a bit of a chat with the Butterworths.

Arthur and Jean seated me at a table in a big bay window once again, and we all had a cup of tea and talked about the Lake District, and keeping a country inn, and how much fun it is to meet new people all the time.

Part of our conversation centered around an article in the British travel magazine, *In Britain.* "The thing that thrilled me," I remarked, "was that the article by Eve MacPherson, which also featured John Tovey of Miller Howe and Francis Coulson of Sharrow Bay, had a large picture of Jean with her smoked mackerel braid."

"I must say I was extremely flattered to be in such great

company," she said. "Francis has long been rated as one of the top chefs in Britain and John Tovey is equally famous. I can't imagine how I happened even to be thought of in the same breath."

"I'll take exception to that right at the start," said Arthur Butterworth, helping himself to a generous scone and some Lake Country jam. "I'll put your cuisine up against anybody's."

These days Jean is sharing her knowledge of cuisine with her son-in-law, Peter Dixon, who has joined her in the kitchen of the White Moss House. "Arthur and I are delighted to have Peter and our daughter Susan join us here at the hotel," she said. "It's wonderful to have members of the family in business with us and it also gives Arthur and me time to do a little more traveling. I hope to be able to come to the States to join in one of your meetings sometime in the near future."

Since my previous visit, a small, old lakeland cottage, situated on the fell-side about five minutes' drive (or energetic walk, according to Arthur), is available to White Moss guests. It has a kitchen, dining room, lounge, bathroom, and a choice of twin bedrooms. It is very pleasant for honeymooners or guests who enjoy their own company.

The living rooms, dining rooms, and lodging rooms of the main house all have Jean's marvelously feminine touch with fresh flowers, gay curtains, and bedspreads. I was delighted to see many books in the bedrooms, especially books on the Lake District. "We try to have them because we realize that many of our guests stop for only a few days, and they would like to have information about this area readily available." Jean said.

"It takes most people at least a day to wind down, but then they like to know more about the entire region," remarked Arthur.

"The best way to enjoy the Lake Country is to get out and walk in the hills. It makes all the difference," he said, "in getting the feel of the place.

"As far as walking is concerned, I think that our English Lake Country is quite unique because it is possible to walk over most all of the hills and not get lost. They are not heavily forested as are your hills in New England."

Advance bookings are normally taken for a minimum of three nights, although where mutually acceptable, one or two nights are taken. In such cases, there is a small surcharge per night. I would suggest that an overseas telephone call directly to the White Moss is well worth the effort, and will relieve the anxiety.

It felt wonderful to be back at the White Moss.

WHITE MOSS HOUSE, Rydal Water, Grasmere, Cumbria, England LA22 9SE. Tel: (096 65) Grasmere 295. A 7-room country house hotel in the midst of the beautiful English Lake Country approx. 14 mi. from Kendal. Dinner served to non-resident guests by reservation only. Resident guests are served full English breakfast, and dinner at 7:30 every night. No children under 11. No pets. Within easy driving distance of every point in the Lake District, including museums, historical and literary landmarks, and Wordsworth's cottage. Excellent center for some marvelous fell walks. Commissions are not paid to travel agents. Arthur and Jean Butterworth, Susan and Peter Dixon, Owners.

Directions: From the south: leave the M6 at Exit 36. Follow A591 through Ambleside. The hotel is at the head of Rydal Lake, 2 mi. north of Ambleside on the right-hand side. From the north: leave M6 at Exit 40, follow A66 toward Keswick, turn left on small country lane B5322. Turn left at A591 for 7 or 8 mi. Arrive at the Swan Hotel, Grasmere; carry on a mile farther. White Moss House is on the left at the head of Rydal Lake.

LOW BANK GROUND GUEST HOUSE
Coniston, Cumbria

Before I could open the door of the Low Bank Ground, Melvyn Smith popped out and greeted me brightly. "I saw you coming," he said, transferring a chef's whisk to his left hand so that we could shake hands. "The window in my kitchen is situated so that I can greet everybody as they arrive."

In retrospect, I realize now that this spirit of cordiality is indeed a key to Melvyn's cottage which has been converted into a very attractive, withal somewhat tiny, guest house. It didn't take us very long to see all four of the attractively furnished and decorated bedrooms, and when we returned to the parlor I had an opportunity to talk with him before he had to return to his preparations for the evening meal.

"Actually there is no one else involved here but me," he said, as we settled down in front of the fire. "I guess the best word for me is 'chef patron,' which is a sort of grand name for somebody who is chief cook and bottlewasher!

"I do all of the preparation and cooking myself. I studied at the Blackpool Culinary School and then went down to London. I've had a chance to travel all over the world, so that I think my menu reflects an international flavor." He handed me a sample menu which started with a salad from France, continued with a Russian kidney and dill-pickle soup, and then offered a choice of Parmesan oven-fried chicken, fresh salmon, or pork cutlet Mandalay. It finished off with sweets that included elderberry syllabub and rum and black cherry cake. Some other dishes in his cuisine are Mexican chicken, Italian fried spring cabbage, and something called bittersweet pancakes.

CLOSED

In addition to Melvyn's culinary expertise, the other main attraction at Low Bank Ground is unquestionably the setting. On the day of my short visit there was an absolutely incredible light show. It is impossible to conceive of a sight more lovely than the sun on the lake, the cloud formations, and the convolutions of the mountains as they seem to tumble down into the water.

"Our situation is ideal for fell walking, rambling, fishing, and boating," Melvyn commented. "Grizedale Forest has deer and other wildlife, nature trails, and it is literally right outside my front door. I think we are off the beaten track and sometimes we take a bit of finding, but guests seem to enjoy this feeling of seclusion."

Melvyn had to return to his kitchen, and I to drive the eight miles back to Ambleside. I did, however, make one resolution, and that was to by all means order a main dish with a most intriguing name on my next visit: "Mr. Pickwick's Pepper Steak."

LOW BANK GROUND COUNTRY HOUSE HOTEL, Coniston, Cumbria, England LA21 8AA. Tel: (096 64) Coniston 525. A restaurant with 4 lodging rooms on the banks of Coniston water (lake), 8 mi. from Ambleside in the English Lake country. Open Mar. to Dec. Price of rooms includes a hearty breakfast and four-course gourmet dinner. No credit cards. Within convenient driving distance of all lake country scenic, cultural, and recreational attractions. Ruskin Museum within a short stroll. Melvyn R. Smith, Chef-Patron.

Directions: From M6 Exit 36. Follow A591 (Kendal Bypass) through Staverley, Windermere to Ambleside. Follow A593 to Coniston, then B5285 (Coniston/Hawkshead Road) to the head of Coniston Lake (northern end). Turn right and follow road ¾ mi. Look for small inn sign on right.

MILLER HOWE
Windermere, Cumbria

I couldn't help but hear the enthusiastic conversation between two other guests as we all stood on the terrace of Miller Howe at sunset. One solitary, silent sailboat was beating its way across Lake Windermere with the aid of a light breeze laden with the perfumes of gardens and meadows.

"I'm going to spend the entire day on the balcony of our room," said a voice. "Right after the morning tea is served, I'm going to settle down in a chair with a book and just let the lake, the hills, and the sky envelop me. It's no wonder that Wordsworth felt such a lift from this countryside."

The focal point at Miller Howe is this exceptional view from the brow of the hill overlooking the lake. Each of the four lounges, most of the guest rooms, as well as the dining room, are dominated by this idyllic scene.

The hotelier at Miller Howe is John Tovey, a man with a reputation for being one of *les enfants terribles* of the English hotel business. He is a first-rate pastry chef, an excellent public relations man, an organizer, a deft conversationalist, an innovator, extrovert, and a really nice guy.

Under his sometimes quixotic direction, Miller Howe has developed a reputation for doing things somewhat differently. For example, it is on a modified American plan, which includes early morning tea (I really learned to appreciate this); a full breakfast; box lunches (very important for the all-day excursions into the fells); and dinner, which many consider the *piece de resistance*.

Here are a few of the dishes on the dinner menu: triple paté including Dutch liver and marjoram in aspic, pea pear and watercress soup, roast loin of lamb with five fresh herbs, and an assemblage of sweets which, of course, are John's own specialties. I'll just mention the apple and orange farmhouse pie. Incidentally, everyone gathers at 8:00 p.m. for seating at 8:30.

At the Miller Howe, each arriving guest is presented with a small booklet, especially inscribed with his name, which contains a diamond mine of information to enhance a three-day stay (the minimum according to the tariff sheet). It contains a rather complete description of each of the four meals served, and a list of attractions in the Lake District, including cinema, public gardens, art galleries, libraries, all of the outdoor recreational facilities, guided walks, and a generous dollop of interesting Lake District statistics about mountain heights and lake dimensions. The booklet concludes with space for a personal Miller Howe diary.

The furnishings and decor are all extremely attractive and the service, which is mostly by young men wearing brown suits, is quick and friendly.

All of this plus that fabulous view.

MILLER HOWE, Windermere, Cumbria, England LA23 1EY. Tel: (09662) 2536. A 16-room country house hotel in the English Lake Country, 1 mi. from Windermere. Open early April to Jan. 2. Breakfast, tea, dinner served to non-residents. (Dinner by reservation only.) Located within convenient distance of all of the scenic, cultural, and recreational attractions of the English Lake District. Not particularly suitable for children. John Tovey, Resident Owner.

Directions: From the south use Exit 36 from M6. Follow A591 to Windermere, then take A592 to Bowness.

OVER KIRKSTONE PASS

It had been three years since I had taken the Kirkstone Pass road from Ambleside to Ullswater, and once again I was blessed with a fairly clear day. "Fairly clear," in England means that its not raining at the moment. Once again I had to pause on the upward climb to allow for sheep on the road. With each twist of the road,

I could look back down into the valley at the village of Ambleside and its lakes.

On each side the grassy fells changed to bare rock near the top, and every so often I could see the silhouette of an adventuresome sheep along the skyline.

The public house at the crest of the paths was still there. I headed down the steep grade to the north, shifting into second gear and hugging the stone wall on the left-hand side of the road as closely as I could to accommodate the buses on their way up. Soon, I was on the floor of the valley which was brilliantly lit by sunlight through the pass. It was late May and there were very few other cars on the road, although there was a bank holiday weekend coming up and I was sure that this section would be much traveled. (It is always best to allow for bank holidays, if possible, when planning a vacation in Britain. All Britons love to go "on holiday" then.)

At numerous small parking areas along the road, a few people had left their cars taking to the nearby footpaths over the fells. They wore heavy boots and knickers, carried raingear, and usually wore wool caps. I noted a few vacancies at the B&Bs, but it was still early in the day and the season was not really under way. Even so, these would be filled before noon, as people from the city arrived in the Lake Country for the holidays.

The road continued on through Patterdale and Glenridding, the latter located on the shores of Lake Ullswater. The road was occasionally overhung by precipitous granite cliffs, reminding me of the lake country in northern Italy. Some mergansers and mallards were making tiny ripples in the otherwise glasslike surface of the lake which faithfully reflected the mountains on each side. Here and there was a beach with coarse sand.

One of the sights that continually amazed me in this country, as well as in the Lancashire Fells, was seeing the stone walls which march right up one side of the mountains and down the other. They are formidable barriers placed, no doubt, to establish boundaries and to keep sheep under control. They are kept in extremely good repair. I understand that it is the custom here, just as it is in rural New England, for people to walk along each side of the walls together, replacing the stones that have been disrupted by frost and weather.

This time, I turned left on the A5901 to the west and went through and over the mountains, once again past several fields of sheep. It's such a wondrous sight to see the care and affection that exists between the mother lamb and her lambkins. Such complete innocent trusting, care, and love.

LOW HOUSE
Hartsop, Patterdale, Cumbria

"I know that you are going to love Low House, and Audrey and Peter are two of my favorite people." Bronwen Nixon and I were taking one of my favorite roads in the Lake Country—up over Kirkstone Pass and down the other side toward Penrith. The beautiful fells were brilliantly lighted by the midafternoon sunshine and countless, neat stone walls, so characteristic of this part of England, disappeared over the tops and down the other side. We were now at the bottom of the pass and Bronwen pointed out Brotherswater to the left, and then the first turn on the right by the phone box.

I was prepared for something unusual, but was delighted by this 17th-century stone farmhouse with its wonderful feeling of antiquity. As soon as we parked, Peter and Audrey Jerram came out to greet us, and I felt as if I had known them for years. As we paused before the fireplace in the low-ceilinged living/dining room, we decided to have a cup of tea in the garden before touring the house.

I learned that a great many of the guests at Low House particularly enjoy bringing their oils and watercolors. "We can accommodate seven persons and our aim is to provide a friendly, informal atmosphere in which guests can enjoy and develop their individual styles of painting. For indoor work, we have a barn studio with such lovely views that even on inclement days artists can paint the nearby fells or the brook. However, many do not paint and just come for the fell walking and peace and quiet."

There followed a delightful tour of the house, including the bedrooms that are reached by a winding Cumbrian staircase. The old walls were all whitewashed and everything looked extremely pleasant with a nice, bright feeling about it.

We talked for a moment about the evening meal and Audrey explained, "I have starters, main courses, and sweets; coffee is served beside the fire afterwards. Sometimes we have a main course with sweets, and biscuits and cheese. Casseroles seem to be my thing; they are very popular and include beef, chicken with wine, and chicken with lemon. We have trout every so often. We usually pack a lunch for our guests, because most of them would prefer to spend the time out in the countryside. Afterwards, everybody gathers here at the end of the day and we talk well into the evening."

Thanks to Bronwen Nixon of Rothay Manor, I can now introduce our readers to Peter and Audrey Jerram at the Low House in Patterdale.

LOW HOUSE, Hartsop, Patterdale, Cumbria, England CA11 ONZ. Tel: (08532) Glenridding 511. A 3-bedroom (shared baths) 17th-century lakeland farmhouse ideally situated in painting country between Windermere and Penrith. The room rate includes breakfast and dinner. Open year-round. Splendid footpaths and excellent back roads through the Lake District fells lead to an endless variety of scenery, as well as cultural and recreational attractions. A car is not necessary; guests can be met in Penrith or Windermere. Audrey and Peter Jerram, Proprietors.

Directions: Hartsop is on A592 between Penrith and Windermere at the northern end of the Kirkstone Pass. Turn east at telephone booth for about 200 yds.

SHARROW BAY COUNTRY HOUSE HOTEL
Lake Ullswater, Near Pooley Bridge, Cumbria

For almost twenty-five years paeans of praise have been heaped upon Sharrow Bay by travel writers and food critics alike. The first group extolled the lake and mountain scenery. (The view from the main drawing room overlooking the lake and the mountains won an award as being the best in Great Britain a few years ago.)

Food guide writers are expansive in their description of chef Francis Coulson's true gourmet offerings. They have rhapsodized over the roast loin of English lamb Doria cooked on a bed of cucumbers and shallots and served with a red currant and orange sauce; the roast sirloin of Scotch beef served with Yorkshire pudding and horseradish cream sauce; and the choux pastry with a filling of partridge, duck, chicken and herbs and served with bacon. When it comes to the sweets, even my masters in this field, the food guide writers, are humbled before the white peaches with grated apple, orange juice and cream; the chocolate brandy cake; and the famous sticky toffee sponge cake served with cream. I would dearly love to introduce my good friend and *chef extraordinaire,* John Ashby Conway of The Farmhouse Restaurant in Port Townsend, Washington, to both Francis Coulson and Brian Sack, and then just sit back and listen to their conversation.

Sharrow Bay is situated on the northwest edge of Lake Ullswater in the English Lake District. It is owned and operated by two men whose interests seemed to have blended beautifully. Francis Coulson does all the cooking and his partner Brian Sack handles the myriad details that are connected with the rooms and

the "front of the house." The real beneficiaries of this partnership are the Sharrow Bay guests.

The main house sits on twelve acres of garden and woodlands, and there's about a half a mile of lakeshore for all the guests to enjoy. In addition to the twelve rooms in the main house, there are other accommodations available, including a converted farmhouse about one mile up the lake where long-staying guests may enjoy peace and solitude.

On my most recent visit, both Brian and Francis reminded me that a few years ago, I had skipped the main course at lunch and had decided on three "starters" and a dessert. In fact, Francis remembered that I had had the French peasant vegetable soup and the purée of carrots and oranges which is the supreme specialty of the house. "I'm sure," he added, "I also served you some chicken livers in a pastry shell."

Talk to anyone who has ever visited Sharrow Bay, and it seems that they inevitably sigh and say, "Ah, yes."

SHARROW BAY COUNTRY HOUSE HOTEL, Lake Ullswater (Nr. Pooley Bridge) Cumbria, England CA10 2LZ. Tel: (08536) Pooley Bridge 301. A 29-room country house hotel (19 with private baths/showers) on the edge of Lake Ullswater. Open from early Mar. to early Dec. Breakfast, lunch, tea, dinner served to non-residents (please reserve). All of the scenic, cultural, and recreational attractions of the Lake Country within a short distance. No credit cards. Not suitable for younger children. Minimum booking for overnight guests includes bed, breakfast, and dinner. Francis Coulson, Brian Sack, Co-Proprietors.

Directions: Use Exit 40 from M6 and follow A66 for ½ mi. Go through the roundabout and turn left on A592 to Ullswater. Turn left at the lake, pass through village of Pooley Bridge, then right at small church at signpost, "Howtown and Martindale." After 100 yds. turn right at crossroads signposted, "Howtown and Martindale." Sharrow Bay is 2 mi. along this road.

THE MILL
Mungrisdale, Penrith, Cumbria

David and Pam Wood had invited me for a morning cup of tea (not another!), and we sat in the very snug, low-ceilinged parlor of this mill cottage which dates back to 1651. On the wall was what I'm sure is the world's largest crossword puzzle. It is necessary to stand on a chair to fill in the top squares and to get down on hands and knees to do the bottom, because it runs from floor to ceiling. "It really gets our guests together," David said.

David is a Devonshire man, and he and his wife Pam moved to this lovely corner of the world a number of years ago to start a whole new career as guest house hosts. "We offer bed, breakfast, and the evening meal," he went on. "Pam does the cooking and she's most particular about her homemade soups and sweets and she serves quite a few regional dishes from Cumbria. Tonight, she's doing a curry and she decorates the dish with at least a dozen tidbits. Sometimes people don't know whether to wear them or eat them. We have an enjoyable time around the dinner table each evening."

The Mill occupies a unique location immediately at the foot of the mountains on grounds bounded by a trout stream. Within the immediate vicinity is a wide range of activities including fell walking, rock climbing, pony trekking, sailing, fishing, and even hang gliding. There are eight bedrooms, six with wash basins and sharing two bathrooms, and two have private bathrooms.

This was a visit in late June, and the roses and honeysuckle, lupin and wisteria, were almost in full bloom. I also observed country birds including the grey wagtail, the dipper, and a spotted flycatcher.

"A lot of our guests take their autos to this end of Lake

Ullswater," David remarked, "walk up to Pooley's Bridge, and then ride the steamer back. It makes a most pleasant trip."

In a letter I received recently, David said, "We are both working extremely hard, but are in good heart and enjoying life."

I think that I should like to add one more line to the giant crossword puzzle at the Mill—a four-letter word meaning: "a comfortable, friendly place to stay when visiting the English Lake District."

THE MILL, Mungrisdale, Penrith, Cumbria, England CA11OXR. Tel: (059 683) Threlkeld 659. An 8-room guest house serving bed, breakfast, and the evening meal, located about 20 mi. from Carlisle in the English Lake Country. Open every day from March 21 to Oct. 31. No credit cards. Mr. & Mrs. David Wood, Proprietors.

Directions: Leave the M6 motorway at Penrith (Junction 40). Take the A66 road toward Keswick (pronounced Kes-ick) and after 10 mi. turn right at the signpost for Mungrisdale Village. It is 2 mi. to The Mill. There are two places here, and it is necessary to drive through the parking area of The Mill Inn which is really a pub, to reach the Mill Guest House immediately adjacent.

THE PHEASANT INN
Bassenthwaite Lake, Cockermouth, Cumbria

"I think that we are best described as being a residential English country pub." I readily agreed with innkeeper Barrington Wilson's evaluation of the Pheasant Inn.

This welcoming inn is set in the countryside at the head of Bassenthwaite Lake with Thornwaite Forest behind. The 16th-century L-shaped building is white with black trim, and there is a very pleasant lawn and extensive gardens in the rear. When I visited, the poppies were out in great numbers, as well as some of the other early summer flowers.

Over the rather rustic entrance are some mounted birds of the region, including several pheasants. There are several other references to this noble bird, including a handsome painting against a background of lakes and mountains. The snug conviviality of the interior is emphasized by low, beamed ceilings, patterned curtains, and comfortable lounges with chintz-covered furniture, log fires, and fresh flowers.

Over the years, apparently both Mr. and Mrs. Barrington Wilson and previous owners had collected a number of Lake Country memorabilia, including a mounted fish with a notice that it was caught in 1921 by one of the hotel guests. I was also interested in a novel collection of prints of old British inns that were at one time included in cigarette packages.

There are twenty spotless, comfortable bedrooms at the Pheasant, many of which have private bathrooms.

The innkeeper thoughtfully provides his guests with an excellent map of Keswick (Kezz-ik) which shows hotels and pubs

in the area serving bar lunches and snacks. This is particularly important, because it's possible to motor all over the Lake District, as well as walk on the fells (hills), and it is good to know where there is a friendly pub. A hearty bar lunch usually includes some specialty of the house such as meat pies and salads, and many of these smaller places have a house paté of which they are very proud.

After a day of motoring and walking in the Lake Country, it is most pleasant to return to The Pheasant and settle down in the lounge where there is a view of the blue mountain peaks and the dark green fir trees. There are many good American and British magazines scattered about.

The dinner menu consists principally of good English cooking, including braised ox tongue, roast turkey with bread sauce, roast capon with bacon and bread sauce, and rhubarb and ginger pie served with cream.

Sailing, boating, fishing, walking, pony trekking, fox hunting (on foot), exhibitions, festivals, visiting the Roman Wall, and touring the Lake Country by car, are just a few of the many things enjoyed by Pheasant Inn guests.

This part of the Lake District is particularly beautiful in spring and autumn when the trees are at their loveliest.

THE PHEASANT INN, Bassenthwaite Lake, Cockermouth, Cumbria, England. Tel: (059 681) Bassenthwaite Lake 234. A 20-room traditional residential English country pub (inn) in the English Lake District. Open Jan. to Dec. All Lake Country scenic and recreational attractions nearby. No credit cards. W.E. Barrington Wilson, Proprietor.

Directions: From Keswick, follow A66 7 mi. on west side of Bassenthwaite Lake.

NORTHERN CUMBRIA

This part of Cumbria closely resembles Scotland with its narrow-passage roads and steep fells, and also Norway, which, in places, has much the same scenery. I decided to go to Scale Hill by way of Keswick and was delighted to find that the road, actually the long way around, was alpine in nature but completely safe. Although it was a Sunday afternoon, the high season had passed and there was a paucity of traffic.

The road winds and twists alongside a lake, continues up over a pass, and drops down into the dales with a descent that is breathtaking. Low gear is the word for both going up and coming down, but it is worth every great inch of it. This is one of those roads where British courtesy is to be commended. Many cars pull off in the lay-bys to let others pass. I only regret that I was unaccompanied and there was no one to share this really wonderful adventure.

The clouds put on a remarkable show. The mist at the top of the fells would shift unexpectedly and let in a little ray of sunshine and a patch of blue sky.

Most spectacular were the great profiles created by the mountain skyline. My mind played tricks as I read various shapes into all of them. The valley widened out and I could see several swift-flowing streams tumbling down from the tops of the hills. It reminded me of just such sights while cruising the Norwegian fjords. Now, after a very pleasant journey I could see the unmistakable outline of Scale Hill Hotel in the distance.

SCALE HILL HOTEL
Loweswater, Cumbria

Much to my delight, Scale Hill turned out to be a small hotel quite resembling the Pheasant at Cockermouth, ten miles to the north. It is a two-story white building with impressive views out over the meadows toward the fells. There is a pleasant garden in the rear, with many benches permitting visitors to quietly enjoy the spectacular scenery. The view from the front is a little more threatening, as the fells seem to be much higher and, under a leaden sky on the day of my visit, more ominous.

However, there was nothing ominous about the tempting Saturday afternoon tea being served by a very pert miss to the many people who happened by to enjoy the warm coal fire, the cups of tea, and the enticing scones with whipped cream and jam.

As is the case with most inns of this type, there is a residents' lounge, separated from the main lobby. It was occupied by a black cat with white paws, who was curled up contentedly by the fire.

Upstairs, the hallways have many photographs, sporting prints, and the unmistakable air of an old British inn. Bedrooms look clean and comfortable and, once again, enjoy the marvelous view.

There is a tiny bar, which was not open during the time of my visit, but I peeked through the window and could well imagine that it provided a pleasant atmosphere for locals and visitors alike.

Innkeepers Michael and Sheila Thompson provide a hearty menu with four courses. Some of the main dishes include shoulder of lamb, local trout, Solway salmon, roast turkey, and roast duck with applesauce.

Overnight visitors are charged for dinner, bed, and breakfast, so be sure to arrive in time for dinner. Picnic lunches are provided for guests who either walk the fells or motor through the countryside.

Michael Thompson explained that there's been an inn here since 1633. The property was originally a farm and, because it was located at the top of the hill, it became customary for the stage drivers to stop and give the horses a rest, and for the farm to provide some hearty bread and cheese for the travelers. This quite naturally lead to the establishment of the inn, or to what would be known then as a pub.

SCALE HILL HOTEL, Loweswater, English Lakeland, Cumbria, England. Tel: (090085) Lorton 232. A 14-bedroom (11 with private baths) traditional country inn in the northern Lake District. Residents must take dinner, bed, and breakfast. Dinners served to non-residents. Advance reservations are accepted for a minimum of 2 nights. Open year-round, although an inquiry would be in order during the deep winter months. Most conveniently located to enjoy all of the English Lake scenery and attractions. Walking, fishing, bird watching, golfing, horseback riding, and many other recreational advantages nearby. Michael and Sheila Thompson, Resident Proprietors.

Directions: M6 to Penrith, A66 to Keswick to Braithwaite; turn left over Whinlatter Pass to High Lorton and on to Scale Hill.

CROSBY LODGE HOTEL
Crosby-on-Eden, Carlisle, Cumbria

"This is, indeed, the Border Country," said Patricia Sedgwick, as we were enjoying a cup of tea in the sunny dining room of the Crosby Lodge Hotel. (I realize that this book sounds as if I subsist on tea, but it is the marvelous British way of expressing hospitality and I've enjoyed dozens of cups of tea and cakes with hoteliers and innkeepers from Inverness to Mousehole and from County Galway to Norfolk.)

"Hadrian's Wall which is just a few miles away, was constructed by the Romans to keep the raiding Scottish tribes from marauding the lands to the south. We are within a day-trip of Edinburgh, both the east and west coasts, the Cumberland and Northumberland country, and the Scottish lowlands. The Lake District is a few miles away to the west."

Until 1970, Patricia and her husband Michael lived in nearby Carlisle where they operated a restaurant. "Michael is an expert chef," she said proudly, "trained in both London and Switzerland. I was born in Carlisle, and I've never moved away.

"In the eight years we've had Crosby Lodge we've gradually upgraded it. You'd be surprised how run down it was when we first saw it in October, 1970. Now we've done all the bedrooms over and added further guest rooms in the stable block. I guess you'd call us a country house hotel and restaurant. Our prices for rooms include a full English breakfast. We have a nice walled garden which is available to our guests. Most of the people who stay here spend the days touring about and return in time for dinner."

It was obvious that the Sedgwicks had done much to improve both the interior and exterior of this country house which was built around 1805. The two towers in front are connected by a crenelated battlement which, of course, has never seen any sieges.

Many trees grace the spacious lawns and meadows are abloom with flowers.

As I made a reluctant departure after a pleasant tour of the house and grounds, Patricia Sedgwick's final words were, "If you get stuck for a room, give me a ring."

CROSBY LODGE HOTEL, Crosby-on-Eden Carlisle, Cumbria, England CA64QZ. Tel: (022873) Crosby-on-Eden 618. An 11-room manor house hotel, 4½ mi. east of Carlisle in the lush Cumbria countryside. Open mid-Jan. to Dec. 23. Breakfast, lunch, dinner served to non-residents. Restaurant closed Sunday evenings. Convenient for tours through the English Lake District, the Scottish lowlands. Hadrian's Wall, Carlisle Castle, Rosehill Theatre, and other scenic and cultural attractions nearby. Mr. & Mrs. G.M. Sedgwick, Resident Owners.

Directions: From M6 use Exit 44. Follow B6264 approx. 2 mi. Turn left at crossroads, still following B6264 sign. Approx. 2 mi. to hotel, just through Crosby village. Crosby Lodge stands on right at the top of the hill.

FARLAM HALL HOTEL
Brampton, Cumbria

"There are other Bramptons in Britain," explained Alan Quinion, "but we're the one near Carlisle. That's why it's necessary to be very careful about fully identifying some of the villages and towns." Alan and I were enjoying a relaxing chat in front of the crackling fire in the residents' lounge in Farlam Hall.

He was telling me the fascinating story about the long search he and his wife, daughter Helen, and son Barry had made, looking for a country house to convert into a hotel. "We had looked for at least two years, and even as tired and rundown as this place was when we saw it, we knew that the location and situation were exactly perfect for us. The house had the right feeling . . . the 'vibes' were right, and we just ached to bring it to life."

And bring it to life is exactly what the Quinion family has done. The departments of the hotel are divided almost equally, with Barry, the chef, being responsible for the kitchen and the food. "He has worked in some excellent restaurants," said his father, "and is very well trained. We're building our strength on his foundations. If the food and genuine comfort are good enough, people will seek you out."

Daughter Helen is mainly responsible for the reception and

running of the dining room. She organizes the tables and looks after parties and various functions.

"Mrs. Quinion takes the responsibility for the decor, the furnishings, the housekeeping, and generally looks after all of us." he smiled. "And I believe we need some looking after. I handle the accounts, supervise the gardens and outside developing, and run the bar."

At dinner, I had ample opportunity to sample some of Barry's cuisine. The starter was avocado mousse, the main course was beef Wellington served in a very crisp pastry jacket, and the cheese selection was one of the most extensive I'd ever seen.

In a moment of complete madness, I accepted Mrs. Quinion's suggestion that I try both a small helping of the raspberry mousse, which was decorated with whipped cream, and the chocolate gateau. Heavenly.

Farlam Hall started life as a 17th-century farmhouse and was enlarged in stages and subsequently became the center of a thriving local community.

FARLAM HALL, Brampton, Cumbria, England CA8 2NG. Tel: (069-76) Hallbankgate 234. An 11-room country house hotel (all with private baths) 11 mi. from Carlisle in the vicinity of the Roman Wall. Open Mar. to Jan. Dinner served to non-residents. Ample Lake Country and Northumbria recreation and sightseeing nearby, including the Roman Wall and three golf courses. Alan Quinion Family, Proprietors.

Directions: Leave M6 at Carlisle, Exit 43; follow A69 (Newcastle Rd.) to Brampton. Leaving Brampton, take right fork (A689) to Hallbank-gate and Alston. Hotel is 2½ mi. along this road on left.

YORKSHIRE
County of York

Yorkshire is England's largest county, comprising two national parks, one hundred miles of coastline and many attractive fishing villages. The county is centered around the ancient city of York with its four great gates, old streets, and world-famous York Minster, a church which contains over half the medieval stained glass left in England. The castle museum is another principal attraction with re-creations of complete Victorian and Edwardian streets and old craft workshops.

Yorkshire is divided into sections called "Ridings," which is a Scandinavian term meaning one-third. The North Riding is famous for its national park, its popularity with walkers, and its lavish display of heather. The West Riding contains the Yorkshire Dales National Park, and is one of the most peaceful and unspoiled regions in Britain.

West Yorkshire is the land of the Brontë sisters, Charlotte and Emily. Many people make a literary pilgrimage to the village of Haworth, located in typical brooding Brontë country among the rolling moors and dark, purple hills. It is situated between Leeds and Blackburn, south of Keighly. The Brontë parsonage has been reproduced to look as it did when the sisters lived there with their father.

The AA Touring Guide to Britain *outlines five most interesting tours in Yorkshire.*

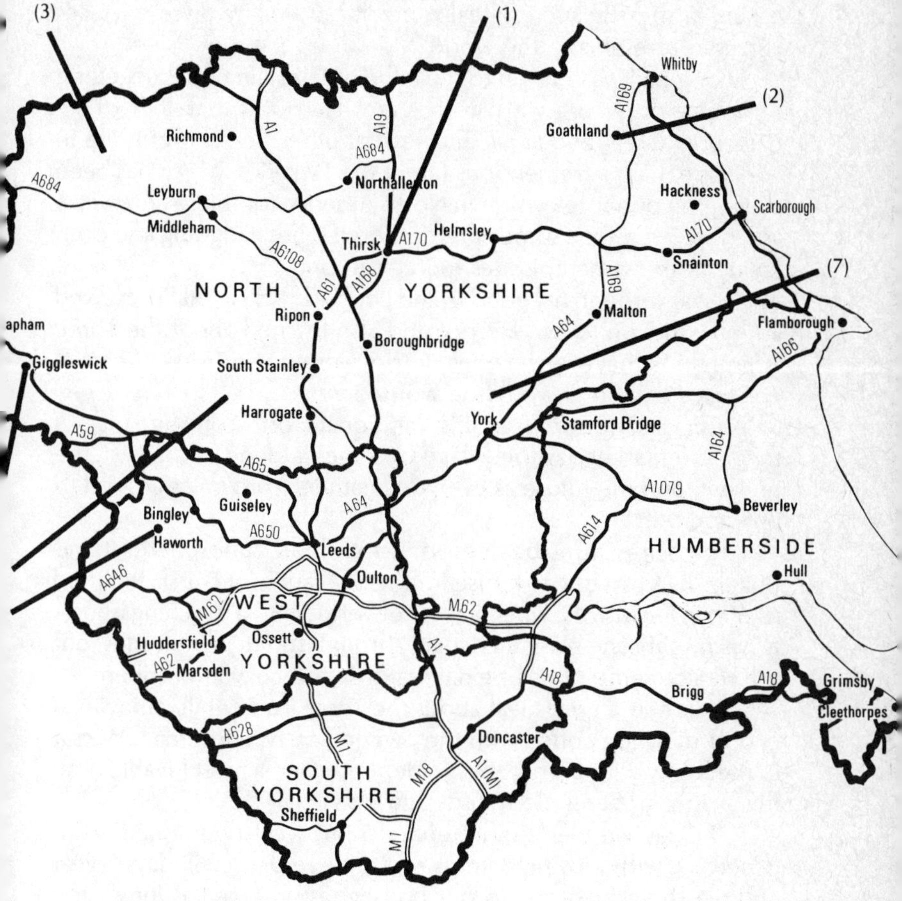

YORKSHIRE

(1) THREE TUNS HOTEL, Thirsk, North Yorkshire, 210
(2) MALLYAN SPOUT HOTEL, Goathland, North Yorkshire, 211
(3) STONE HOUSE HOTEL, Sedbusk, North Yorkshire, 214
(4) OAKROYD HOTEL, Ingleton, Yorkshire, 215
(5) OLD SILENT INN, Stanbury, West Yorkshire, 216
(6) WOODLANDS, Settle, North Yorkshire, 218
(7) WHITWELL HALL, Whitwell-on-the-Hill, York, 220
(8) AMERDALE HOUSE HOTEL, Skipton, North Yorkshire, 221

THREE TUNS HOTEL
Thirsk, North Yorkshire

The more I traveled in Yorkshire, the more fascinated I became, and the more I realized just how many different faces Yorkshire presents to the world.

I originally journeyed to the town of Thirsk in hopes of getting a glimpse or even a word with James Herriot, the author of *All Creatures Great and Small* and several other books on his life in Yorkshire. I am a tremendous fan of the TV series, which has been playing on public television in North America for the last few years and have even seen some episodes three times, laughing and even crying at the same episodes more than once.

It was through my good friend Lou Satz that I actually received an introduction to Mr. Herriot and also learned about the Three Tuns. I think that even if James Herriot were not in Thirsk, the town and the small hotel would be worth a visit.

It sits in one corner of this traditional North Yorkshire market town. On market day the village becomes a blend of the past, the present, and the future as everyone gathers from miles around to buy and sell.

The Three Tuns belongs in just such an atmosphere. It was built in 1698 as a dower house for the Bell family of Thirsk. It started its public life in 1740, when it was converted into a coaching house. It has undergone several changes through the many decades, but still retains some of its original features and cozy atmosphere.

I learned a great deal about the Three Tuns while enjoying a cup of morning coffee with the owner, Mr. Ivan Redman. We sat in the lobby with Barney, his golden retriever, a most lovable dog, hospitably greeting old friends and new.

"I'd say we were unpretentious, but well intentioned" Ivan observed, with a twinkle in his eye. "We're open 365 days a year and we serve breakfast to our houseguests, as well as lunch and dinner. We have twelve bedrooms, eight of which have private baths, and the others have wash basins in the room. They are all equipped with color TV, radio, and telephone service."

While he excused himself for a moment, I could hear the tick-tock of the large, old clock from Paterson & Son hanging on one wall. It was obvious that the lobby was also a meeting place for townsfolk, because there were many tables and chairs, suggesting congenial gatherings of coffee or tea drinkers.

Glancing at the menu I noticed that for the most part the Three Tuns serves traditional English food, including beef and roast duckling and the like. There were a few Continental dishes as well, because this part of Yorkshire also has quite a few visitors from the Continent.

I found both the Three Tuns and Ivan Redman a very warm and generous experience, and Thirsk, a Yorkshire town with a natural, unaffected feeling.

Now a word or two about James Herriot. Ordinarily he is quite willing to see visitors at his Surgery, and if you arrive between 2:30 and 2:45 on either Wednesdays or Fridays, he's happy to have a word with you and perhaps autograph one of his books. I was fortunate to be there at the approinted time. We did have a very splendid, short talk as he explained: "I cannot guarantee that I am going to be here on those two days and I hope that no one makes a special trip. However, if I am here, I'm delighted to meet anyone. You see, I'm still very much a country veterinarian."

The Surgery is located on the little road off the square next to the Royal British Legion Club and the signs says, "Sinclair & Wight."

THREE TUNS HOTEL, Market Place, Thirsk, North Yorkshire, England Y07 1LH. Tel: (0845) No. Thirsk 23124. A 12-bedroom (8 with private baths) traditional town hotel overlooking the square. Serving breakfast, lunch, and dinner 365 days a year. An ideal center for touring the Yorkshire Dales, the North Yorkshire Moors, National Park, and the city of York. Pony-trekking, gliding, fishing, golfing nearby. Market days are Monday and Saturday. Within walking distance of Dr. James Herriot's surgery. Ivan Redman, Proprietor, Hotelier.

Directions: From south, take M1 and A1 to Dishforth; turn right on A168 to Thirsk. From York, take A19 direct to Thirsk. From north on A1, turn left on A61 at the Ripon/Thirsk intersection. Nearest railway station—Thirsk 1½ mi. Phone hotel to arrange transport.

MALLYAN SPOUT HOTEL
Goathland, Whitby, Yorkshire

"Cozy" and "bustling" are two good words to describe the Mallyan Spout Hotel which sits in the heart of the Yorkshire moors. The note of coziness is underscored by the decoration and furnishings of all of the three spacious lounges which have welcome fires most evenings and wide windows overlooking the spectacular moorland.

I arrived at the end of a rather stormy day and was immediately taken in hand by Judy Heslop. She ensconced me in a room at the top of the house with an impressive view of the countryside, and after a welcome tub and a bit of rest, I joined her in the main lounge before dinner.

Again I was struck with the thought that inns and pubs in England provide an opportunity really to get acquainted with the people of the surrounding area. All around me were the sounds of distinctive Yorkshire accents and faces which seemed to be crinkled up in good humor much of the time.

The hotel is an ivy-clad stone building that, in some ways, typifies British solidarity. For the comfort of the guests, a fully equipped sauna and health club have been installed. This is an experience that would be quite welcome after a day of exploring the moors or perhaps enjoying a dip in the ocean nearby.

Because this part of Yorkshire is really not on the main tourist route, Judy pointed out that Americans are not readily apt to find their way here. "We love to see them," she said, "because there is so much to do out-of-doors here that appeals to the American 'get-up-and-go' spirit. Besides the moors, there's tennis, golf, horseback riding, and also some good trout and salmon fishing in the River Esk."

For dinner, I ordered a grilled Whitby plaice, a local fish garnished with sliced bananas and served with a special sauce. Other dishes included Goathland broth, another local tradition, and moorland trout, of which I had two bites from Judy's plate. Super.

I was up early the next morning for a brisk walk in the freshly washed moors which today gave promise of being blessed with

sunshine. Filled with American "get-up-and-go," I would have enjoyed several days at the Mallyan Spout.

MALLYAN SPOUT HOTEL, Goathland, Whitby, North Yorkshire, England YO22AN. Tel: (094786) 206. A 24-room traditional country inn (13 with private baths-shower), 35 mi. from York. Open all year. Breakfast, lunch, tea, dinner served to non-residents. Horse riding, golf, walking the Yorkshire moors, all within a convenient distance. Judith Heslop, Innkeeper.

Directions: From York take A64 to Malton by-pass. At Malton take A169, signposted: Pickering/Whitby. After passing Flying-Dales radar station, take first turning to Goathland. It is 3 mi. to hotel.

MORNING ON THE MOORS

I'm always an early riser and sometimes that's the very best time to take walks. On this Sunday morning I found myself wandering through a parish churchyard, considerably in advance of the eight o'clock service. It was located right across the road from the Mallyan Spout Hotel in a small triangular park where several roads all came together. Among the headstones in that churchyard was one marked 1695.

A signpost by the road said thirteen-and-a-half miles to Pickering, and four miles to Edgeton Bridge, which is where the Roman Road is. Still another sign said nine miles to Whidbey-on-the-Sea.

Dominating everything and stretching out into all distances are the low fells of the York moors where the heather will bloom madly at the height of the season.

Carefully making my way among a flock of sheep, I climbed to the top of one of the fells where I could see the splendid farms tucked into their own fields, which were now serenely verdant. I could imagine what it would be like here in January and February with the snow swirling, and the winds off the moors rattling the windowpanes and shaking the buildings—a time for sitting-by-the-fire.

These are not the dramatically deserted heaths of Northumbria, nor the gentler hills of Lancashire. Here, the earth is convoluted with twists and folds. Above a certain line, the shrubs are low, and the grazing meager.

The sun climbed higher and shown brightly off the wet surface of the road. I stopped to look at a plaque on a big chestnut tree behind a stone wall which announced that "His Majesty's Manor of Goathland commemorates the Silver Jubilee of His Majesty King George V." The tree was planted by Captain Smalass on the sixth day of May in 1935. The fence around the tree kept the sheep from getting inside. I couldn't help but wonder what happened to the good Captain . . . did he see action at Dunkirk, or perhaps in the jungles of Burma? The peaceful years between the wars were all too short.

On my way back, I passed in front of the Mallyan Spout Hotel and two young lads lying on a bench at the bus stop. I asked them if they were waiting for the first bus to Whidbey, and they said no, they were resting—they had been up all night at a party.

STONE HOUSE HOTEL
Sedbusk, North Yorkshire

The British love to unravel mysteries, whether they be literary or real. Witness the great success of the Agatha Christie books and Sherlock Holmes.

Enter now the *dramatis personae* of our mystery. They are P.G. Wodehouse, the very popular British novelist and creator of *the quintessence* of the English gentleman's gentleman, "Jeeves"; an unknown real gentleman's gentleman named Robinson; and a Yorkshire cricketer named Percy Jeeves.

And what has all this to do with a beautiful stone house in North Yorkshire, an ideal setting for a relaxing holiday in the heart of the Yorkshire Dales National Park?

We must now introduce the final member of the cast: Mr. H.A. Crallan, racehorse owner and cricketer. Mr. Crallan is important to us, because he was the man who built the Stone House in 1908.

According to my information, newspaperman Rowland Ryder determined that P.G. Wodehouse actually hired a butler from an agency in order to study him for the character in his book. However, this man's name was Robinson, which lacked the comic overtones for which Wodehouse was searching.

The ideal name was discovered by Wodehouse as he watched a man named Jeeves play in a cricket match.

Now for the final connection: it seems that in 1909 this self-same Jeeves worked as a gardener on the grounds at Stone House for Mr. Crallan!

Aren't you amazed! May I add that Jane and Peter Taplin, host and hostess at Stone House, have all the documentation to make this a jolly literary adventure. They also have many other things that make staying at Stone House a North Yorkshire holiday adventure, including this lovely, comfortable house with its garden, and two Yorkshire terriers.

There is also an impressive collection of miniatures, including pocket watches, thimbles, toys, and vintage automobiles. These are all carefully arranged to provide an enjoyable diversion for the viewer. The public rooms and bedrooms are all comfortable and accommodating.

The evening meal emphasizes homecooked, plain English food, such as roast beef and, of course, Yorkshire pudding. There are usually seven or eight main choices. The Taplins also have a butcher shop in a nearby Yorkshire town.

Incidentally, Stone House sits in the middle of the setting for the James Herriot TV series ("All Creatures Great and Small"). The area provides marvelous walking and motoring throughout the magnificent Yorkshire Dales.

STONE HOUSE HOTEL, Sedbusk (near Hawes), North Yorkshire, England DL8 3PT. Tel: (09697) Hawes 571. A 12-bedroom (most with private baths) country house hotel in the heart of North Yorkshire. Breakfast and dinner served daily. Open year-round. Most conveniently located to enjoy many of the historic towns, castles, abbeys, waterfalls; bird watching, walking, and motoring through the nearby Dales. Tennis on grounds. This is James Herriot country. Jane and Peter Taplin, Hoteliers.

Directions: A684 runs east and west between Kendall and A19. In Hawes, turn north toward Muker; follow the road over the bridge and make the first right turning. Continue about 500 yds. to Stone House Hotel.

OAKROYD HOTEL
Ingleton, Yorkshire

This was another of several very pleasant U.K. surprises. I was motoring down the A-65 from Kendal in the Lake District, and something made me turn into the town of Ingleton. It is the place where two rivers come together, and before entering the town there is a rather spectacular viaduct, and a most picturesque waterfall among limestone caves.

In fact, the scene was so attractive I thought how nice it would be if there were a pleasant small hotel or guest house to make the experience even more enjoyable.

Well, I found the Oakroyd Hotel right on the main street and, even though I walked in unannounced, the proprietress, Pearl Brown, proved to be a very lovely young woman and we got along famously.

The Oakroyd has a very happy feeling that was evident as soon as I stepped inside. Formerly the vicarage, it's a typical small British hotel, where some of the bedrooms have private baths and others are shared; however, all of the bedrooms have basins.

Room D on the top floor would be a good choice because of its view, although Room 1 is convenient to the bathroom and to the telephone.

There is a most agreeable lounge with an open fire, where the optional evening meal is served at individual tables of polished oak. Mrs. Brown assured me that everything is homecooked and the portions are "ample."

Ingleton is well situated for touring the Yorkshire Dales and the lakes.

OAKROYD HOTEL, Main Street, Ingleton, via Carnforth, Yorkshire England, LA6 3HJ. Tel: (0468) 41258. A 7-bedroom (shared baths) quiet hotel in a pleasant resort town in North Yorkshire. Breakfast served; dinner available on an optional basis. Open all year. Bowling, swimming pool, fishing, golf, fell-walking, and dancing nearby. Ideal for touring the Dales, the lakes, or the coast. Children and pets welcome. John and Pearl Brown, Proprietors.

Directions: A65 runs diagonally northwest from Leeds to Kendal in the Lake District. Ingleton is on A65, a few miles southeast of Exit 36 on the M6.

OLD SILENT INN
Stanbury (near Haworth), West Yorkshire

There are now two reasons to visit this part of Yorkshire; the first is to experience the Bronte presence, and the other is to visit the Old Silent Inn.

The Brontë presence is experienced by visiting the Parsonage in Haworth; once the home of the Brontë family, it is now an intimate museum cared for by the Bronte Society. The rooms of this small Georgian parsonage are furnished as in the Brontës' day, with displays of their personal treasures, pictures, books, and manuscripts. Visitors can see where the writers of *Jane Eyre* and *Wuthering Heights* lived.

Now to the Old Silent Inn, located a few miles out in the West Yorkshire countryside, which would be a curiosity no matter where it was located.

You can see it at a distance, all right. It is a whitewashed building, and the chances are that there will be a vintage Rolls Royce in the parking lot. This belongs to the owner, Mr. Joseph Proctor, who could have had a second career at any time playing an English pub-keeper in the films.

Mr. Proctor is a proclaimed self-made man, and I believe him. In a country that produces colorful characters *ad infinitum*, Mr. Proctor is a standout. He certainly worked his way up through life, and the Old Silent Inn is a testimonial to some of his interesting and bizarre ideas. It is jammed from top to bottom with knickknacks and photos and prints of the monarchs of England, including the Queen and Duke of Edinburgh and now the Prince and Princess of Wales. The first thing I saw was a brass bird cage with a plaster parrot in it. Around the inside of one of the dining rooms are display cabinets with wonderful collections of hand-painted dishes.

The bedrooms are traditional pub-inn rooms—rather small with shared baths. Morning coffee is served, as well as lunches. The bar areas are closed from 3:00 to 6:00, and open until late into the evening. There are dozens of little tables and chairs everywhere.

The menu is extensive, including soup, country paté, individual dishes of homemade steak and kidney pie and chicken pie. There is also the plowman's brunch, with two cheeses, potatoes, a hard-boiled egg with pickles, lettuce, and tomatoes.

I have an earlier connection with the Old Silent Inn. I first met Mr. Proctor's son, Nigel, when he was on the staff of the Red Fox Tavern in Middleburg, Virginia. After a pleasant conversation, he gave me a book of matches from the Old Silent Inn and I vowed to pay a visit the next time I was in West Yorkshire.

Well the day came and I found that Nigel was keeping the

Grouse Inn, a sort of sister inn to the Old Silent Inn, but located high on the fells a few miles away. I had a very pleasant reunion with Nigel as we talked over the many things that had happened to each of us since our last visit.

As I drove away from the Old Silent Inn, Joseph Proctor came out of the door and, just before stepping into his Rolls Royce, said that he was off to an auction. "Perhaps to buy another inn nearby," he said.

OLD SILENT INN, Stanbury (nr. Haworth), West Yorkshire, England BD22 8DR. Tel: (0535) 42503. A 7-bedroom (shared baths) free house in the heart of Bronte country in West Yorkshire. Breakfast included in room rate. Light lunches and evening meals also served. Closed from 3 P.M. to 6 P.M. Make arrangements ahead if checking in between these times. Conveniently located to enjoy all of the recreational, cultural, and scenic attractions of this section of Yorkshire, including a visit to the famous Brontë Parsonage, open year-round except for three weeks in December. Joseph Proctor, Publican.

Directions: From London take the M1 north and M62 west to Bradford, then M606 to Bradford city center. Follow signs for Keighley. Haworth is signposted from Keighley. Follow main road to Stanbury.

WOODLANDS
The Mains, Giggleswick, North Yorkshire

Afternoon teatime at Woodlands. I was enjoying a splendid solitary moment on the terrace, allowing my eye to play the game of following the course of the seemingly endless stone walls that wind their way down into the valley of the Ribble River and continue on up the green, rugged countryside, now joining other walls and finally disappearing over the top of the fell into some kind of Yorkshire eternity.

A little earlier, coming from the Lake District, I turned off A65 and found my way to the top of the hill for my first glimpse of this Georgian-style country house, serenely master of all it surveys. The view is of wooded slopes and grassy fields dotted with sheep, the Ribble River rushing over pebble and rock, and the Dale itself dotted with stone houses and barns.

The house, built of local stone, was originally designed as a private estate around the turn of the century. The bedrooms and public rooms are well appointed and many helpful amenities, such as television, radio, and electric blankets, are provided by Roger and Margaret Callan, the hosts. Almost every bedroom shares this marvelous view.

There are many different plans available for the traveler, but by all means do arrange to have dinner at Woodlands. You must make your table reservations by noon that same day.

Woodlands is within easy driving distance of the Lake District, James Herriott country, Haworth (home of the Bronte family), and the city of York. The footpaths wind up the famous limestone fells and along the bank of the Ribble. The unspoiled Yorkshire Dales provide ample diversions for a two- or three-night stay.

WOODLANDS, The Mains, Giggleswick, Settle, North Yorkshire, England BD24 0AX. Tel: (072 92) Settle 2576. A 10-bedroom (shared bathrooms) Georgian-style country house in the Yorkshire Dales district. Open all year except Christmas and New Year. Bed and breakfast, as well as dinner, available. Most conveniently located for walking and automobile tours of this section of Yorkshire. Many castles, abbeys, halls, and distinguished houses nearby, as well as the Yorkshire Dales National Park. Margaret and Roger Callan, Proprietors.

Directions: The A65 runs from Skipton northwest to the edge of Cumbria. Woodlands is actually located in the village of Giggleswick, next to the larger town of Settle. Once in Giggleswick, look for the signpost for the Mains. Continue to the top of the rise for Woodlands.

THE NATIONAL PARKS OF BRITON

It was while crossing the North York Moors and the Yorkshire Dales that I became aware of the National Park System which was established in the 1950s by what is now the Countryside Commission, and is administered by local planning authorities who have the double duty of conserving the fine landscape and then ensuring that people can get there to enjoy it.

Fortunately, these parks will preserve some of the remaining forest lands of Britain which, over the past five centuries were all but decimated for the building of ships and for fuel.

In my journeys for this book, I have traveled in Dartmoor Park in Devon, which is the biggest area of elevated moorland and wilderness remaining in southern England; in Exmoor with its wild red deer in Somerset; Brecon Beacons in Wales; Snowdonia, which is an unusually large park in North Wales, containing high bleak passes and valleys that were scoured by glaciers; the Lake

District which contains England's highest mountains; as well as the North York Moors and the Yorkshire Dales.

There are National Park Information Centres throughout Britain. Extensive and valuable literature on each park is available.

THE WHITWELL HALL COUNTRY HOUSE HOTEL
Whitwell on the Hill, York

I'd been told that Whitwell Hall was very impressive, but I never expected anything like this. It was almost as if some genii had rubbed his magic lamp and suddenly created a gracious and expansive country house hosted by a former Naval type and his beautiful wife. It was worthy of a motion picture setting.

Set in its own park at the end of a curving gravel drive, the front entry to the hall is made through a stately porte cochere and into a center hall with a cantilevered staircase and balcony framed by an elegant wrought iron balustrade. It is two-and-a-half stories high with a skylight that creates a gentle even glow. It all reminded me somewhat of Inverlochy Castle in Scotland.

Lieutenant Commander Peter Milner, formerly of the Royal Navy, turned out to be a very entertaining, voluble man with a keen interest in many different areas. He joined the Navy when he was seventeen and went to Dartmouth School, which also provided Prince Philip's naval training.

Both the Lt. Commdr. and Mrs. Milner obviously share a great interest in art, because the hotel is enhanced by many oil paintings, some quite heroic in dimension.

The furniture and decorations in the graceful, spacious drawing room have been chosen with care to blend with the numerous works of art.

"We actually like to feel that this is a real house party," he said, as we strolled through the gardens and grounds. "We have eighteen acres of grounds here, and if I do say so myself, we keep the gardens in fairly good condition. It is not easy, because at one time there were half-a-dozen gardeners; now we get along with just one. The Americans who come here enjoy our tennis court, as well as fishing and bicycling. Croquet is something we feel rather serious about, too."

Whitwell Hall is quite convenient to many of the beautiful natural attractions of Yorkshire, as well as being only twelve miles from the city of York. In fact, the famous tower of the Minster is visible from the terrace. In the adjacent woodland areas there are beeches, sycamores, and yews, and delightful walks overlooking

the Vale of York. Close by are the River Derwent and Kirkham Abbey.

All the guest rooms have their own bath or shower, and all overlook the gardens and spacious lawns.

For years I've been looking for the perfect place where I can stride into the drawing room in my white flannels and utter the now-famous line, "Anyone for tennis?" I believe Whitwell Hall is the place.

WHITWELL HALL COUNTRY HOUSE HOTEL, Whitwell on the Hill, Yorkshire, England Y067JJ. Tel: (065 381) 551. A country house hotel 12 mi. from York. Open every day of the year. Breakfast, lunch, tea, dinner served to non-residents. (Please ring in advance.) Castle Howard, York, North Yorkshire Moors nearby. Tennis, fishing, bicycles, croquet, and garden walks in grounds. Not suitable for children under 12. Lt. Commdr. P.F.M. Milner, Resident Owner.

Directions: Exit A1 for York. Follow A64 bypass signposted "Scarborough." Leave A64 and turn into village of Whitwell on the Hill. Turn left in village at telephone box.

THE AMERDALE HOUSE HOTEL
Arncliffe, North Yorkshire

In all of North America I have never found anything quite resembling the serene Dales of North Yorkshire. This great, rolling countryside is inhabited by countless sheep separated by countless walls, and the motorist now and then will find it necessary to stop the car to open a gate and drive through and then close the gate once again. This is true even on principal roads through the countryside. To stop and be alone is to listen to the sounds of lambs bleating. It's the landscape seen in the TV series "All Creatures Great and Small."

The road from Giggleswick to Arncliffe has a roller coaster effect and it is quite possible to drive for a considerable time without seeing another car. It is a single-passage road with "lay-bys" and occasional cattle grids, which are placed on the road to keep the cattle from wandering between fields.

The Amerdale House Hotel was quite a surprise to me. I didn't expect such a sophisticated, appealing accommodation this far into the Dales. Dating back to Elizabethan times, this old manor house undoubtedly has had its ups and downs, but someone obviously has invested quite a bit of money recently in restoring and refurbishing it, and has succeeded in converting the Amerdale House into a very pleasant residential hotel.

The reception area is most inviting and the well-furnished dining room looks out over the lawn and the meadows beyond. An attractive pub serves bar lunches at noon.

The bedrooms have been pleasantly furnished with flowered sheets, and furniture that is somewhat contemporary in fashion, and not necessarily quite in the spirit of the architecture of the house.

The village is rather interesting. It's mentioned in the Domesday Book and I understand a Norman Church stood there in the 11th century. The area itself is crisscrossed with public footpaths, which are found throughout England. These follow along beside the River Skirfare or meander along the sides of the Dales to the topmost craigs, which afford a splendid view of the countryside.

One footnote: I leafed through the hotel register rather extensively, and I don't believe many Americans have visited there in the past two years. The Amerdale House Hotel provides the kind of holiday that Britons enjoy very much.

THE AMERDALE HOUSE HOTEL, Arncliffe, Littondale, Skipton, North Yorkshire, England, BD23 5QE. Tel: (075 677) Arncliffe 250. A 10-bedroom hotel (share 4 bathrooms) in the North Yorkshire Dales, 15 mi. from Skipton. Morning tea, breakfast, and dinner served daily. Bar lunches available. Closed Nov. 1 to March 31. Splendid footpaths and excellent Yorkshire Dales roads lead to an endless variety of scenery, abbeys, castles, and stately homes. Jack and Noreen Vaughan, Innkeepers.

Directions: A65 and A59 meet at Skipton; take B6265 north to the National Park Center at Grassington. Then ask directions for Arncliffe.

NORTHUMBERLAND

There is a marvelous system of very fast roads in the United Kingdom; those running from London, north, can be divided into two basic roads. The M6 goes as far north as Carlisle and then breaks up into a series of good routes to both coasts, as well as to Glasgow or Edinburgh. The M1, when it is not a Motorway, becomes the A1. The A1 continues north through York, Durham, Newcastle-upon-Tyne, and into Edinburgh by way of Berwick-upon-Tweed. Of the two roads, the M1 (A1) is the least used north of Newcastle. In Northumberland it provides one of the most scenic routes in Britain. In this edition I have provided some accommodation suggestions on and just off the A1 which would be ideal for an overnight visit and even longer, as there are literally hundreds of castles, beaches, and nature preserves along the Northumberland coast.

There are three tours for Northumberland in the AA Touring Guide to Britain.

NORTHUMBERLAND

(1) LINDEN HALL HOTEL, Longhorsley, 224
(2) MARINE HOUSE HOTEL, Alnmouth, 225
(3) BLUE BELL HOTEL, Belford, 226
(4) TUGGAL HALL, Chathill, 227

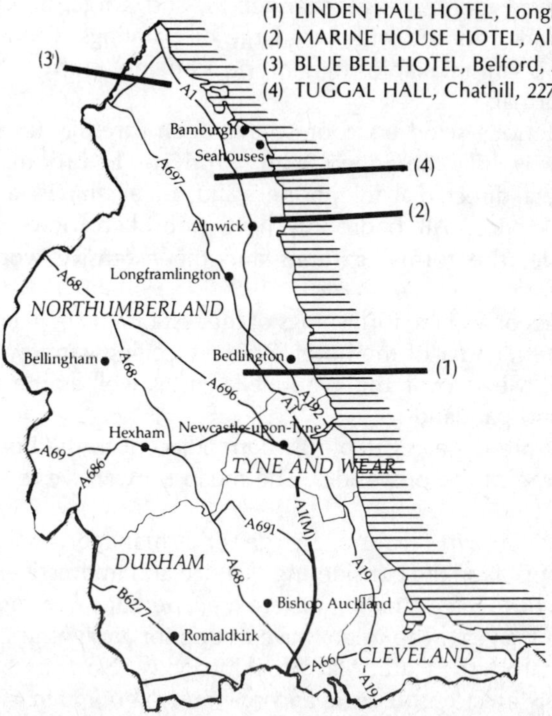

LINDEN HALL HOTEL
Longhorsley, Northumberland

This magnificent country house, set in 300 acres of breathtaking parkland and woods, was originally built in 1812 for Charles William Bigge, a local industrialist and banker. Recently rescued from ignominy, Linden Hall has been converted into a most impressive hotel.

Newly planted linden trees flank some stretches of the almost-mile-long private drive to the hotel.

The drawing room and inner hall have a sweeping staircase, a magnificent dome, huge chandeliers, and gorgeous carpets. The walls are adorned with very large oil paintings. The aura of grandeur is unmistakable. It is proper, but not stuffy; elegant, but not formal.

The various-sized bedrooms have been carefully furnished, and each is fully equipped with a private bathroom, color television, a direct-dial telephone—and, of all things, a baby-listening service. All bedrooms have unbroken views of the countryside, the formal gardens and the extensive woodland walks.

The decor and the furnishings of the restaurant are in keeping with the remainder of the hotel. Floor-to-ceiling windows allow panoramic views over the croquet lawn, as well as the formal gardens and parklands.

There are large vegetable gardens adjacent to the hotel that supply some of the provender. The menu is extensive to say the least.

I was shown around by general manager, Mr. Alan Blenkinsopp. Frankly, considering the size and impressiveness of the hotel, I expected a rather austere man, perhaps wearing white piping on his vest, who might have a superior air. Nothing could be farther from the truth. Alan Blenkinsopp is a Northumberland man and is most enthusiastic and obviously very much at home with his guests.

In contrast to the Georgian opulence, the Linden Pub, converted from the old granary, conveys a complete change of mood and atmosphere. It has exposed beams, an open fire, and a most interesting inner gallery. A collection of enamelled advertising signs of a bygone age adorn the walls. The sheltered courtyard has barbecue facilities and such outdoor pub games as quoits, boule, and draughts.

On the day of my visit there was a formal wedding party being held in another part of the hotel, and male members of the wedding party were wearing the famous grey top hats so fashionable at Wimbledon and Ascot. This was England at its 20th-century best, with ladies and gentlemen "dressed to the nines." The air was warm, the sky was clear, and the expectations for the marriage were obviously very high. They were certainly off to a great start.

LINDEN HALL HOTEL, Longhorsley, Morpeth, Northumberland, England. Tel: (0670) 56611. U.S. reservations: 800-223-5581. A 45-bedroom (private baths) luxurious country house hotel in a former 1812 Georgian mansion, set in 300 acres of parkland and woods. Breakfast, lunch, and dinner. Open year-round. Billiards, table tennis, outdoor tennis, and croquet on grounds. Many museums, stately homes, foot paths and backroading nearby. All modern amenities. Alan Blenkinsopp, General Manager.

Directions: Take A1 north out of Newcastle-upon-Tyne and turn onto A697 just above Morpeth. Linden Hall is just a short distance north of the village of Longhorsley.

MARINE HOUSE HOTEL
Alnmouth, Northumberland

Continuing on the A1 my next stop was Alnmouth, an attractive small seaside village that was once a small seaport not particularly noted for its righteousness. These matters, I am told have receded into the past and the village is now a very popular resort.

The Marine House Hotel is a large, comfortable stone house built on the edge of the village golf links with fine views of Alnmouth Bay. The seaside sands are of a very fine consistency and bathing, boating, sea and river angling, and pony trekking are much favored.

I think the real point about stopping off here is that it is a very natural small hotel that would be quite popular with the British because of its location and because of its relatively reasonable tariffs. It isn't the kind of place that the visitor to England would be likely to find, because it is a little out of the way. It affords an opportunity for an English seaside hotel experience with very friendly and affable proprietors. Four of the bedrooms face the sea and there is a pleasant little terrace and a garden, which also shares this pleasant view.

Proprietress Sheila Inkster does all of the cooking and this includes roast beef, Yorkshire pudding, roast turkey, and creamed potatoes.

If the reader stays here, please send me a card with your impressions. It had an appeal for me.

MARINE HOUSE PRIVATE HOTEL, Alnmouth, Northumberland, England. Tel: (0665) 830 349. An 8-bedroom traditional small seaside hotel (some shared baths). Open all year. Breakfast and dinner served daily. Overlooking a 9-hole seaside golf course. Seabathing, yachting, pony trekking nearby. Sheila and Gordon Inkster, Proprietors.

Directions: Alnmouth is on the Northumbrian coast between Berwick and Newcastle, and east of Alnwick, off the A1. Can be reached by London-Edinburgh railway, 1 mi. away.

BLUE BELL HOTEL
Belford, Northumberland

During the "high season" there is a good chance that the traveler in England may run into some difficulty in booking a room along the Northumberland coast because, during July, August, and September, this is a very popular holiday area for Britons. That is why I was particularly glad to discover the Blue Bell Hotel in Belford, with fifteen bedrooms. It is ideally located to enjoy the

region's attractions, including Holy Island, the wild, white cattle at Chillingham, the many magnificent castles, the bird sanctuaries of the Farne Islands, and the extensive sandy beaches of the coast.

Some eleven miles south of Berwick-upon-Tweed, the Blue Bell is a full-service hotel, open year-round. The beautiful brick building and the most tasteful furnishings, including attractively decorated bedrooms and a sheltered garden in the rear, make it a very agreeable stop for the tourist. The menu is quite extensive for a relatively small place, and it is possible also to enjoy bar snacks or luncheon, as well as afternoon tea.

The feature that appealed to me the most about the Blue Bell is that, like the Three Tuns in Thirsk and other non-tourist-oriented small British hotels, it has an easy, unhurried atmosphere.

The A1, continuing north to Berwick into Scotland, has some really spectacular views and seascapes. It's a good idea just to take one of the side roads (shown on the map with four numbers) down to the sea and discover the pleasant little harbor and countryside for yourself.

THE BLUE BELL HOTEL, Belford, Northumberland, England NE70 7NE. Tel: (066-83) 543. A 15-bedroom (most with private baths) pleasant, unassuming hotel, 11 mi. south of Berwick-upon-Tweed. Breakfast, lunch, dinner, afternoon tea served daily. Open all year. Conveniently located for a more extensive holiday on the Northumberland coast. Sadie Patterson, Manager.

Directions: The Blue Bell is located directly off the A1 in the middle of the village, which recently has been by-passed.

TUGGAL HALL
Chathill, Northumberland

"Perhaps the most surprising aspect of this part of Northumberland is the numerous superb, sandy beaches all along the unspoiled coastline. The nearest one is just a fifteen-minute walk from us and there is marvelous bird watching and also a seal colony on the Farne Islands."

Naomi Barrett had joined us after dinner in the attractive drawing room—also a guest dining room—of Tuggal Hall, a distinguished country house that traces its origins back to the 13th century. We were all seated around the fireplace, where a coal fire burned brightly.

Naomi poured coffee and continued extolling the virtues of Tugall Hall as a center for a pleasant holiday: "There are seven golf

courses nearby, excellent fishing on several different rivers, as well as sea fishing off the coast, sightseeing on the many islands, marvelous walking in the Cheviot Hills, and more castles and historic sites than could be visited in a week, all within a short drive."

Tuggal Hall is a part of the Wolsey Lodge Consortium and, like the other two I visited and have included in this book, it is of first-class quality. There are two very large double bedrooms sharing one bathroom, and dinner is available by advance request. Naomi pointed out that guests who stay more than one night might prefer to take the evening meal at one of the several good restaurants in the area.

The house faces south, surrounded by trees and gardens overlooking farmland with eastern views to the sea. It is only about seventy miles to Edinburgh by car on the A1. It's possible to make a day trip to that famous Scottish city by taking the train in the morning and returning on the 5:00 p.m. train, arriving in Chathill at 6:30.

TUGGAL HALL, Chathill, Northumberland, NE67 5EW England. Tel: (066 589) Chathill 229. A 2-bedroom (shared bath) country house accommodation just a short distance from the seacoast. Open year-round. Breakfast included in room rate; evening meal on request. Ideally situated with miles of sandy beaches for walking and exceptional bird watching; golf courses, fishing, sightseeing, and many castles nearby. A Wolsey Lodge accommodation. Mrs. Naomi Barrett, Proprietress.

Directions: Coming north on A1, exit at the Alnwick Bypass. Turn off at Denwick and follow B1340, watching for a very simple sign on the side of a barn that says Tuggal Hall. It is on the left-hand side of the bend, 10 mi. north of Alnwick. If you pass a sign that says Tugall Grange, you have gone too far.

SCOTLAND

*Welcome to Scotland, or as it is expressed in Gaelic: "*Ceud Mile Fáilte.*" It translates into "a hundred thousand welcomes." (Try pronouncing it* Cute Mela Falsha.*)*

Scotland has some of the most beautiful and rugged scenery in the world—mountains, firths, glens, lochs, and islands. Scotland is tartans, haggis, oat cakes, pipes, kilts, trews, grouse-on-the-wing, Highland games, hundreds of ruined castles and abbeys, golf, monsters, sheep on narrow roads, hidden fishing villages, and rich farmland.

Scotland is also history, a history intertwined with heroes and villains. One of the best ways to prepare for a trip to Scotland is to read the history and identify with some of the personalities: Robert the Bruce; Mary Queen of Scots; Rob Roy MacGregor, Flora MacDonald, and Bonnie Prince Charlie. Read about the Campbells, MacDonalds and Bloody Glencoe, the Glorious Revolution, Bannockburn, and Culloden.

Return to Sir Walter Scott's poems and novels. He perhaps unknowingly became Scotland's best press agent.

To further enrich a Scottish experience, dip into the poetry of Robert Burns, the novels of Robert Louis Stevenson, and the famous trip to Scotland by Doctor Samuel Johnson written by his biographer James Boswell, himself a canny Scot.

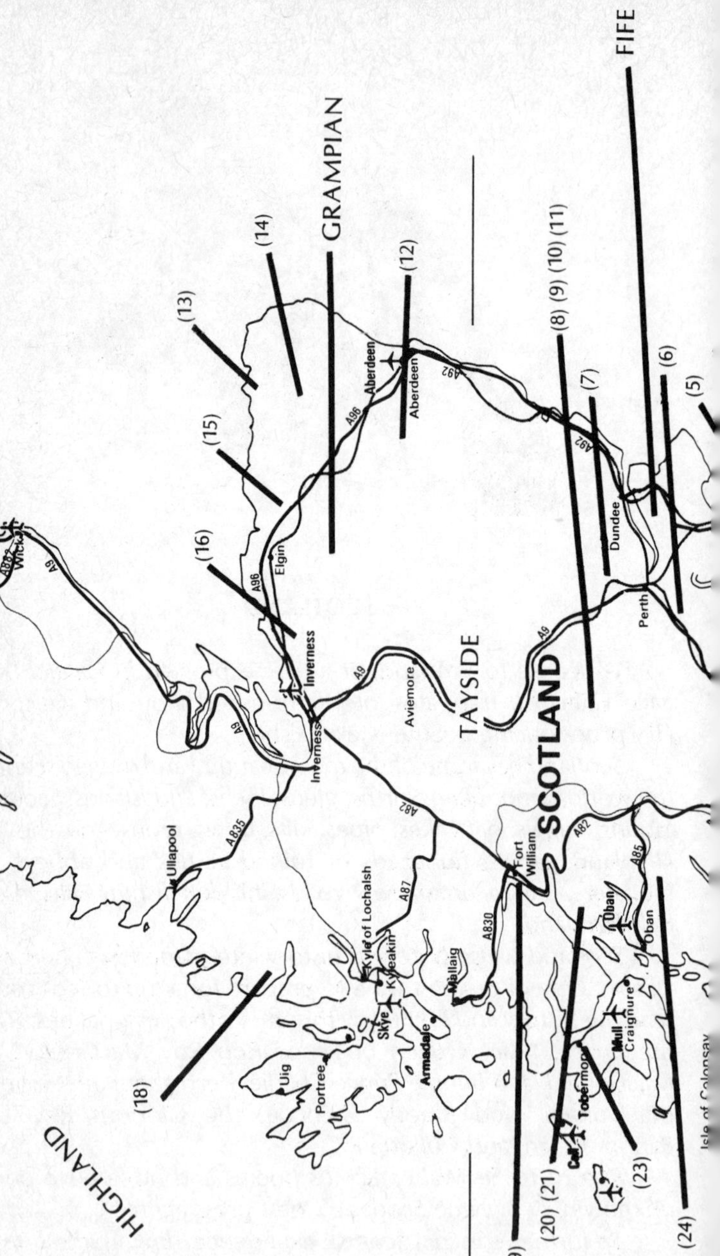
HIGHLAND
GRAMPIAN
TAYSIDE
FIFE
SCOTLAND
Scrabster
Thurso
Wick
A882
A9
A96
Elgin
Inverness
Aviemore
Aberdeen
A92
Dundee
Perth
Ullapool
A835
A82
A87
Kyle of Lochalsh
Kyleakin
Skye
Uig
Portree
Armadale
Mallaig
A830
Fort William
A85
Oban
Mull
Craignure
Tobermory
Coll
(5)
(6)
(7)
(8) (9) (10) (11)
(12)
(13)
(14)
(15)
(16)
(18)
(19)
(20) (21)
(23)
(24)

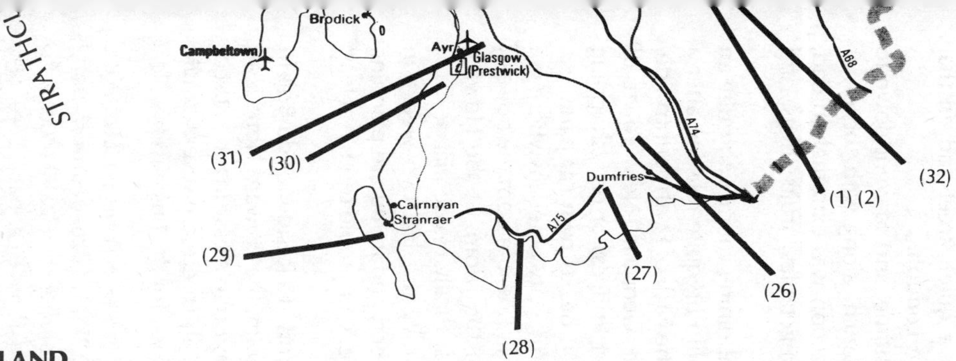

SCOTLAND

(1) THE HOWARD HOTEL, Edinburgh, 232
(2) HOUSTOUN HOUSE, Uphall, Lothian, 233
(3) OPEN ARMS HOTEL, Dirleton, Lothian, 234
(4) GREYWALLS, Gullane, East Lothian, 235
(5) PRESTONFIELD HOUSE RESTAURANT, Edinburgh, 237
(6) BALGEDDIE HOUSE HOTEL, Glenrothes, Fife, 238
(7) BALLATHIE HOUSE, Kinclaven by Stanley, Perthshire, 240
(8) DUNKELD HOUSE HOTEL, Dunkeld, Tayside, 241
(9) THE KENMORE HOTEL, Kenmore, Aberfeldy, Tayside, 243
(10) ROSE VILLA, Fortingall, Highland Perthshire, 245
(11) PORT-AN-EILEAN HOTEL, Strathtummel, Tayside, 246
(12) TULLICH LODGE, Ballater, Grampian, 248
(13) COUNTY HOTEL BANFF, Banff, Grampian, 250
(14) PITTODRIE HOUSE HOTEL, Pitcaple, Grampian, 251
(15) ROTHES GLEN HOTEL, Rothes, Grampian, 254
(16) THE CLIFTON HOTEL, Nairn, Invernesshire, 255
(17) DUNAIN PARK, Inverness, Highland, 256
(18) TIGH-AN-EILEAN, Shieldaig, Highland, 258
(19) INVERLOCHY CASTLE, Fort William, Highland, 259
(20) ARDSHEAL HOUSE, Kentallen of Appin, Strathclyde, 261
(21) ISLE OF ERISKA HOTEL, Ledaig, Connel, Strathclyde, 263
(22) ISLE OF COLONSAY HOTEL, Isle of Colonsay, Strathclyde, 267
(23) WESTERN ISLES HOTEL, Tobermory, Isle of Mull, Strathclyde, 269
(24) TAYCHREGGAN HOTEL, Kilchrenan, Argyll, 272
(25) THE CREGGANS INN, Strachur, Strathclyde, 274
(26) AUCHEN CASTLE HOTEL, Beattock, Dumfriesshire, 276
(27) THRUSHWOOD B&B, Mouswald, Dumfriesshire, 277
(28) BALCARY BAY HOTEL, Auchencairn, Dumfries and Galloway, 277
(29) KNOCKINAAM LODGE HOTEL, Portpatrick, Wigtownshire, 278
(30) MARINE HOTEL, Troon, Ayrshire, 280
(31) GLEDDOCH HOTEL, Langbank, Strathclyde, 281
(32) THE PHILIPBURN HOUSE HOTEL, Selkirk, 282

THE HOWARD HOTEL
Edinburgh

Edinburgh has many great and luxurious hotels; however, I was looking for a good, small, conservative, well-run, personal hotel where I thought our readers would be able to feel at home after a long drive north. Imagine my delight on learning that Arthur Neil of the Open Arms in Dirleton had acquired just such a hotel. I was happy to follow his fairly simple directions and to see it for myself.

The Howard Hotel attracted me immediately in that it is situated in a former townhouse on a quiet street and, in that respect, resembles Number Sixteen in London.

By coincidence I arrived at lunchtime, and so went down to the first floor to have a good bar lunch, along with the other business people of the city. The selection was extremely broad, including various types of salads, vegetables, fruits, eggs, and cheeses.

The hotel also has a more formal dining room with quite an extensive menu, and dinner here could be quite relaxing after a day of seeing the sights of the city or the Firth of Forth countryside.

The Howard is located in the Georgian New Town of Edinburgh, close to the George and Princess Streets shopping district. One of its advantages is that it has its own car park.

One of the things I strive to find in a city hotel anywhere is a bedroom that is quiet and as far away as possible from the noise of trucks and traffic. Fortunately, all of the rooms at the Howard fill that bill, because the area is almost totally residential.

The Edinburgh Festival is generally the last two weeks in August and the first week in September, and if you are planning to stay at the Howard during that time, you should reserve at least six months in advance.

Just like the Algonquin in New York, La Residence du Bois in Paris, and the Hotel Reisen in Stockholm, the Howard Hotel is an ideal city hotel, providing a quiet, comfortable base in the midst of a busy metropolitan center. Incidentally, there are several single rooms that make it a very canny stopover for the business traveler.

THE HOWARD HOTEL, 32 Great King Street, Edinburgh, EH3 6QH, Scotland. Tel: (031-556) 1393. Telex: 727887. A 26-bedroom hotel (private baths) in a quiet section of Edinburgh, ideally situated to enjoy the many attractions of the town. Private car park. Breakfast, lunch, and dinner. Open all year. Reservations may also be made for the Open Arms at Dirleton and vice versa. Arthur Neil, Proprietor.

Directions: From George Street in the center of Edinburgh turn down the hill at Hanover Street; Great King Street is the 5th street down, turn right and the Howard is on the left. Park in front of the hotel to check in.

HOUSTOUN HOUSE
Uphall, Lothian

Houstoun House enjoys the distinction of being both a restful place to stay, and just a few minutes from Edinburgh's new air terminal. Convenient to one of Scotland's great cities, it is also just a few miles from the direct route north into the Eastern Highlands and the Grampian region.

Keith Knight, who owns and operates Houstoun House with his wife, is a former architect. He has restored this white lofty-gabled Lowland home into a most comfortable hotel, preserving the quality of this former ancient laird's house, and combining it with the comforts of the 20th century.

In a brief chat with me, Keith pointed out that Houstoun House has a choice of accommodations. "For short stays, we have rather simple, newer rooms, each of which has its own private bathroom, central heating, and telephones. In the tower and in the small and ancient "Woman House," the atmosphere is more traditional, many rooms having 18th-century paneling and several with four-poster beds. A lot of these additions and the redecorating have been done since your last visit."

Our conversation turned to the menu and his supervision of the kitchen. "We try to provide what we think is some of the best,

and certainly the most interesting food in Scotland. To that end we offer a limited choice in our four-course dinner, preferring to concentrate all of our efforts on preparing unusual dishes from all over the world into a carefully balanced meal."

By way of illustrating his point, my dinner that evening was cream of lettuce soup, a hot salmon mousse with a tomato and mushroom sauce, chicken with parsley stuffing, and for dessert I had a whim-wham—a cross between a sherry trifle and a syllabub.

Houstoun House stands in its own parkland and gardens, considerably away from the noise of the highway. There is a "hedge-sheltered garden" laid out in the 18th century with clipped yews, enormous copper beech and cedar trees.

HOUSTOUN HOUSE, Uphall, Lothian, Scotland. Tel: (0506) Broxburn 853831; Telex 727148. An elegantly appointed 29-room country house hotel 13 mi. from Edinburgh. The garden was laid out in 1722. Most convenient to all of the cultural and sightseeing in Edinburgh. Open all year. Breakfast, lunch, and dinner served to non-residents. Mr. & Mrs. Keith Knight, Resident Owners.

Directions: From Newbridge Roundabout (the end of M8 and M9) take A89 (signposted Bathgate/Broxburn). Turn right at traffic lights after 3 mi., and a sharp left at T-junction, up drive to house.

OPEN ARMS HOTEL
Dirleton, Lothian

"Our guests find that the Open Arms is perfectly suited for the visitor who wants to be near Edinburgh, but who prefers to stay in the country."

Arthur Neil, the managing director of this village hotel was explaining some of the interesting sights and activities of this corner of Scotland which borders on both the North Sea and the Firth of Forth.

"We have eight golf courses within an easy driving distance," he commented. "The sandy local soil enables the golfer to play in almost any weather, summer and winter. There are also many beaches and numerous beauty spots nearby."

We were enjoying a chat in the drawing room and he noticed that my attention was drawn to the ruins of the famous Dirleton Castle which is literally just across the quiet village street.

"Our guests love to roam inside of those walls," he said. "It's one of the most famous ancient monuments in the British Isles.

Time has dealt most graciously with the old 11th-century castle—it has taken on a great mellowness of age."

I had seen quite a few of the carefully kept bedrooms, each with its own private bath. Mr. Neil made a point of mentioning that service is available in the rooms at no extra cost.

We did have a moment or two to talk about some of the items on the menu, including a mussel and onion stew, something which I must confess I had never heard of until visiting the Open Arms.

Mr. Neil spoke at some length of his interest in encouraging the young people of Scotland to become involved in the hotel business; he has set up some standards for industry practice and training programs that I found most admirable.

Arthur Neil is also the proprietor of the Howard Hotel, located in a very pleasant residential area of Edinburgh. When telephoning either one or the other hotel, arrangements can be made for either place.

Incidentally, the symbol on the stationery and brochures for the Open Arms is a stylized version of a young lady in a colorful costume with long hair curling over her shoulders holding her arms out with such bountiful offerings as oranges, apples, pears, grapes, other vegetables and fruits. The motto of the house is, "Where welcome ever smiles and farewell goes out sighing."

THE OPEN ARMS HOTEL, Dirleton, East Lothian, Scotland, Tel: (0620 85) Dirleton 241. U.S. reservations: 800-243-1806. A 7-room village hotel 20 mi. east of Edinburgh. Open every day in the year for breakfast, lunch, tea, and dinner. Within a short drive of many historic and scenic attractions and adjacent to active sports such as tennis, golf, fishing, walking, and riding. Arthur Neil, Managing Director.

Directions: From Edinburgh: follow A1 to Musselburgh and watch for A198 which is on the left. The road passes through Gullane to Dirleton.

GREYWALLS
Gullane, East Lothian

Greywalls is the American's "golf club away from home." It's a mashie-niblick shot from the fairways and greens of the world-famous Muirfield golf links. The great and near-great of golfdom have played Muirfield, and the hotel guestbook includes such names as Palmer and Nicklaus.

To avoid any misunderstanding, the proprietor of Greywalls,

Giles Weaver, points out that being in residence at the hotel does not automatically provide an introduction to Muirfield. "To play, one has to make one's own arrangements with the Secretary." So come prepared with letters from your home club and other documents—they take such things seriously at Muirfield. Not everyone can be accommodated.

So much for golf. I can assure any golfers that even if they cannot play Muirfield, the ten other courses in East Lothian contain some surprises and challenges.

As suggested earlier, Greywalls has a definite clublike atmosphere. Several of the drawing rooms are lined from floor to ceiling with books, and have cheery fireplaces. The furniture is deep and comfortable, inviting conversation with new acquaintances.

The rather opulent lodging rooms overlook the fairways and greens of Muirfield and the Firth of Forth beyond. On the opposite side of the hotel there are some gorgeous gardens with many roses and beautiful delicate purple iris which were in bloom during my visit.

Greywalls is a luxurious, highly reputable country house hotel. Guests are made to feel as if they are in a private home, and there is a casual and natural atmosphere.

The amenities are numerous including fresh fruit and good books in the rooms, as well as telephones. There is a call button in both bedrooms and bathrooms to summon the bellman, if needed. Everything has been done, as the saying goes, "to the nines."

GREYWALLS, Duncur Rd., Gullane, East Lothian, Scotland, EH31 2EG. Tel: (0620) 842 144. U.S. reservations: 800-243-1806. An elegant 24-room country house hotel immediately adjacent to the famous Muirfield golf links on the Firth of Forth and 19 mi. from Edinburgh. Breakfast, lunch, dinner served to non-residents. Open every day in the week. Closed during the winter. It is wise to check in advance for accommodations at any time. In the historically rich and beautiful natural area of scenic beauty in East Lothian. Golf and many other sports available nearby. Giles Weaver, Proprietor.

Directions: From Edinburgh take the A1 through Musselburgh and then watch carefully on the left for A198 which leads eastward to Gullane. Turn left at the end of Gullane Village at the signpost; Greywalls is 300 yds. further on.

PRESTONFIELD HOUSE RESTAURANT
Edinburgh

The peace and quiet was so deafening and the scene so sylvan, that I found it hard to believe I was only ten minutes from the center of Edinburgh. Here at Prestonfield House, a 17th-century manor which stands in 23 acres of its own lawns, parkland, and landscaped gardens, I marvelled at the bucolic setting, with peacocks and pheasants feeding diffidently on the lawns.

Once inside the rather austere entrance with its Doric columns, the entrance hall sets the scene for a series of truly impressive public rooms. The Italian Room is so named because it is paneled with 17th-century paintings in the style of Italian capriccios. The ceiling of the Tapestry Room is richly ornamented with cupids and heraldic beasts. The paneled doors are from Spain, and the room is furnished lavishly with antique furniture, Chinese porcelain, Persian carpets, and Mortlake tapestries. The Leather Room has leather panels which were brought from Cordova, Spain, in 1676. These escaped destruction in a later fire.

Other public rooms are decorated with landscapes by G.A. Williams, and there are many oil portraits of past proprietors and inhabitants of Prestonfield House, some of which have been presented to the National Gallery.

Except for the basement and the old staircase, the present house dates from 1687. About 1815, the twin dining rooms, one formerly a ballroom, were added, and the main hall redesigned to achieve a harmony between the old and new. The black and white marble floor is of the 17th century, and the Doric columns and pilasters are of the later date.

Aside from the truly elegant interior embellishments, the history of Prestonfield House is tremendously interesting. Some of the personalities involved include Sir James Dick, who acquired the property in 1677, and whose descendants are still associated with the hotel. King James II was a frequent visitor at Prestonfield, often arriving from neighboring Holyroodhouse Palace on foot by a path which came to be known as Duke's Walk. In 1681, the students of Edinburgh University burned down Prestonfield House as part of a protest.

Boswell and Johnson stayed here after returning from their journey to the Western Isles, and Benjamin Franklin was a guest in 1759.

Bonnie Prince Charlie, who apparently slept in as many beds as George Washington, was also a guest.

Fortunately, the visitor to Scotland can enjoy either lunch or dinner at Prestonfield House, and the trip out from the center of the city is a short one. In addition to standard fare, the menu offers game dishes such as pheasant, grouse, woodcock, teal, snipe, wood pigeon, and venison. The remarkable public rooms and grounds make it a memorable experience.

PRESTONFIELD HOUSE RESTAURANT, Priestfield Road, Edinburgh, Scotland EH16 5UT. Tel: (031) 667-8000. One of Scotland's most famous "great houses" in rural surroundings, but within the city limits of Edinburgh. Breakfast, lunch, and dinner served every day. Convenient to Hollyrood Palace. Pleasant walks on grounds.

Directions: All access to Priestfield Rd. and Prestonfield House is from A68 (Dalkeith Rd.). At center of city, ask for Dalkeith Rd.

BALGEDDIE HOUSE HOTEL
Glenrothes, Fife

James Crombie, the director of Balgeddie House, arrayed in a very dashing tattersall vest, was telling me about some of the pleasant recreation nearby. We were having a chat in the lounge of this beautiful country house hotel.

"Do you play golf?" he asked. "The Royal & Ancient Club at St. Andrews is only thirty minutes away and Glen Eagles is just a bit farther. We have many North Americans who stay here mainly for the golf.

"If your readers are truly adventurous of spirit, there's a gliding club nearby and a horse riding stable. In the town of Glenrothes, there's a swimming pool and a sports center."

Crombie proved to be a gentleman of ready wit with a great fund of information, all of which he imparted with a most engaging Scottish accent. "Is croquet your game?" he asked, with a twinkle in his eye. "We happen to indulge in it frequently here during the

summer months. I even play myself on occasion." I can well imagine Mr. Crombie plays a cracking game of croquet.

The view from the lounge is out over an impressive sweep of lawn that extends past the brow of the hill and into the meadows beyond. The grounds have many spruce, fir, and copper beech trees, and a glorious profusion of rhododendron.

Most of the large bedrooms in this elegant house have their own private bathrooms, and all have color television, radio, and telephones.

On my most recent visit I was quite impressed with the handsome new lounge restaurant called the Paddock, which Mr. Crombie pointed out was formerly a garage. On the day of my visit it featured an inviting buffet lunch, which proved to be popular with the "locals."

Mr. Crombie was not at all reticent about speaking of his menu. "The *pièce de résistance* is probably the *cordon bleu* artistry of our *chef de cuisine.* We also feature steak Fergusson served with stovies, fresh Scottish salmon, and Aberdeen Angus beef."

The Balgeddie House Hotel is a little more contemporary than other country house hotels I've visited in England and Scotland. It is nonetheless comfortable and accommodating.

It also has Mr. James Crombie who, among many different careers, has also been an opera singer.

BALGEDDIE HOUSE HOTEL, Leslie Road, Glenrothes, Fife, Scotland. Tel: (0592) Glenrothes 742511. A 19-room country house hotel (13 rooms with private baths/showers) about 9 miles north of Kirkcaldy. Open every day in the year except Jan. 1 and 2. Breakfast, lunch, tea, and dinner served to non-residents. Located approx. 30 mi. from Edinburgh and within a short drive of many prestigious golf clubs. James Crombie, Director.

Directions: From Edinburgh leave the M90 at Intersection #5 towards Leslie and Glenrothes. After passing through Leslie, approx. 300 yds. on the left there's a large signpost indicating the hotel entrance.

BALLATHIE HOUSE
Kinclaven by Stanley, Perthshire

It's not very often that I find fireplaces with a merry fire crackling away on the *second-floor* hallway of country house hotels. However, this was exactly what was happening at Ballathie House. In fact it is somewhat indicative of the entire atmosphere of this French baronial Victorian country house, built on the west bank of the River Tay around 1850.

The dimensions of the entryway, the main lounge, the elaborate staircase, the dining room, and particularly the spacious lawns leading down to the banks of the river were most impressive. The master bedrooms, originally designed to provide the owner and his guests with plenty of room to spread out, could well accommodate a paddle-ball court. I give you my word that one has a bathroom in which you could hold a dance. Most bedrooms on the back of the house look out over the lawns and the river bank and there are few scenes anywhere in the world as idyllic. Incidentally, there are also smaller bedrooms that have been adapted from the original staff quarters. All have the same amenities, views, and rates.

The atmosphere here is sophisticated but friendly, with French and German spoken, in addition to English. The menu is a combination of British and French cooking with a generous taste of Scotland. Leg of lamb, beef Stroganoff, salmon steak, cold game pie, and grilled Scottish beef steak were offered during my stay.

This might be a good place to say that almost every British country house hotel has off-season and special "breaks" (rates) available in the spring and late autumn. All the more reason to plan your trip during these times.

Staying on for extra days is quite enticing. For instance, there's salmon fishing on the River Tay right at the hotel—this requires advance reservation. Trout fishing is also available nearby. Please make inquiries about the local rules and regulations. Tennis, practice golf, putting, croquet, and trap shooting can be enjoyed at the hotel.

I seldom have time for any of these wonderful diversions, but I would certainly enjoy just spending the entire day relaxing on the lawn overlooking the River Tay and looking forward to dinner in the candlelit dining room.

BALLATHIE HOUSE, Kinclaven by Stanley, Perthshire, PH1 4QN. Tel: Meikleour (025 083) 268. U.S. reservations: 800-323-5463 or 800-243-1806. A 21-room luxury country house hotel (private baths) in the heart of the scenic Perthshire country. Bedrooms of varying size available in main house. Breakfast, lunch, tea, and dinner. Open Mar. 1 thru Nov. 31. Within a very short drive of Pitlochry and Perth. Excellent recreation on grounds. Mrs. P.E. Brassey, Managing Director.

Directions: The best way is to go north from Perth on the A93 and look for the hotel sign on the left just after crossing the River Tay. There are lots of wonderful back roads on which to get lost.

DUNKELD HOUSE HOTEL
Dunkeld, Tayside

It was a lovely, quiet moment here on the banks of the River Tay, which at this point was deep and swift-flowing on its eastward journey to Dundee.

Directly behind me the soft yellow lights of Dunkeld House were glowing more brightly in the deepening Highland dusk. Along both sides of the river the many flowers, dominated by the rhododendrons, heralded the arrival of a Scottish summer. Kingfishers, ospreys, and an occasional merganser flitted perilously close to the river's surface looking for young wayward salmon.

I sent a pebble skipping across the water and turned back on the footpath toward the hotel. The pleasant discord of the orchestra tuning up drifted through the dining room windows, and as I got closer, I could see great preparations were being made for the weekly Saturday night dance at Dunkeld House.

On this particular evening, the occasion would be even more festive because there was a wedding party in progress in the garden, with several Scotsmen decked out in their dress kilts. The bride, of course, was quite evident from her radiant beauty, and the groom, from the beaming happiness on his face.

I wandered on by the putting green, tennis court, and croquet court which were momentarily inactive, but I was certain the next day would find them in use again.

Dunkeld House is situated in over one hundred acres of gardens and woodlands, and is reached by a long drive leading off the road just north of Dunkeld Village. For the naturalist, it is an ideal area for the study of many wild animals and birds.

The pine-paneled hall lounge is a popular meeting place for guests, even more so in cold weather when an open fire provides additional welcoming heat. Other comfortable lounges and the dining room all have views of the lawn and river.

Salmon fishing, particularly in the late winter and early spring, is one of the principal attractions, and hotel guests have fishing privileges along one and a half miles on the River Tay.

Golfing enthusiasts may play on a number of very good and well-known courses in the surrounding district. In addition, the Pitlochry Festival Theatre is nearby, as well as an unusual number of nature reserves, and several castles, including Glamis which was the inspiration for Shakespeare's *Macbeth*.

All twenty-six bedrooms have been individually and tastefully decorated. Most overlook the river or gardens.

Tay River salmon and trout head up the menu, also venison, Angus beefsteak and Scottish roast beef.

At dinner that evening, the members of the wedding party cut very fancy figures dancing in their kilts and enjoying frequent toasts to the bridal couple. There was one braw Scottish lad, about twelve years old, with the most angelic face and the handsomest black eye to be found south of Inverness. I was dying to ask him how he got it, but I restrained myself.

DUNKELD HOUSE HOTEL, Dunkeld, Perthshire, Scotland PH8 OHX. Tel: (035 02) 243. A 27-room hotel overlooking the famed salmon River Tay, located about 12 mi. north of Perth in the beautiful Tayside section of Scotland. Open Jan. 14 to Oct. 31. Breakfast, lunch, tea, and dinner served to non-residents. Conveniently located for trips to beautiful lochs and mountains of central Scotland, as well as the Pitlochry Theatre, Scone Palace, Blair Castle, Dunkeld Cathedral. Tennis, bowls, pitch-and-putt golf, croquet, and river fishing (salmon) on grounds. Championship golf and riding nearby. No credit cards. Mrs. G.B. Miller, Managing Director.

Directions: Follow A9 (Perth-Inverness Road) 12 mi. due north, turn right at signpost for Dunkeld. Turn left over river bridge to Dunkeld town, through town ¼ mi., turn left through turreted gateway 1 mi. through hotel grounds.

THE KENMORE HOTEL
Kenmore, Aberfeldy, Tayside

On November 2, 1572, Sir Colin Campbell gave the first lease of the Kenmore Hotel to his servants Hew Hay and spouse, thereby establishing what is said to be the oldest hotel in Scotland.

All of this information, including a translation from the original language of the lease, is included in a most interesting book, *Four Hundred Years Around Kenmore,* written by Duncan Fraser, and presented to me by the innkeeper of the Kenmore Hotel, Ian McKenzie.

Despite the fact that numbering among its visitors over the past four hundred years have been royalty, foreign dignitaries, and possibly the most revered guest of all, Robert Burns, the Kenmore Hotel does not put on any airs! It's a jolly place where the local farmers and countrymen stop in at the pub and, no doubt, raise many a toast to Bobbie Burns, who spent the night of Wednesday, the 29th of August, 1787. He wrote a tribute to Kenmore on the wall which can still be seen, now under a protective sheet of glass. This room has been named the "Poet's Parlour."

Ian McKenzie pointed out that the Fifteenth of January Festival, celebrating the opening of salmon season, is "verra important." Almost every Scot enjoys fishing and the River Tay is one of the most famous fishing streams in Scotland.

"The River Tay actually starts right here in Loch Tay," he explained, "and a great many of us gather on the banks of the river here at the hotel and then we march down to the river shore, where a bottle of Scotch whiskey is broken over one of the boats and everybody toasts the season. It's really a most convivial idea and then we come back here and continue the festivities. As you can imagine, there's very little fishing done that day, and there's a big party that night."

Today, the Kenmore consists of the original building and two more adjacent structures. There are 48 rooms at this ancient inn; 35 with private baths or showers. Rooms look out either over the village, or the River Tay to the rear.

"I believe it could truthfully be said that we are in the very heart of Scotland," he declared. "We're very convenient for trips to Edinburgh, Aberdeen, Inverness, Oban, and Glasgow. We're open all year and there's skiing on Ben Lawers, or on the slopes of Aviemore, Glencoe, or Glenshee. Our walking is some of the best in the Highlands."

As might be expected in this part of Scotland, the menu is headed by Tay salmon and Aberdeen Angus beef dishes.

Ian proved to be an excellent host and was kind enough to take me on a brief tour of a nearby castle where there is a golf course. We drove around the castle and then strolled down to the banks of the River Tay. "This is a very popular salmon pool," he said. "Fishermen who come here have their own ideas about fishing and they have their favorite pool. That bridge over there is called the Chinese bridge. Last week we had ninety-odd rafts floating down the river which is another annual event. Today, it seems terribly quiet by comparison."

Ian advised me that June would be a most pleasant month to come to Kenmore, because the weather is very pleasant and it is in advance of the more popular months of July and August. Fishing months are April, May, and early June, and then September and October.

THE KENMORE HOTEL, Kenmore, Perthshire, Scotland PH15 2NU. Tel: (08873) Kenmore 205. U.S. reservations: 800-243-1806. A 48-room traditional village inn (35 with private bath/shower) in the beautiful lake area of Scotland's Highlands. Open all year. Breakfast, lunch, tea, dinner served to non-residents. Hill walking, fishing, skiing, golf, riding, and pony trekking available. Pitlochry Festival Theatre and many museums, art galleries within a short drive. Ian H. Mackenzie, Manager.

Directions: From Perth take A9 (Inverness Road) to Ballinluig (23 mi.). Turn left for Aberfeldy on A827 (10 mi.). Continue to Kenmore on A827 (6 mi.). Kenmore Hotel is in village square.

For room rates and times for last dinner orders see Addendum-Index.

ROSE VILLA
Fortingall (Aberfeldy), Highland Perthshire

My good friends, Michael and Maureen Turner, formerly of the Fortingall Hotel, have embarked on a new venture that bids fair to be of great interest to the readers of this book.

Fortingall, as can be seen by looking at the map, is almost in the dead center of the Scottish Highlands. This convenient location makes it the hub for a series of wonderful trips in all directions.

As Michael says, "We are ideally located for people who would like to have a true Highlands experience with the convenience of returning to the same warm, snug home every night."

They have converted their lovely home in Fortingall into just such an experience. A part of the house was the original village schoolhouse, dating back to 1720. There are three guest bedrooms, all named after choice roses. There is electric central heating and also open log fires when the weather is cold.

Rates at Rose Villa include dinner, bed, and a full Scottish breakfast, and the dinners include many international dishes and Scottish specialties served on a table d'hote basis.

Perhaps the most unusual feature is the chauffeur-driven Scottish tours that Michael refers to as his "Dram" ("Daily Roundabout and Meander"). They begin when you're collected from a nearby airport or railroad station and driven back to settle in at Rose Villa. From then on daily tours can be arranged, some long and some short, with either Michael or Maureen doing the driving and guiding.

"We are convinced that our central situation, allied to our local knowledge, will give those guests who opt for our 'Dram' a truly unique holiday," Michael observed. "I think if your readers would get in touch with us by telephone I can explain it most adequately.

"For outdoor-minded guests we can provide information on all types of local fishing (mainly salmon and trout), golf courses, pony trekking, nature walks, and climbing."

I'm looking forward to visiting Michael and Maureen in the near future. It sounds very much to me as if Michael's "Dram" might be an excellent solution for getting the most out of a visit to the Scottish Highlands.

ROSE VILLA, Fortingall (Aberfeldy), Highland Perthshire, Scotland PH152LL. Tel: 088 73 335. (International: 4488 73 335.) A 3-bedroom private home, originally a 1720 village school house, in the Scottish Highlands. Rates include dinner and a full Scottish breakfast. Open from spring to fall. Please telephone for full details. Con-

venient to golf, salmon and trout fishing, stalking and shooting, pony trekking, walking, climbing, and nature. Chauffeur-driven tours available. No credit cards. Michael and Maureen Turner, Proprietors.

Directions: Take A9 north (Inferness Road) 23 mi. to Ballinluig. Turn left onto A827 to Aberfeldy. Turn right just beyond square onto B846 (Tummel Bridge Road) to Coshieville (5 mi.). Turn left on road marked Fortingall, 3 mi. to thatched village and Rose Villa. Pickup from airport or rail station available.

PORT-AN-EILEAN HOTEL
Strathtummel, Tayside

The leading sailboat had reached the buoy marking the far end of the course and was now coming about, ready to sail a broad reach on the final leg of the course. "Sometimes," said Gordon Hallewell, "they set their spinnakers."

Gordon and I were seated in the lounge of the Port-an-Eilean country house hotel, the bow window providing us with an excellent view of Loch Tummel and the almost daily sailboat race. The hotel, standing in twenty acres of natural woodland and formal gardens with magnificent views of lochs and mountains, was once the Duke of Athol's shooting lodge. It is at the start of the legendary, "Road to the Isles" and at the geographic center of scenic Scotland.

"We are open from the beginning of April to the end of October," he said. "Many of our guests find that a holiday in early spring or autumn finds the countryside most beautiful. The roads are less crowded and log fires are most welcome in the evening after a good dinner."

From the very moment I had stepped through the front door I was impressed with the unusual number of contemporary oil paintings. Gordon explained that he and his wife Evelyn are collectors; I believe they have successfully blended some landscapes by modern painters among the more traditional works of earlier periods.

The general architecture and design of the building can be characterized as Scottish Victorian baronial, and the high-ceilinged drawing rooms and dining rooms are very elegant, with handsome wallpapers and many framed prints and originals providing a rich compliment to the rugs and furniture.

"We're quite well situated for the guest who would enjoy a few days of rest and relaxation," he remarked. "It's possible to tour both the west and east coasts within a day, or take a short drive to

Edinburgh, Inverness, or Aberdeen. We have facilities available for shooting, stalking, and fishing. There are several beautiful walks which start right here at the hotel."

Gordon then suggested that we take a tour of the bedrooms and perhaps even look at the kitchen. As we wound our way up the handsomely paneled open staircase, Gordon told me that there are twelve rooms, five of them with their own private baths. Many of them have a magnificent view of the loch. "The Duke wanted to provide his sporting guests with the best of accommodations," he said. The Hallewells have taken great pains to furnish the rooms in an appropriately Victorian style.

Returning to the first floor, Gordon handed me the menu for the evening, saying, "We always have trout and salmon from the loch, and venison and Scotch lamb in many different variations. Our approach to cuisine concentrates on the good cooking of a limited menu. Besides offering breakfast, lunch, tea, and dinner to non-residents, we can also supply hearty packed lunches for our houseguests who want to spend a day out-of-doors."

As we strolled on the lawn next to the loch, Gordon noted that the sailing dinghies were all at the far end of the loch and told me the view was so admired by Queen Victoria that it has since been called "The Queen's View."

The newest activity at Port-an-Eilean is a sweater-knitting business run by Julia Hallewell. In fact, I purchased one of her sweaters myself, and very handsome it is.

PORT-AN-EILEAN HOTEL, Strathtummel (Nr. Pitlochry), Perthshire, Scotland. Tel: (088 24) Tummel Bridge 233. A 12-room lochside country house hotel almost in the geographical center of the Scottish Highlands, 10 mi. from Pitlochry. Open from April through Oct. Breakfast, lunch, tea, and dinner served daily to non-residents. No credit cards. Fishing, sailing, and boating available at the hotel; 5 golf courses and hill walking nearby. All of the delights of Scottish highlands are within an easy driving distance. Mr. and Mrs. Gordon Hallewell, Resident Proprietors.

Directions: Follow A9 3 mi. north of Pitlochry, then turn west on B8019 to Kinloch Rannoch. Hotel is 7 mi. along this road on left.

THE NORTHEAST CORNER OF SCOTLAND

Scotland isn't really very large, but there is so much to see! For instance, the entire Grampian region, and in particular the northeast corner, is tucked away from the busy through routes.

Looking toward the sea, it's virtually undiscovered by visitors. It's a land of fishermen and farmers, with fishing villages nestling under the cliffs along the coast and small farm villages and market towns dotting its rolling interior. There are miles of peaceful main roads, and quiet little side roads for excursions and picnics.

Robert Bruce was here and it was the home of many a character in fact and fiction. There are many castles, great and small houses, gardens and countryside areas, many maintained by the National Trust for Scotland.

I visited this area in late June, which is supposed to be the threshold of the "high season." I found it uncrowded, very comfortable, and largely undiscovered by the overseas visitor to Britain.

TULLICH LODGE
Ballater, Grampian

It was bar-lunchtime at Tullich Lodge. We were all sitting on bar stools, at tiny tables, or on the seats in the bay window.

Neil Bannister and Hector Macdonald, the proprietors, kept bringing in platters of good things to eat, and by the time we had finished the cheese soup, many of us were on a first-name basis.

I talked to an English couple who were staying here for two weeks and were planning to do some of the "marvelous walking nearby."

This inn sits above the Aberdeen Road about a mile east of the village of Ballater on five acres of woodland gardens and has an excellent view of the Highlands and the River Dee.

Besides the bar lunch which included a lamb chop and some delicious homemade paté, what remains in my mind about Tullich was a really outstanding resident lounge located on the second floor. As soon as I stepped inside, I was tempted to sit down in front of the windows and pick up one of the many magazines and spend the afternoon reading and relaxing with the view. There is even a piano in one corner.

On the first floor there is a large glass Victorian telephone booth which is elegance personified. The dining room is richly paneled with spacious bay windows, again with an impressive view.

That was in 1976. On my most recent visit, I found very little had changed. I remained overnight in one of the tower rooms which was most comfortable. I also had another opportunity to talk to both Neil and Hector, and even make a short visit to their wonderfully immaculate kitchen.

"You mentioned our steak and kidney pie and roast beef and

baked lemon sole in the 1976 book," said Hector. "I hope that you'll point out our baked chicken which has been stuffed under the skin with cream cheese and chives, vension, local cheese, and game dishes served in season.

"There are several castles in our area," said Hector. "Balmoral Castle is open to the public when the Royal Family is not in residence. We also have very popular Highland Games. There are also five golf courses within twenty miles. It's a pleasant drive to Inverness."

Our conversation lasted well into the evening. The big thrill for me came when I received a telephone call and had an opportunity to use the glass telephone booth.

Once again Tullich Lodge was a most memorable experience.

TULLICH LODGE HOTEL, Ballater, Aberdeenshire, Scotland AB35SB. Tel: (0338) Ballater 55406. U.S. reservations: 800-243-1806. A 10-room country house hotel 40 mi. from Aberdeen. Open from April to Nov. Breakfast, lunch, dinner served to non-residents. Meals in dining room must be booked in advance. The scenic Dee and Don

Valleys and the Grampian mountain ranges nearby. Golf, skiing, pony trekking, salmon fishing available. Hector Macdonald, Neil Bannister, Resident Proprietors.

Directions: Ballater is on the A93 (Aberdeen-Braemar Rd.). From the south, watch for Ballater Bypass, hotel signpost on left.

THE COUNTY HOTEL BANFF
Banff, Grampian

Frederic Symonds and Michael MacKenzie, the proprietors at the County Hotel, were explaining to me why Banff has an appeal to the traveler. "It's a peaceful place," said Michael, as we settled down in front of the fire in the drawing room. "It's tucked away from the busy through-routes and it's virtually undiscovered by visitors. It's a land of fishermen and farmers with villages nestling under the cliffs along the coast and small farm hamlets and market towns."

"There's a wide range of things to do in this area," Michael declared. "We have many natural resources and historic connections. Robert the Bruce was here and it was the home of James McPherson. There's good trout fishing in the Deveron, the river that flows through the town, and excellent sea-angling offshore."

Frederic and Michael have assumed proprietorship of this pleasant Georgian townhouse, which was converted a few years ago into a small, comfortable hotel. There have been a few changes since my previous visit, and now all of the bedrooms are provided with private baths. To further enhance the traveler's stay, Fred and Michael have adorned the walls with most impressive original paintings.

"Your countrymen frequently find their way here for a rather unusual reason." Fred commented. "They are interested in tracing their roots back to Scotland, particularly to this part of Scotland. This is very strong Gordon country.

"Many people come here, not necessarily because it may be *the* place, but because it is *a* place with which they can identify. They are, like you, aware of the fact that some of their ancestors were Scottish, and even with just the family name they get a real thrill out of the idea that their forebears might have walked the streets of Banff, Macduff, Fraserburgh, or any of our small, nearby villages. Sometimes they even go to the town hall and check the records."

I think one of the notable changes at the County Hotel is the food. I had a simple, but uncommonly tasty tomato soup that was garnished with orange, and breast of chicken that had been cooked with brie. The cheese blended into the sauce and, even though chicken is not one of my favorite things, it was absolutely scrumptious. I asked Michael, who is the cook, for a few of his thoughts on cuisine.

"We provide a well-balanced meal, both in quality and texture, using only fresh local produce. For instance, the chicken you had tonight was alive yesterday. We have a limited menu so we can concentrate on doing just a few dishes extremely well, which vary according to what is best at the market. We make certain that we serve a limited number of guests each evening and there is only one sitting. We don't try to turn the tables over."

Both of these young men have found life in Banff extremely stimulating and interesting. It is a career change for each of them. "Our purpose is to make our guests feel relaxed and happy and to enjoy themselves," explained Fred. "We've made the bedrooms as comfortable as possible (they are), and we ourselves are here to provide service and information but prefer to remain unobstrusive. After all, while our guests are here, this is their home."

I'm sure you'll enjoy this part of Scotland; in particular, a stay at the County Hotel. I did.

THE COUNTY HOTEL BANFF, High Street, Banff, Scotland, AB4 1AE. Tel: (02612) Banff 5353. U.S. reservations: 800-243-1806.

[Since the first printing of this edition of this book, the above inn has had a change in ownership (one of the built-in dangers of guidebook writing). In all but the most exceptional circumstances, it is my policy not to continue to list an accommodation that has changed hands unless I have had the opportunity to meet the owners/managers personally and to ascertain the prevailing conditions and policies.

Therefore, I am unable to recommend this hotel at this time; however, should you decide to give it a try, I would appreciate any comments you might have about your stay.]

PITTODRIE HOUSE HOTEL
Pitcaple, Grampian

I hope that everybody who visits Scotland will take a few extra days to spend in Aberdeenshire. This area to the north of Aberdeen and south of the Firth of Moray has the largest group of ancient castles and historic houses in Scotland, and the rolling countryside with its busy farms, sweeping horizons, vast meadows and woodlands is a joyful experience. Along the coastline are old fishing villages where hearty Scotsmen still ply their ancient endeavors.

The Pittodrie House Hotel is wonderfully located to visit all of Aberdeenshire. It sits in an estate of 3,000 acres of mixed arable forest and hill land, with the peak of Bennachie providing a dramatic backdrop.

In June, the private road leading through the parkland to the hotel was lined with Queen Anne's lace and the rhododendron was in glorious profusion. I emerged from the forest, following the sweeping curve to the left, and there sat Pittodrie House, dominated by a three-and-a-half story, vine-covered tower with additions on both sides.

The entrance is through a massive door and into a reception area which features an almost overpowering staircase. "Perfect," I thought, "for a descending bride or a nude."

My host, the owner Theo Smith, told me that his grandfather had purchased the property in 1900, and he had opened it in 1977 for the first time as a hotel. "The family paintings and antique furniture have remained in the reception rooms and bedrooms, and I hope we have kept the atmosphere of a family home rather than a hotel."

As one might expect of a castle in Scotland dating to 1480, Pittodrie House has some interesting history. The original building was burned down by the Marquis of Montrose; he was eventually executed in 1650. The main building was a Z plan castle and this

was rebuilt in 1675; the traces of this early history lend an air of antiquity to the place.

The lounges have very high ceilings and many oil paintings that date back two or three hundred years—there is even one of his Royal Majesty, George III. There are gorgeous tapestries, many sporting prints, highly decorated mirrors, rugs that seem almost priceless, and furniture I would expect to find in either a castle or a museum.

Many of the bedrooms have four-poster beds, and enjoy views of the meadows, forests, and parkland. It is really quite romantic.

Pittodrie House seems to run off in all directions because there have been many new sections added over the years. Theo grew up in this house and he said it was a great place to play "hide and seek."

One of the bathrooms contains a Victorian shower which I'm certain must have been a marvelous feat of engineering in its time, and is still in use today. The water spray comes not only from overhead, but from three sides as well.

Theo excused himself to attend to a wedding party and suggested that I might be interested in seeing the walled garden. In typically British fashion, he said, "It's really quite nice, actually." This was the understatement of the day.

The walled garden is one of the most extraordinary I've ever seen. It covers three acres divided into a series of small gardens, each about the size of two tennis courts. There were gardeners wearing rubber boots working among garden pools, rose gardens, and a lavish display of flowers of every type and description. Part of the garden was devoted to vegetables which are served at the hotel.

At Pittodrie House, in addition to the incredible setting, the extensive acres, the Billiard Room, the fantastic gardens, and that incredible bathtub . . . they also make their own ice cream!

PITTODRIE HOUSE HOTEL, Pitcaple (by Inverurie), Aberdeenshire, Scotland AB5 9HS. Tel: (046 76) Pitcaple 202. U.S. reservations: 800-243-1806. A 14-room (7 rooms have private baths) country house hotel in a restored 15th-century castle 20 mi. from Aberdeen. Open every day of the year except Christmas Day and Boxing Day. Lunch and dinner served to non-residents. Tennis, squash snooker, and croquet available on grounds. Fishing and hill walking nearby. Pittodrie House is convenient to all of the National Trust properties and other great houses and castles in Aberdeenshire. Theo Smith, Owner.

Directions: From Aberdeen take the A96 toward Inverness to Inverurie. Continue on, taking the first turning to the left (1½ mi.) signposted to Chapel of Garioch. At the village take the first right fork at the shop and follow signs for hotel.

ROTHES GLEN HOTEL
Rothes, Grampian

I had cut across the Morayshire countryside from Banff deserting the coast for the back roads which would eventually lead me to Craigellachie and then north to the village of Rothes. The late June day was providing a perfect ambiance for this lovely section of Scotland which is peaceful farming country and, from the look, quite prosperous.

After passing through the village of Rothes, I could see the silhouette of the Rothes Glen Hotel on the left side of the road, its Victorian turrets, towers, and crenelated battlements overlooking a group of Highland cattle with their long curved horns and russet shaggy coats.

Once inside, I was struck by the similarity in design to other castle-like hotels scattered throughout Scotland. The imposing main entrance hall had a skylight and a winding staircase to two floors. The carpeting was rich, and rooms were hung with many oil paintings of Scottish scenes, and an abundance of Victorian tables and chairs, and other ornamentation. The ceilings of the dining and drawing rooms were ornamented.

From Elaine Carmichael, proprietor with her husband Donald, I learned that they have almost fully modernized this old building which was designed by the architect who built Balmoral Castle. All the bedrooms are equipped with electric blankets, shaver sockets, radios, intercoms, and a child-listening service.

The menu features the best Scottish beef and freshly caught shellfish and fish from the Moray Firth.

Golf and salmon fishing are the principal pursuits of Rothes Glen guests, with ten golf courses within twenty miles and ten large fish pools in the 2-mile stretch of the Spey River, which is the hotel's beat.

Guests who wish to see the surrounding countryside, in less than an hour, can be in Inverness, the gateway to the scenery and lochs of the Highlands. Winter sports areas are also nearby.

Mrs. Carmichael pointed out that Rothes Glen was "quiet and low key" and there were no "night porters or any activities that would keep people up late in the evening." It impressed me as being comfortable, well-kept, conservative, and neat—all in the tradition of Scottish country house hotels.

ROTHES GLEN HOTEL, Rothes, Morayshire, Scotland IV33 7AH. Tel: (03403) Rothes 254. A 19-room country house hotel in the beautiful glen of Rothes 63 mi. west of Aberdeen. Open from Mar. through Nov. Breakfast, lunch, tea, dinner served to non-residents. Putting green on grounds. Many golf courses and salmon fishing nearby. Donald Carmichael, Owner.

Directions: Turn off the main Aberdeen/Inverness highway at Elgin onto A941. Rothes is just south. Hotel is clearly signposted.

THE CLIFTON HOTEL
Nairn, Invernesshire

J. Gordon Macintyre, the hotelier at the Clifton Hotel in Nairn, is a man of many gifts. Among them is the mastery of the simple declarative sentence. With this in mind I'm going to use his prose to describe this hotel. Let me say that Mr. Macintyre himself is a very elegant gentleman, and on the occasion of my meeting him he was wearing an absolutely smashing beige suit with champagne-colored shoes. As we toured all of the bedrooms and public rooms I realized that the decorations, furnishings, and ambience were really an expression of his individuality. But enough of that. Let's hear what he has to say.

"The Clifton Hotel, with only grass and trees between it and the sea, overlooks the whole stretch of the Moray Firth and commands an unrivalled view of the Ross-shire and Sutherland hills. The beach, tennis courts, and swimming baths are only two-minutes' walk away, and the hotel is equidistant to both golf courses. We can obtain fishing, shooting, and riding by arrangement, given advance notice.

"Many things go towards the unique atmosphere of this small, charming, and very personal hotel—a Victorian house, most decoratively revived and carefully restored, abounding with flowers, paintings, colour, and an interesting collection of objets d'art. A sense of the theatrical, backed up by cleanliness, really good food, and masses of hot water, make this an ideal establishment in which to relax and unwind from the stresses of modern living.

"The hotel has only seventeen bedrooms on two floors. Each room is individually designed and decorated. Second-floor rooms are slightly less exotic. The public rooms include a writing room, a television room, a bar and the drawing room, where a log fire is always burning, except in the very warmest weather. The restaurant is the cornerstone of our cardinal reputation.

"During the winter months, from October to May, a number of plays, concerts, and recitals are staged in the hotel.

"The evening meal includes six to eight main courses. The dining room also serves as a theatre and recital hall during the winter months."

Believe me, the Clifton Hotel in Nairn is one of the most singular experiences in the British Isles.

THE CLIFTON HOTEL, Viewfield Street, Nairn, Scotland. Tel: (0667) Nairn 53119. A 17-bedroom elegant hotel in a resort town on the shores of the Moray Firth. Lunch and dinner served daily. Open from late Feb. to the end of Nov. Conveniently located to enjoy day trips to the north and western Highlands, as well as golf and recreation nearby. J. Gordon Macintyre, Proprietor.

Directions: Nairn is on the A93, which runs east and west between Inverness and Banf. The best procedure is to make inquiries in the center of town for the Clifton Hotel.

DUNAIN PARK
Inverness, Highland

Anyone seriously considering a stay at Dunain Park should by all means write to Michael and Judith Bulger and request one of their extremely interesting and most informative brochures. Furthermore, the arriving guest receives a small booklet with complete notes about all of the meals served, the description of the public rooms in the house; information about the telephone, the laundry, the hair dryer, and how children and pets are accommodated.

An amusingly written list is included of all of the Highland activities—scenic, cultural, and historic—which are available nearby. Here's a note about the walking:

"We can point you in the right direction for some good walks, but be honest about the extent of your ambitions before you set off and make sure you have some sensible shoes. For the gentle stroller, we can offer six acres of garden and a woodland just outside the door. Have a look at our kitchen garden, we usually manage to grow lettuces in the open until February. The hens are not averse to the odd slice of toast and may lay double-yolked eggs for you, and if you come at the right time of year, the pigs always enjoy being scratched. Unfortunately, we cannot commend the manners of either the goat or the geese."

Michael and Judith are the kind of people who are easy to like immediately. I arrived unannounced, at an inconvenient early part of the morning, but they took it all in good spirits and we hit it off very well from the start. We chatted for awhile in the comfortable drawing room which had a wonderful friendly atmosphere with a fireplace and lots of magazines and books.

Lodgings are in six cozily and individually appointed double bedrooms, four with private baths. Rooms in the front of the house have a superb panorama across the fields and the Caledonian Canal to the Cairngorm mountains beyond.

All Britons love their gardens, both flower and vegetable, however, I have seldom seen such an impressive vegetable garden as the one at Dunain Park. It's behind a high wall which means the rabbits can get in only by burrowing. Naturally, it produces all of the vegetables for the table, and this goes hand-in-glove with the Bulgers' intense desire to use as many natural things as possible at mealtime.

"In addition," explained Judith, "we really try to get away from the mundane as far as our cuisine is concerned. We do things like salmon mousse and a lot of quiches. Cabbage and apple soup is very popular. We usually have a basic roast for every meal. For example, tonight we're doing leg of lamb which is roasted on a bed of herbs and onions with garlic slipped under the skin."

Speaking of natural things, while Michael and I were strolling through the grounds, I noticed the large flock of sheep and I asked him whether or not anybody felt squeamish about eating lamb which may have been running around in the park the day before. "Not really"; he said, "however, we have one gentleman from southern California who was so taken with one of our sheep named Gertrude, that he decided to sponsor her for life. We regularly receive a stipend from him which guarantees that Gertrude will never appear on anyone's table."

DUNAIN PARK, Inverness, Highland, IV3 6JN, Scotland. Tel: (0463) Inverness 230512. A 6-room (4 with private bath) country house hotel approx. 3 mi. southwest of Inverness in the heart of the Scottish Highlands. Breakfast, lunch, tea, and dinner served to non-residents. Open every day in the week from mid-March to end of Oct. Advance bookings accepted only for a two-night minimum stay. Ideally situated for longer stays in the Highlands where cultural, scenic, and historic attractions are within a half-day's drive. No credit cards. Judith and Michael Bulger, Partners.

Directions: Dunain Park is off A82. From Inverness follow High Street across the River Ness and pass through one set of traffic lights. Continue about 1 mi. farther across the Caledonian Canal, past the golf course on the left and Craig Dunain Hospital on the right. The entrance to Dunain Park is located on the left-hand side, ½ mi. past the hospital entrance. From the south (Fort William and Loch Ness—keep your eye out for the monster): Look for the signpost on the right just before the hospital.

TIGH-AN-EILEAN
Shieldaig, Highland

The northwest Highland villages on the shores of lochs and firths are a bonnie sight indeed. Shieldaig is just such a village. Stretching around the shores of Loch Torridon, it is a little larger than a hamlet, but smaller than a town.

Tigh-an-Eilean has changed considerably since my first visit in 1976. The proprietors, the Wilkinson family, have added several more bedrooms. According to their most recent letter, they are "continually improving decor and standards. Many of our guests bring your book with them, and also every year we have visits from one or more parties of the Sierra Club.

"The nearest civilization of any sort is in Inverness. The attractions here are for the country lover and explorer by car. We have splendid hill walking and magnificent mountain climbing."

Tigh-an-Eilean is a modest but growing accommodation, somewhat similar to the Mill Inn in Mungrisdale. The rates quoted are for lodgings with breakfast and dinner, and there is fresh-poached loch salmon and haggis with turnips on the menu. As they say, "We have good home cooking all the time."

TIGH-AN-EILEAN HOTEL, Shieldaig, Strathcarron, Ross-shire, Scotland. Tel: (052 05) Shieldaig 251. A 12-room family-run hotel 72 mi. from Inverness on the seashore in a small village in the Scottish highlands. No private baths (6 shared bathrooms). Open mid-April to mid-Oct. Dinner served to non-residents. Shieldaig is on the shore of Loch Torridon and set amidst the grandeur of magnificent mountain scenery. Hill walking, mountain climbing, car touring. No credit cards. Not suitable for children under six. The Wilkinson Family, Resident Proprietors.

Directions: From Inverness take the A9 over the Kessock Bridge towards Wick. At the first roundabout take the Ullapool road—at the second roundabout a hard right to Dingwall; follow the Ullapool signs until the road forks just after Garve; fork left and follow the Gairloch road 25 mi. to Kinlochewe (A 832). Coming up the west coast from Fort William, follow A82 north to Invergarry, then fork left on A87 to Kyle of Lochalsh and Skye for 43 mi.; 7 mi. before Kyle, turn right onto A890 for the north and Lochcarron (18 mi.), then turn right again after Lochcarron on A896 for Shieldaig (15 mi.).

INVERLOCHY CASTLE
Fort William, Highland

Inverlochy Castle—I'd heard of it long before I had followed A82 south alongside Loch Ness and seen for myself the incredibly gorgeous mountains, lakes, and firths of western Scotland. Other hoteliers spoke with awe about Inverlochy, almost as if it were a kind of heavenly reward for a lifetime of hard work. "Oh, you'll admire it," was the almost constant comment.

Now—as I turned through the imposing entrance past the gatehouse, following the gently curving private road lined with huge rhododendron bushes, and then emerged into the open for a first look at the castle with its imposing porte-cochere and tiered battlements and towers—I knew why.

There it stood, with Ben Nevis in the background, surrounded by rhododendrons and azaleas. On this soft, gentle June afternoon the bonnie blue flag of Scotland rippled smartly in the breeze and the windows reflected the lowering sun to the west.

In Scotland, the word "castle" means a great many different

things. Sometimes it means a fortress which may have withstood many attacks. However, Inverlochy Castle is a totally benign place, built by the first Lord Abinger in 1863 near the site of a 13th-century fortress. Turrets and battlements aside, it resembles a sumptuous Italian villa or an elegant French chateau.

The two-story-high great hall has lavishly frescoed ceilings, large oil paintings, and opulent furnishings; all dominated by a crystal chandelier which seems suspended in space. Inverlochy played host to Queen Victoria in 1873, and in her diary, she wrote, "I never saw a lovelier or more romantic spot."

The dining room and other drawing rooms, as well as the unusually large bedrooms, are all beautifully decorated and fitted with fine, elaborately fashioned furniture.

Such a castle should have a princess to preside over it, and indeed there is one: Mrs. Grete Hobbs. This attractive, sophisticated woman is the owner and is originally from Copenhagen. We talked about what is involved in providing hotel accommodations in a castle.

"I try to run this just like a private home, because it is the only way that I know how to do it," she declared. "There is no other way. All of our guests are introduced to each other. I completely supervise everything that is served in the dining room and I'm very much against gimmicks. Our menu is made according to what I can get fresh each day. We're particular about things like vegetables, and we're quite proud of our game paté which is made from venison.

"Tonight the main dish will be freshly caught salmon, although some guests may order chateaubriand if perchance they don't eat fish. We have a five-course menu, and dinner is served at eight-thirty.

"I've been fortunate enough to travel to a great many different countries in the world. And this house has many things I found most attractive while traveling."

I'm sorry to say that I could not stay at Inverlochy Castle either for dinner or overnight, although one or two of the other guests with whom I've chatted spoke of it as being an almost ultimate experience. One comment: "The rates are above average, but it's worth it."

The house and grounds of Inverlochy Castle are entirely private, and are not open for viewing to non-residents.

INVERLOCHY CASTLE, Fort William, Inverness-shire, Scotland PH33 6SN. Tel: (0397) 2177. A luxurious 13-room private castle-cum-hotel located about 3 mi. north of Fort William. There is limited provision made for non-residents. The west Highlands scenery and other impressive centers of natural beauty are within a pleasant drive. Tennis and fishing are available at the castle; golf, riding, and walking are available nearby. Open from March to Nov. A member of the Relais de Campagne. Mrs. Grete Hobbs, Proprietor.

Directions: Inverlochy Castle is 3 mi. from the center of Fort William on the A82, and approx. 6 mi. from Spean Bridge. The entrance is set back from the road, but is well-signposted.

ARDSHEAL HOUSE
Kentallen of Appin, Highland

"That is Loch Linnhe, and beyond are the hills of Morvern. Strontian Pass leads out to a point that is about as far west as you can get on the British mainland."

Bob Taylor, resplendent in kilts, and I were standing in the window of the billiard room of Ardsheal House looking down across the broad meadow to the loch and the mountains beyond. We were enjoying the absolutely magnificent show being put on by nature, presumably for our special benefit. Overhead, the deeply stratified clouds were parting and closing, allowing un-

expected bars of brilliant sunshine to spotlight the hills and the loch, a sight truly beyond words.

He continued my geography and history lesson: "This is an area known for bloody battles and feuds among the Highland clans," he said. "There are many tales of Bonnie Prince Charlie. In fact, this house, built in 1545 by the Stewarts of Appin, was totally sacked by the Duke of Cumberland during the uprisings of 1745. What is here was rebuilt on the old foundations in 1760. Later sections were built in 1814, and this wing with the billiard room, in 1850.

"Ardsheal plays an important part in Robert Louis Stevenson's *Kidnapped.* It was only a mile or so from here where the infamous murder of Appin took place, providing Stevenson with a great deal of material for his book."

It comes as a surprise to many of the guests at Ardsheal House that Bob, a Princeton graduate, and his wife, Jane, and their sons, Brigham and Jason, are from the United States. Previously they had been pursuing successful careers in banking and advertising, but decided that they wanted to try something as a family that provided them with a greater opportunity for expression—a broader challenge.

To make a long story short, on a trip to Scotland, they discovered this historic house, and the family decision was made to convert it to a country house hotel. They are at Ardsheal from April to November. In the winter, they return to their home in New Paltz, New York.

The reception hall is paneled in oak and there's usually a cheery fire blazing on the old stone hearth. A glassed-in porch on the lochside is made for watching sunsets, seals (or monsters), or for enjoying the peace and beauty of the Scottish highlands. The dining room faces the garden and another glassed-in extension brings the flowers and sky even closer.

Most of the spacious bedrooms have private baths, and all the beds are provided with electric blankets.

"Because we are Americans, we can appreciate the fact that our overseas guests frequently enjoy lots of activity. We have our own tennis court and there's good golfing at Oban. We also have fishing, sailing, and boating, as well as horseback riding. We try to persuade Americans to enjoy the British sport of hill walking, and I think we've got some of the best starting right at our doorstep."

At dinner that evening, which included Loch Linnhe salmon, I made the acquaintance of Ray and Mary Rendall from Northumberland, and we discovered that Ray and I had both been in India at the same time and had a few "old soldier" stories to exchange. They had been there for a three- or four-day holiday, and Mary was particularly complimentary about the menu, which has received a glowing review by Craig Claiborne in the *New York Times.*

Ardsheal House is just off A82, the principal road from Oban to Inverness, a few miles south of Fort William. Due west is Mallaig and the Isle of Skye.

There's a postscript to my pleasant stay at Ardsheal House, which took place the following winter, when Bob and Jane drove from New Paltz and I drove from the Berkshires, all meeting at the Redcoat's Return Inn in Tannersville, New York. It was a most enjoyable reunion and another chance to talk about Ardsheal House. It would be just another month when the Taylors would be heading back to their beloved Kentallen of Appin, enthusiastically looking forward to another season. Jason and Brigham would be there, too, and the Scottish adventure would continue.

ARDSHEAL HOUSE, Kentallen of Appin, Argyll, Scotland PA384BX. Tel: 063-174-227. A 13-room country house lochside hotel overlooking the spectacular view of the western Scottish Highlands. Approx. 17 mi. south of Fort William. Breakfast, lunch, tea, and dinner served every day in the year from Easter through end Oct. Minimum stay of 2 nights with advance booking. Tennis on the grounds. Hill walking, beach walking, sailing, riding, pony trekking, fishing, and golf nearby. No credit cards. Jane and Bob Taylor, Proprietors.

Directions: From Glasgow take the A82 to Crianlarich. Continue on A82 to roundabout at Ballachulish Bridge; then follow A828 toward Connel and Oban. Ardsheal is about 4 mi. on the right. Well signposted.

ISLE OF ERISKA HOTEL
Ledaig, Connel, Strathclyde

Robin Buchanan-Smith leaned back in his chair and raised his eyes to heaven. Because he is the Reverend Buchanan-Smith, it occurred to me that this particular attitude was not unusual for him at all. However, this time he was pondering a question I had put to him about his innkeeping philosophy.

He returned for the moment to more terrestrial environments, "I believe that it's 'taking care of people.' Looking after people means personal attention, and I drill this into our small, youngish staff at every opportunity.

"My wife Sheena and I keep an eye on everything, and

fortunately, the staff is quite dedicated. It's really like a house party. Eriska combines the two oft-forgotten ideals of the modern world—Romanticism and Realism."

He paused for a moment to add a dollop of cream to my cup of tea and continued, "One of our guests stayed here and then went back to California, saying that he had seen everything. He was referring to the fact that there was a British prime minister seated in our parlor, smoking a nine-inch cigar and reading Jane Austen. The prime minister was Harold Mac Millan."

Eriska's setting on the shores of the Firth of Lorne is superb. It is on a small island one mile by half a mile, and is reached by a private bridge—this little bridge is important, because it does create a marvelous feeling of being set apart.

On this sylvan island, the hotel stands in the middle of a lovely green lawn dotted with maple and copper beech trees, and accented with rhododendron, wild orchids, sea pinks, and iris.

The building is Scottish Victorian baronial, and true to its tradition, has turrets and battlements from which there are additional and revealing views of the mountains and firths. I was intrigued to learn that there were trekking ponies available from stables right on the hotel grounds, as well as tennis and fishing. The English-style croquet, played with great politeness, was for blood. The feeling of being on a Highland estate is heightened by the presence of roe deer, badgers, heron, and even, on occasion, golden eagles. The milk and cream are from a herd of Jersey cows and there are well-tended vegetable gardens.

The interior is characterized by log fires, wood-paneled walls, and elegantly decorated plaster ceilings. The drawing room where the P.M. smoked his cigar, enjoys a view of the lawn and firth. The bedrooms all have their own private bathrooms.

At tea that afternoon, I joined four other Americans who had just returned from an excursion to the islands of Mull and Iona.

Oddly enough, it was Jim Mellow from St. Louis who first recommended that I visit the Isle of Eriska. He particularly made note of the roast pheasant and the breakfasts which would have pleased Pangloss.

Later as I was walking on the shores of the firth, I caught a snatch of conversation from a young hand-holding couple . . . "This is the most romantic place I could ever imagine. It far exceeds my greatest expectations."

ISLE OF ERISKA HOTEL, Ledaig, Connel, Argyll, Scotland PA37 1SD. Tel: (063 172) Ledaig 205. U.S. reservations: 212-371-1323. A 24-room elegant country house hotel on an island in Scotland's western Highlands 100 mi. from Glasgow. Open early April to end of Nov. Lunch, dinner served to non-residents. Fishing, riding, croquet, tennis, beach walking on grounds. Sailing, golf nearby. Stunning views of Loch Linnhe and the Atlantic Ocean. Many castles and places of historic and natural interest nearby. Robin and Sheena Buchanan-Smith, Resident Owners.

Directions: From Glasgow, take A82 past Loch Lomond to Tyndrum, then A85 to Oban, turning left onto Fort William Rd. at Connel on A828. Cross Connel Bridge, proceed 3 mi. to Benderloch and look for hotel signs.

DRIVING IN THE SCOTTISH HIGHLANDS

Motoring in the Highlands is marvellous. It is also very different. Fortunately, by the time I had reached this incredibly beautiful country I had quite a few days of driving on the left-hand side of the road so that my reactions were good.

The entire experience from the broad expanse of the extraordinary scenery to the minutiae of the individual plants, flowers, trees, houses, rocks, animals and clouds, make it sensational back roading.

Like the fjord country of Norway, the White Mountains of New Hampshire, the Grand Canyon of Arizona, and the Himalayas of Tibet, the Scottish Highlands have a wildness completely their own. One of the qualities I like is that, with all of the ruggedness, there is a certain gentleness, because almost everything is covered with green grass and heather. It is only the mountain crags which are without vegetation.

Sheep and cattle in the road are a way of life. The roads in the Highlands are so curvy and twisty that when I took a moment to look at a loch or a glen I frequently found myself confronted by a cow in the road.

Much of the time I was traveling on roads only wide enough to accommodate one car. However, they were all paved and in good shape. There are turnouts every 50 or 100 yards, and the courtesy of the road determines which car going in either direction would pull over and wait for the other car. The question naturally comes as to what happens when two cars meet in the middle between two turn-off places? My experience was that everyone was quite considerate and very frequently there would be two cars backing up, each expecting to allow the other car to continue. Cars traveling at a leisurely pace also pull over to the side allowing those who are traveling faster to pass. Ninety per cent of the time great courtesy is shown by all concerned and everyone acknowledges with a friendly wave of the hand

Quite a few Scottish innkeepers will hold a telephone reservation only until 5 o'clock in the afternoon. Some of the popular American credit cards are only good in the more luxurious hotels, although traveler's checks are accepted. I carried British traveler's checks and had no problems. I was never able to buy gasoline (petrol) with anything except cash.

Watch out for bank holidays; change money or traveler's checks the Friday before; I got caught on a few Mondays with no pounds sterling.

There is a lot of sunshine and also a lot of "Scottish Mist." I was glad to have a lightweight nylon jacket with a hood.

THE ISLE OF COLONSAY

Anyone looking for a truly "different" travel experience, where there is practically no commercial intrusion and where it's possible to feel the thrill of being alone and secluded, will enjoy the Isle of Colonsay.

Although visitors are very much encouraged to come to Colonsay and to enjoy its special attractions, it does not offer any synthetic entertainments. There are no tourist traps, no amusement arcardes or fun fairs. Nor are there day-trippers, because the ferry only runs every other day. Caravans (camping vehicles) are not allowed, and only educational and scientific organizations are given permission to camp in tents.

There is one general store, which is used by all of the islanders. The arrival of the ferry is an Event, and guests of the Isle of Colonsay Hotel invariably hurry down to the dock to watch the unloading.

However, for anyone who is content with a holiday built around the natural amenities and social life of a small Scottish island, Colonsay has plenty to offer. In the summer, there are a dozen beaches for bathing and picnicking. The walking is superlative along the beaches, roads and paths, and among the rocks and cliffs and several caves which were probably inhabited as long as six thousand years ago. There is much of interest to the archaeologist and antiquarian, including various standing stones and ancient ruins.

Colonsay is the larger of two islands in the outer Hebrides, joined at low tide by a narrow sandy beach called The Strand. The second is Oronsay Island, which lays claim to a most important event in history—it is said to have been where St. Columba landed on his way to Iona from Ireland in the middle of the 6th century.

ISLE OF COLONSAY HOTEL
Isle of Colonsay, Strathclyde

This story began in Ireland a few years ago when I first met Kevin and Christa Byrne, who are now the hoteliers at the Isle of Colonsay Hotel. At that time, these two attractive young people, graduates of Trinity College in Dublin, had enthusiastically embarked on a carreer of hotelkeeping.

A short time later I received a letter from Kevin, who is a tall red-bearded man with a fascinating gift of conversation, to the effect that they were moving to the Isle of Colonsay to take over the hotel.

So I found myself on the ferry from Oban arriving at the wharf where the self-same Kevin was waiting in a former London taxicab to drive me to his small hotel which is in sight of the ferry dock.

Kevin immediately enveloped me with his enthusiasm. "I'm glad you're coming here now," he said. "We've put things in beautiful shipshape order, but it's been a lot of work. Christa has really been magnificent, being both mother and hotelier. Ah, here we are." He pulled into the small parking lot scattering some of the ubiquitous sheep.

Kevin was right, the additions were shipshape and the accommodations were clean, comfortable, and without a doubt, cordial. Furthermore, he had a very good chef, and the menu included Colonsay oysters and other local seafood, as well as hearty and tasty native lamb.

Guests become involved with each other almost immediately, exchanging experiences at the end of the first day and joining forces on subsequent days. There's ample opportunity to meet the islanders because the hotel has the only pub on the island.

I spent almost a whole day on a walking excursion of one portion of the island with two American women. We climbed over fences (legally) and followed rocky roads over cliffs and moorland, sandy beaches, and lily-filled lochs, rhododendron woods, cultivated lands, farms and hills. It was a day to be remembered.

During one of my long conversations with Kevin, I remarked that someone ought to write a book about Colonsay.

"Somebody already has," he replied with great glee, whereupon he presented me with a copy of a book entitled, *The Crofter and the Laird,* by John McPhee (Farrar, Straus and Giroux, New York). Author McPhee visited the island in the late 1960s because he, like so many other McPhees, McAfees, and other permutations of the name, have ever been drawn back to the land of their ancestors. The people he wrote about still live on the island, including the schoolmistress with whom I visited on the very last day of school.

Because the railroad station in Oban is right next to the ferry dock, it's possible to reach Colonsay using public transportation from any point in England or Scotland. The ferry ride around the islands is also a singular experience. Automobiles are not necessary, and the hotel has bicycles.

Please check all sailing schedules and other important details with Kevin Byrne when making bookings.

I believe I've presented Colonsay as it really is. Incidentally, the hotel is the only such accommodation on the island. If it's "your kind of place," you'll love it.

ISLE OF COLONSAY HOTEL, Colonsay Island, Argyll, Scotland PA 61 7YP. Tel: (095 12) 316. An 11-room village inn located on an island 37 mi. from Oban.(Some rooms with private baths.) Open every day in the year. Breakfast, lunch, tea, and dinner served. Exceptional hill and muir walks. Bicycles and boats available. Primitive and challenging golf course; fishing. Kevin and Christa Byrne, Resident Proprietors.

Directions: Colonsay is, with the aid of the railroad and the ferry, available to all parts of Britain. The train station is a few steps from the ferry dock. All sailings are from Oban (Railway Pier). Check with hotel for days and hours of sailing (2½ hrs.); meal service provided on board. Cars may be left on mainland; really not needed on island.

WESTERN ISLES HOTEL
Tobermory, Isle of Mull, Strathclyde

What a beautiful, glorious, fantastic day! Once again, I was strolling through the golf course at Tobermory with Derek McAdam, the innkeeper of the Western Isles Hotel.

Our talk covered a wide range of subjects, including reminiscences of my first visit to Mull a few years ago, and his subsequent visit to the United States in 1978, when we met with a number of American innkeepers in Annapolis, Maryland. At that time Derek showed slides of Mull and the Highlands which everybody thought were magnificent.

We reached the highest point of the course and turned to look back over the hills of Morvern and the Bay of Tobermory. Gesturing with a stout walking stick, Derek said, "Although the history of Mull and Iona really starts much earlier, you might be interested in something of a more recent nature that took place right down in the bay.

"In 1588, a galleon from the defeated Spanish Armada sailed north around the top of Scotland and came down along the

western side. It sank right out there after being blown up by a Scottish hostage. For centuries, there have been unsuccessful attempts to find the great treasure which is supposed to be in the galleon's hold. Even now it is still going on with some controversy as to who really owns it if it is recovered."

Derek went on, "Dr. Johnson and James Boswell visited Mull in 1773, but I guess they happened to be here on one of the few days when we didn't have sunshine, because they gave us a bad notice." This was said with a wink.

The Western Isles Hotel has a truly commanding view of the Bay of Tobermory. The scene from the sunporch is magnificent, with sailboats scudding across the harbor and the more sedate fishing boats following in their wake. Tea on the terrace is delightful, as I discovered on my first trip.

The hotel is of Victorian vintage built back in the days when whole families repaired to Tobermory for weeks at a time. Over the years there has been much remodeling and renovation, but the original facade has been preserved. It's a very comfortable, casual place. The informal tone is set by Derek and his wife Kathy, both of whom are warm, enthusiastic people.

The hotel is on the headlands above the town with the shops and houses of the village jostling each other on the bayside street below.

On this trip I took a leisurely stroll and found quite a few craft shops, including one where I could watch scarves and sweaters being knitted.

This particular part of Tobermory by the waterside has a most pleasant aspect. I also visited the historic museum which is in the Masonic Hall and is really a "people place," displaying everyday utensils and tools that were used more than a hundred years ago by the people of the island. There were pitchers and bowls, spinning wheels, old-fashioned chairs, maps, and photographs taken during Queen Victoria's visit.

At dinner that evening I asked Derek and Kathy what guests did besides gaze in rapture over the Bay of Tobermory. She responded, "Our nine-hole golf course is free to our guests, and there is fishing and boating on the lochs, tennis, pony trekking, sailing, deer stalking, and cruises to nearby islands by the dozens. During the off-season, we have a series of special weekends including a golf weekend, a gourmet weekend, a bridge weekend, a winter birds weekend. I suppose you already know that the Gulf Stream supplies the Hebrides with very mild winters.

"One recurring problem we have is that our guests frequently fail to set aside enough time to visit both Mull and Iona. The absolute minimum should be three nights, and for a good night's rest and a proper holiday, it should be four or five."

WESTERN ISLES HOTEL, Tobermory, Isle of Mull, Argyll, Scotland. Tel: (0688) Tobermory 2012. A 47-room (13 with private bath/shower) cliff-top hotel overlooking Tobermory Bay on the Isle of Mull. Open all year except Christmas. Breakfast, lunch, tea, dinner served to non-residents. Golf course on grounds. Tennis, fishing, riding, boating, sea angling, stalking nearby. Derek McAdam, Resident Proprietor.

Directions: From the south, the Isle of Mull is reached by ferry from Oban to Craignure. Automobiles may be left in Oban as buses to Tobermory frequently meet ferry. [R.R. station car park locked on Sundays.] From the north, take the ferry from Lochaline to Fishnish and then motor to Tobermory. (No buses.) Check hotel for other ferry schedules.

MULL AND IONA

The roads on the Isle of Mull provided my first experience with single-passage Highland driving. The island is very beautiful and for the most part unspoiled. One of the main roads follows the eastern contour of the island which is separated from the mainland by the Sound of Mull. There were a few fishing boats and quite a few pleasure sailboats. The water on this sunny day was almost turquoise. There were very few houses along this road, a few campers, and just one sizable community called Salen, where there were a couple of restaurants, a hotel, and a few crossroads shops.

As I proceeded north toward Fishnish, the higher peaks of Morvern were plainly visible, and the cattle were dots on the hillside.

I could now look ahead and see where the road was going up and over the top of one of the heather-clad hills, at least three or four hundred feet high. Here and there were piles of stones. The road crested the hill and I was so far above the water that the sailboats seemed almost toylike.

The sign for Fishnish Point led me off through the forests on a very bumpy, rugged dirt road and I found that the ferry would be leaving within ten minutes of my arrival.

Before we leave the Isle of Mull, I would like to take a few minutes to consider Mull in retrospect. I can enthusiastically

recommend a visit for anyone who is interested in unspoiled natural beauty, history, walking, fishing, golf, sailing, painting, photography, botany, geology, and sea life.

Don't plan on remaining in Mull less than three days. I could have remained a week.

It takes a whole day to enjoy a visit to the neighboring Island of Iona, which has been a focal point of the Christian world for fourteen centuries. In 563 A.D., St. Columba and a handful of followers landed there bringing the hope of Christianity and tremendously influencing, not only the history of Scotland but that of Western Europe, because missionaries from this community traveled everywhere. Iona attracted men of religion and learning, and during the Dark Ages it was instrumental in keeping the flickering candle of knowledge and Christianity alive.

Furthermore, Iona became the final resting place of forty-eight kings of Scotland, seven kings of Norway, and four kings of Ireland. It is Scotland's oldest Christian burial place.

Today, the oldest remaining relics are the many sculptured stones carved by the early monks on the island. In fact, it was known as the "Island of Sculptors." Many of the ancient buildings, including the Abbey, have been restored.

Iona can be reached directly by ferry from Oban, or by ferry and bus from Mull.

TAYCHREGGAN HOTEL
Kilchrenan, by Taynuilt, Argyll

Even if you will never visit Taychreggan Hotel, please write to the proprietors, John and Tove Taylor, and tell them I suggested you ask for the brochure of the hotel. With many excellent full-color photographs and an engaging personal description, it is one of the best I've seen anywhere. As I was on my way from Connel across A85 toward a luncheon at Creggans Inn, I saw a sign for Taychreggan Hotel leading down a country road. It was just on a whim that I decided to see what was at the end of the road.

What I found was the little village of Kilchrenan, a cluster of houses and a post office, and a little farther on, the Taychreggan Hotel.

It is situated on the shore of Loch Awe, which, at twenty-four miles, is the longest fresh-water loch in Scotland.

The older part of the building was originally a drovers' inn; in subsequent years, substantial additions were made to the old stone house and further imaginative construction has created a three-sided cobbled courtyard. The fourth side of this very sunny environment is a glassed-in passageway connecting the old house with the new.

I was quite disappointed that Mr. and Mrs. Taylor were not in residence during my brief visit, but I was much impressed with the cordiality of the staff.

There are traditional bedrooms, as well as some that have been more recently created. The decor is plain and simple; good, straight colors and pine. The overall effect is one of light and warmth.

One of the great advantages of staying at the Taychreggan is the opportunity to meet and perhaps engage the services of the local gillie for a fishing guide. Of course he knows all of the waters and islands of Loch Awe and is ready for serious fishing with a generous dollop of humorous anecdotes.

I was not there for dinner, but the menu included Scottish as well as Continental main courses. My whim to visit Taychreggan turned out to be a good one and I would recommend that travelers plan on spending two nights, not only to enjoy the hotel, but also the many outdoor diversions within a few miles, at most, of the hotel.

A departing young American couple were enraptured with Taychreggan and full of regret that they had engaged a room for only one night.

TAYCHREGGAN HOTEL, Kilchrenan, by Taynuilt, Argyll, Scotland PA35 1HQ. Tel: (08663) Kilchrenan 211. U.S. reservations: 800-243-1806. A 17-bedroom (14 with private bathrooms) lochside hotel in the western Highlands. Open from Easter to mid-Oct. Rates include dinner. Breakfast, lunch, tea, and dinner served. Riding, sailing, fishing, shooting, walking, gardens, and historic places, as well as many day trips. John and Tove Taylor, Proprietors.

Directions: From A85 turn off at Taynuilt onto B845 for Kilchrenan. Follow B845 to the village; the hotel is just beyond.

THE CREGGANS INN
Strachur, Strathclyde

I believe that one of the biggest thrills in my life was being mistaken for Sir Fitzroy Maclean. It happened on my last visit to Creggans Inn, where a group of American ladies were taking a very special tour of Scottish gardens. With a big smile, one of them spoke to me.

"Oh, Sir Fitzroy," she exclaimed, "we're all so thrilled that you happened to be here at Creggans Inn during our visit!" Then all of the ladies clapped their hands. Can I tell you that for about three seconds I stood there basking in my false glory, wondering how I was going to get out of this situation, when the *real* Sir Fitzroy Maclean appeared. Somewhat sputteringly I explained that *he* was the man to whom they were referring. Well, there was lots of general laughter and then he was kind enough to introduce me.

I couldn't have chosen a lovelier day for my second visit to the Creggans Inn, and the panorama of mountains, sky, and loch was absolutely glorious. My first visit had been in considerable contrast—a showery afternoon with great rolling clouds occasionally allowing a shaft of golden sunlight to brilliantly light Loch Fyne and the village of Strachur.

This time, coming from the north, I had driven from Oban and stopped at the village of Inveraray, just across Loch Fyne from Strachur. Oddly enough, Creggans Inn was plainly visible across this narrow stretch of water, but in order to reach it, I had to drive up to the far end, and down the other side, following a hairpin-curved course. There's a famous castle at Inveraray where, among other things, a cannon from the Spanish Armada ship,

Florida, is on display. The ship itself is supposedly still under the sands and silt in the harbor of Tobermory on the Isle of Mull.

Sir Fitzroy traces his family well back into both Scottish and American history. During World War II, he was Winston Churchill's personal liaison with Marshall Tito of Yugoslavia. Later, he served in Churchill's cabinet and was a member of Parliament. In America, he is well known as an author, with three books on the Balkans to his credit.

Lady Maclean is also an author in her own right and is particularly well known as a travel journalist.

Creggans is an old West Highland inn with a tradition of homey comfort and individual attention to the visitor. It is ideally situated amidst magnificent scenery for walks and excursions by land and water. It serves the needs of local people as well as the tourist.

Mrs. Laura Huggins, the innkeeper, and I had time for a nice chat in the reception area of the inn where there are numerous brochures, folders, and booklets about all of the historic and natural attractions within a short drive of Strachur. Some of them, including *Castles and Gardens of Argyll* and *Woodland Walk, Strachur* are by Lady Maclean.

"We've had quite a few visitors who have come from your book, *Country Inns and Back Roads, Britain and Ireland,*" said Mrs. Huggins. "Some of them have come back a second time. We're beautifully located for people to stay a few days and enjoy trips to Inveraray, Benmore, the Isle of Bute, Eckford, Easdale, Loch Lomond, and Glencoe. We can arrange deer stalking, fishing, and boating. Swimming, wild-life watching, and pony-trekking are available. We have our own private woodland walk as well."

I thought the menu was quite extensive for what Sir Fitzroy insisted was a "humble Highlands inn." It included rainbow trout, honey-baked ham, various kinds of beef and lamb, mackerel, and duckling Montmorency. "Lady Maclean completely supervises the menu," he remarked. "It's a sort of interesting combination of English, Scottish, American, French, and northern Italian cooking."

A permanent marker outside, just a few paces from the dining room of the inn (which has a gorgeous view of the loch), commemorates the visit of Mary, Queen of Scots, who landed here 400 years ago on her way through the Highlands. I tried to imagine that perhaps the incredible beauty of the loch brought a few moments of joy to that ill-fated lady.

THE CREGGANS INN, Strachur, Argyll, Scotland. Tel: (036986) Strachur 279. U.S. reservations: 800-243-1806. A 22-bedroom (all private baths) lochside country hotel 50 mi. from Glasgow in the Scottish highlands. Open all year. Breakfast, lunch, tea, and dinner served to non-residents. Very convenient for tours into the Highlands as well as visits to innumerable Scottish castles and gardens. Sea and loch fishing, boating, bathing, woodland walks, birding, stately homes, archaeological and garden tours, pony trekking nearby. Just across the loch from the town of Inveraray, and its castle. Sir Fitzroy and Lady Maclean, Proprietors; Laura Huggins, Manageress.

Directions: From Glasgow: follow road to Loch Lomondside, Arrochar, the 'Rest and be Thankful,' the A83 and A815. Also by Gourock, take the car-ferry across the Clyde to Dunoon and follow the A815.

For room rates and times for last dinner orders see Addendum-Index.

AUCHEN CASTLE HOTEL
Beattock, by Moffat, Dumfriesshire

The traveler headed north from the Cotswolds to the western highlands might find this castle hotel an ideal midway stop. It is located just off the A74 in the beautiful Scottish Borders. I must say that I visited at least four other accommodations in this particular area and found this by far the most satisfactory for our purposes.

Auchen Castle Hotel is a very impressive former country house, built in the mid-19th century and retained by the same family for about a hundred years. It has a most advantageous position on a hillside, with views of the surrounding landscape and an attractive loch, which I understand is well stocked with trout.

Almost all of the bedrooms were of a comfortable size and sensibly furnished, with views of the surrounding countryside.

The dining room also had an admirable view and a rather extensive menu, including roast grouse and roast venison.

In many ways the countryside is "Scotland in miniature," with rolling hills, lochs, river, historic houses and gardens, and many sporting and leisure activities. It is the land of both Robert Burns and Sir Walter Scott, and provides a most enjoyable stay for more than one night.

AUCHEN CASTLE HOTEL, Beattock, by Moffat, Dumfriesshire, Soctland. Tel: (06833) 407. U.S. reservations: 800-645-7462. A 28-bedroom country house hotel; Carlisle, 41 mi.; Edinburgh and

Glasgow, 55 mi. Open Feb. 1 thru Nov. Breakfast, lunch, and dinner. Convenient for several golf courses, river and loch fishing, splendid hill walking and back-road touring. Mr. and Mrs. Robert Beckh, Proprietors.

Directions: The hotel is signposted off the A74 near Moffat.

THRUSHWOOD BED & BREAKFAST
Mouswald, Dumfriesshire

There are lots of B&B signs in the British Isles and it's impossible to check them all. However, this one had such a pleasant name and the garden out in front looked so attractive, I thought I'd stop.

I'm glad I did. Isabel Grant has a very pleasant bed-and-breakfast establishment with three nice, big bedrooms. Breakfast is served in a sunny room overlooking the garden.

This is another place with good value for the money and excellent for an overnight stay, particularly if you're on the Lake Country-Glasgow route and you want to get away from traffic.

THRUSHWOOD BED & BREAKFAST, Carrutherstown Road, Mouswald, Dumfriesshire, Scotland. Tel: Mouswald 220. A very pleasant 3-room bed and breakfast (shared baths) between Dumfries and Annan. Breakfast the only meal served. Conveniently located for travelers on route between Carlisle and the west coast of the Scottish lowlands. Open April to Sept. Isabel Grant, Proprietor.

Directions: On the A75 between Dumfries and Annan, look for sign for Dalton and continue on, looking for Thrushwood sign.

BALCARY BAY HOTEL
Auchencairn, Dumfries and Galloway

I was standing for a moment at the edge of Solway Firth, looking out from the terrace of the Balcary Bay Hotel, listening to the insistent sounds of the sea birds, and watching the tide creep up the beach. Soon, the half-dozen or so boats that had been lying on their sides in front of the hotel would be riding on the water, probably ready to venture out into the bay for fishing or perhaps for carrying people on excursions.

This is the southern part of Scotland known as Dumfries and Galloway, and here at the end of the road I accidentally discovered this trig, natural Scottish hotel.

Behind me, in the rather austere white stuccoed building, the lounge and many of the bedrooms had a fine view of the Firth.

The hotel is quite old, and back in the 17th century it was used as a headquarters for smuggling. The goods were stored in underground passages reached via a door in the back of the fireplace in the cellar. Some of this atmosphere has been retained in the "Raiders Cave" bar, created from the original cellars.

It does take a bit of finding; however, I think that once guests locate the hotel, they'll return again.

The menu has salmon taken right out of the nets, as well as lobsters from the Firth.

The thing that I enjoyed most about this rather quiet hotel was its "natural" feeling. It is an old-fashioned Scottish hotel, the kind of place where the local people have met and chatted with visitors for many years.

It also has a ghost, but it would be more fun if you learned about that for yourself.

BALCARY BAY HOTEL, Auchencairn (near Castle Douglas), Dumfries and Galloway, Scotland, DG7 1QZ. Tel: 055-664 217. A 12-bedroom (half with private baths) hotel on the Solway Firth, 33 mi. west of Carlisle. Breakfast, lunch, and dinner served daily. Open all year. Splendid walking and excellent roads lead along the Solway Firth and throughout the Robert Burns country. Many golf courses nearby. Julie Barclay, Owner.

Directions: From Carlisle follow the road (A75) to Dumfries and continue on (A711) through Dalbeattie to (A711) Auchencairn.

KNOCKINAAM LODGE HOTEL
Portpatrick

Even now I can close my eyes and experience once again the sunset at Knockinaam. The setting is breathtaking, for the lodge sits in its own little, naturally created row of rugged cliffs, and the broad expanse of lawns invites a walk toward the sea among the box hedges and the wild flowers and roses.

I was reminded of the Pacific Ocean coast of Northern California—Carmel, Monterey, and even farther north. The entire experience of the sea, sky, and the rugged cliffs impressed itself upon me forever.

The owners of Knockinaam are two very attractive people, Simon and Caroline Pilkington. They both have a wonderful, outgoing way that I think would be particularly attractive to North American visitors. They've done a perfectly splendid job of infusing the entire hotel and the staff with their enthusiasm.

Simon puts it this way: "Most people come to Knockinaam for the peace and relaxation, but the guests who feel so inclined can walk, fish, play golf, visit the gardens at Logan and Castle Kennedy, or simply explore one of the few areas of Scotland as yet largely undiscovered."

Caroline joins in, "Yes, I should say quite undiscovered, particularly by North Americans. There are many larger, smarter hotels offering more facilities, but what we have is unique and we think that our guests enjoy the homey feeling, as well as the really serious attention given to our food. Furthermore, in these difficult times when everything is very expensive, you can still

rely on a friendly smile and a good word. When guests arrive, we do our best to make them feel welcome. Their spirits are lifted when they catch the first glimpse of Knockinaam and its beautiful setting. Once inside, they need to relax, so we offer them something refreshing, explain to them how the telephone works, and carry their luggage upstairs."

I would hope that many of the readers of this book will break away from the standard practice of many first-time visitors to Scotland and make a real effort to visit this southwest corner. It is actually less than two hours' drive from Prestwick, and passengers on the night flight from North America can be here at Knockinaam between 10 and 11 a.m., allowing them an almost two-day stay, even though they may remain for only one night. The car ferry to Ireland is just a few moments away and not likely to be as crowded as some of the better-known terminals.

Knockinaam Lodge is a little out of the way, but it is a rewarding, relaxing experience and travelers should plan to spend a minimum of two nights.

KNOCKINAAM LODGE HOTEL, Portpatrick, Wigtownshire, Scotland, DG9 9AD. Tel: 077-681-471. USA: 1-800-323-3602. A 10-bedroom (8 with private baths) seaside country house hotel on the extreme western end of the Scottish Lowlands. Breakfast, lunch, and dinner served. Open Easter to end October. Excellent walking, fishing, golfing, swimming, and driving nearby. Convenient for a first overnight stop after landing at Prestwick. Member: Pride of Britain. Mr. and Mrs. Simon Pilkington, Proprietors.

Directions: Portpatrick is 119 mi. from Carlisle (A75) and 101 mi. from Glasgow (A77). From Stranraer, travel south on the A77 toward Portpatrick and 3 mi. after the village of Lochans, turn left at the main hotel sign.

MARINE HOTEL
Troon, Ayrshire

If you are flying in or out of Prestwick Airport, the Marine Hotel can provide sensible accommodations either the night before your departure or the day of your arrival.

Actually, the building is rather impressive for its size alone. It's a big, multistoried, red sandstone building that provides holiday accommodations for Britons and their continental neighbors who enjoy the game of golf. It stands between the Royal Troon and the Portland golf courses and I saw many golfing holiday-makers arriving and departing, complete with their golf bags.

There are three restaurants at the hotel, although I personally favored L'Auberge de Provence, which offers very acceptable French cuisine.

I believe that you can be assured of getting some kind of a meal at the Marine Hotel if you arrive by 10:00 p.m.

Bedrooms are comfortable but unimaginative for the most part; however, all have private bathrooms and the other British hotel amenities.

MARINE HOTEL, Troon, Ayrshire, Scotland KA10 6HE. Tel: (0292) 31-4444. A large, conventional hotel a few minutes from Prestwick Airport. Open year-round. Breakfast, lunch, and dinner served daily. Quite convenient to many nearby golf courses. Located in Robert Burns country; his cottage at Alloway and other Burns memorabilia nearby.

Directions: Troon is to the west of M6. Follow any of the roads to the middle of town and make inquiries.

GLEDDOCH HOUSE
Langbank, Strathclyde

I could see why Gleddoch House has acquired an excellent reputation, particularly among American travelers who are accustomed to a resort experience.

The hotel stands on 250 acres of land which provides trout fishing from two small, well-stocked streams and also golf on an eighteen-hole course. There are riding stables and other country-club amenities, including a squash court, a sauna, a small swimming pool, changing rooms, and a professional golf shop.

Among the lodging rooms in the main house there are some impressive, mansion-sized rooms overlooking the rolling country. I was attracted to one corner tower room with a four-poster bed and a telescope which provides a closer view of the ships plying the River Clyde, as well as the mountains to the north.

Rooms in the original house have been augmented by a group of more modern bedrooms in a newer section. All of the rooms have been named after birds, and each has a sprightly drawing of the bird next to the door.

My dinner at Gleddoch House began with a melon and prawn salad, followed by baked filet of sole. For the main course I chose a grilled pork chop stuffed with apple and served with caraway seed sauce. Other main courses included poached Scotch salmon served with cucumber and lemon, and a sirloin of beef. There were several puddings from which to choose for dessert, and also a cheese board and fresh fruit.

Within an hour's drive of Prestwick Airport, the Gleddoch House provides a convenient stop for the first or last night in Scotland.

GLEDDOCH HOUSE HOTEL, Langbank, Renfrewshire, Scotland, PA14 6YE. Tel: (0475 54) 711; U.S. reservations: 800-323-5463 or 800-243-9420. An 18-room luxurious country house hotel on the outskirts of Glasgow overlooking the Clyde River and a distant view of the Scottish Highlands. Breakfast, lunch, and dinner served every day except Saturday lunch. Open all year except Dec. 26 and Jan. 1 & 2. Golf, swimming, fishing, riding, walking on the grounds.

Directions: From Glasgow follow the M8 to Langbank and Exit B789 following the signs to Gleddoch House.

For room rates and times for last dinner orders see Addendum-Index.

THE PHILIPBURN HOUSE HOTEL
Selkirk

It is possible to drive from London to Edinburgh in one day, but please don't do it. A much more enjoyable, maybe even a more *civilized,* way is to take it in easy stages and spend two nights at each stop along the way. This book is based on that premise.

After an enjoyable trip through the lovely Scottish Lowlands (I'm sure you will agree they have been misnamed), one of the stops might well be the Philipburn House in Selkirk, located south of Edinburgh in the Borders.

This country house hotel is set in the heart of Sir Walter Scott country in the Dale of Ettrick and Yarrow. The original house was built in 1751 and the exterior has that wonderful feeling of Scottish austerity that at times can be most attractive.

The interior has obviously been well designed and co-ordinated, and the lounges, poolside restaurant (oh yes! I said poolside), and public rooms all have a wonderful glow about them, partially provided by some extremely attractive pine woodwork.

I was seated at one of the tables in the poolside restaurant talking with Anne Hill, who, with her husband Jim, is the owner of Philipburn House, about what Americans would find entertaining and diverting while on a holiday in Scotland.

"Just imagine that it's morning now and the sun is already warm—slanting over the nearby Border hills, and the scents of pine, heather, and peat are in the air. Your American friends can spend a day in the hills with Davy Fordyce, our resident guide, who is a sort of craggy person with a warm and friendly personality and a grand sense of humor. A walk with Davy provides a rich insight into the history and romance of the Borderland, the hills, the forests, the rivers, the lochs, the ancient towers, the poetry, the legends, the songs, and the rich wildlife that abounds in our territory. How's that for starters?"

I had to admit that I was already convinced. Other activities that provide a holiday atmosphere include horseback riding in all seasons (because there is an indoor riding school nearby), 200 miles of trout and salmon fishing, which can be arranged, garden and woodland walks, golf, and swimming in the pool, quite a rarity for Scotland.

Each accommodation is different, including spacious country house bedrooms, family suites, poolside suites, and cottages. All of these look over the lawns and woodlands to the hills beyond. All have private bathrooms and color television.

"We believe that dinner here is the highlight of the day and, perhaps after a last dip in the pool, I meet all the guests and help them with the difficult task of trying to choose from the menu items. We have such traditional dishes as freshly caught fish, as well as pheasant stuffed with raspberries and wrapped in bacon, roast pork stuffed with apple, fillet of sole, mallard duck, and venison served with poached pears, cherry port, and cranberry sauce."

During my stay I saw no other Americans, but lots of British families with children, and since my idea of travel is not only to look at the scenery but to meet the people, here's a wonderful opportunity to meet our British cousins as they enjoy a good holiday. By the way, there is much entertainment and diversion for children with provisions for serving them at teatime, giving their parents an opportunity to relax for a few moments. The Hills have three children of their own and believe that people need a holiday as much as, if not more than, the children, so they provide as many things as possible to entertain the younger generation.

THE PHILIPBURN HOUSE HOTEL, Selkirk, Scotland TD7 5LS. Tel: 0750 20747/21690. A 16-bedroom (mostly private baths) country house hotel about an hour from Edinburgh. Breakfast, lunch, tea, and dinner served daily. Open year-round except two weeks following New Year's. Swimming pool on grounds. Ample facilities to amuse young people. Golf, fishing, and hill walking. Jim and Anne Hill, Proprietors.

Directions: Locate Selkirk, south of Edinburgh. Coming from the south on A7, ignore the right turn in the middle of Selkirk and continue on over the river towards A708. A sign for Philipburn House is at a T-junction.

ACCOMMODATION RESERVATION SERVICE

For bookings in hotels, guesthouses, farmhouses, and cottages, contact your nearest travel agent or contact the Central Reservation Service, Bord Fáilte, P.O. Box 273, Stephen Street, Dublin, Ireland. Tel. Dublin (01) 607344, Telex 33125. Here you can book all types of accommodations, including cabin cruisers and horse-drawn caravans.

Throughout Ireland you will see a sign displayed by farmhouses and houses in town and country which offer accommodation that has been inspected and approved by the Irish Tourist Board.

IRELAND

ROAD MAP OF IRELAND & LOCATION OF HOTELS

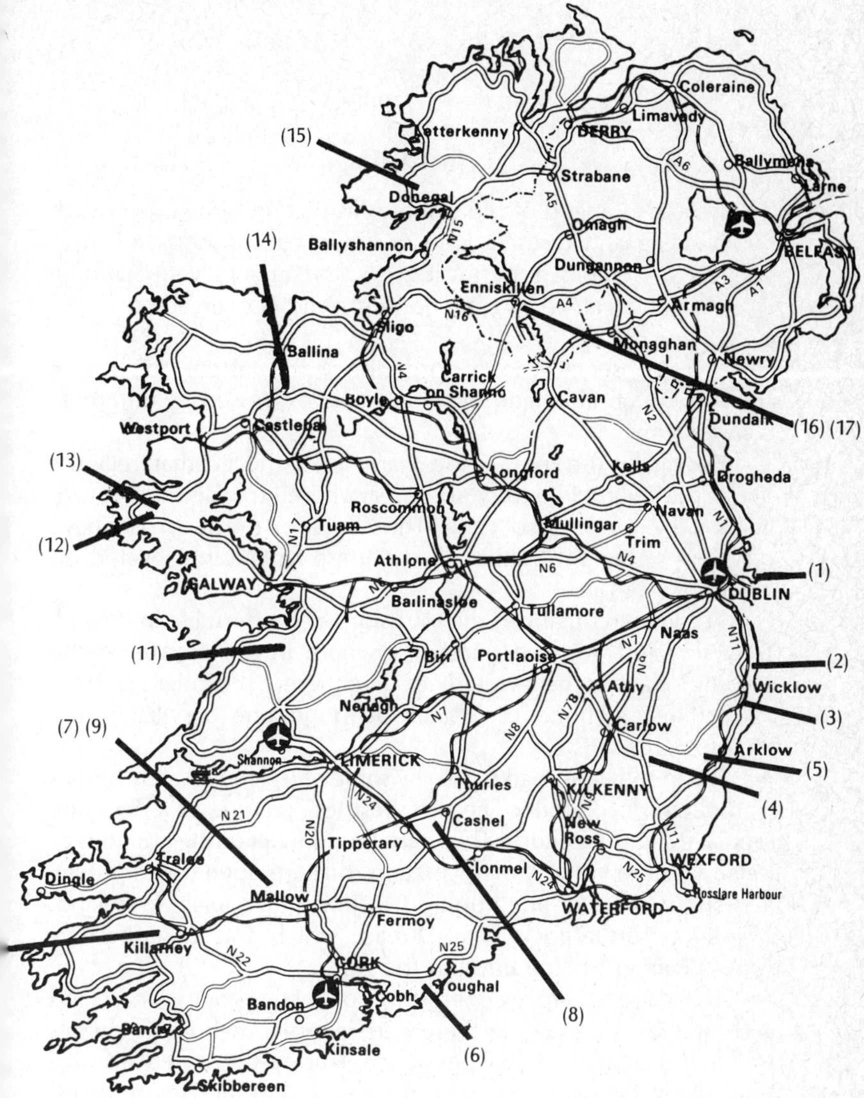

IRELAND

Ireland is a land of old stone walls that are grown over with honeysuckle and roses; a land of fields, farmhouses, and small villages. In Ireland it is possible to find an old gate standing abandoned because the great house that it once served no longer exists.

It is a conservative land, bordering on the austere. The houses are very much alike and individuality is expressed by different-colored trims.

Essentially, the countryside charm lies in the fact that Ireland is still an agricultural country and everywhere I traveled there were fields with either crops or cattle. The villages on the back roads have very few restaurants, although there are restaurants located on main highways.

There aren't many of the intrusions of modern life in Ireland. Television and radio are found everywhere, but only in a few of the accommodations that I visited did I find them in the lodging rooms.

Public telephones can usually be found, one to a village, near the post office.

Frequently the road passes by some of Ireland's stately homes with their decorated ceilings, tapestries, picture galleries, fine fireplaces, and furniture. These are found in all of the counties of Ireland. There are also many gardens that are open to the public.

There are over one hundred 18-hole golf courses in Ireland, including Portnarnock near Dublin, which was described by Arnold Palmer as "the finest in the world."

There are very many interesting connections between Ireland and America. For example, there were several Irish-born signatories to the Declaration of Independence. During the American Civil War nearly 150,000 natives of Ireland served in the Union forces. The first-recorded celebration of St. Patrick's Day was in 1762 in New York City. In 1779, the first St. Patrick's Day Parade was held in New York City. Apparently, the Irish have always been fond of coming to America; one legend says that the first Celtic arrival in North America was St. Brendan, the Navigator, around A.D. 550.

More than 200 recipients of the U.S. Medal of Honor were born in Ireland, and even before California became a state, Irishman Topper O'Farrell laid out the first street survey of San Francisco. Men of Irish birth and descent are calculated to have formed about one-third of the forces during the Revolutionary War. Fifteen generals on the American side were born in Ireland.

Irish-Americans have also had significant influence on literature and drama in the United States. The Nobel Prize went to playwright Eugene O'Neill in 1936, and novelists with an Irish heritage include F. Scott Fitzgerald, James T. Farrell, and John O'Hara.

Accommodations and Food in Ireland

Basically, I found two kinds of accommodations in Ireland. The first type is converted country houses, mansions and castles which are similar to those I saw in England and Scotland. However, the menus are frequently both English and French-oriented.

These somewhat luxurious country mansions and castles are really resort-inns. Most of them have rooms with private baths and serve an elaborate meal. In most cases, I found them owner-operated and comfortably informal. There are usually quite a number of recreational facilities on the grounds, and since they are located in resort areas, there are plenty of additional sports and recreational activities nearby.

The second type of accommodation is the farm and country houses. The main difference between the two, as far as I understand it, is that the farmhouse actually has land that is being used for farming. In both instances the traveler is in a private home.

Those that I saw had five or six rooms and resembled the American farmhouse with the individuality and creativeness of the owners expressed in terms of bright curtains, multi-colored sheets, flowered wallpaper, and very comfortable living rooms where the guests and family gather to watch TV or talk. In all cases cleanliness is very important. I understand that the Irish Tourist Board checks the farm and country houses to make certain that high standards are being maintained.

The food was generally right off the farm at all farm accommodations that I visited, and this is one of the main points of pride. Meals are very informal and everyone sits around a big table, very often with the family.

Incidentally, all of these offer bed and breakfast. Partial or full board is also obtainable for a longer period of time.

Traveling in Ireland

Sooner or later anyone traveling in the Irish countryside has to get directions from one village to another. Irish signposts are in two languages. Most of the time one of them is English. The main problem is that the signs only direct the traveler from one village to the next and very seldom to villages beyond. I found that when the village I was looking for was not on my map I had to stop and ask directions. These directions were given in a wonderfully charming, polite, melodious manner and always ended up with the assurance that "you can't miss it." Well, "miss it" I did—quite a few times in spite of some of the most intricate detail that accompanied each direction.

The most frequent direction was "straight on." One of the problems was that "straight on" usually led to another four-way crossroads and it was necessary to go through the whole process again.

As in Scotland and England, driving is on the left-hand side of the road. I found very few traffic tie-ups even in the larger cities.

EGAN'S HOUSE
Glasnevin, Dublin

Johnny Eagan was fullback captain of the Irish Gaelic football team that played in New York, Boston, and Philadelphia in 1970. In fact, he made three trips to America as a footballer.

This is one of the interesting bits of information I learned during a pleasant evening at Egan's House, which is a guest house in a very quiet section of downtown Dublin called Iona Park. In a city that has many impressive hotels, Egan's is rather modest in demeanor, but big on friendliness and service. There are twenty-six rooms in all and each room has its own private bath—quite unusual for a small hotel.

I was also impressed with the international clientele from Norway, Austria, and France at Egan's. We all gathered in the TV room to watch "Dallas," which was popular in Dublin.

The hotel consists of two Dublin townhouses that have been connected, and so there are several different stairways to the second floor. Dinner, which is available to residents only, except by special arrangement, is served at six o'clock, and as Betty Egan explained, besides roast beef, there is roast lamb, pepper steak, pork chops, chicken in a white wine sauce. "We only serve fresh vegetables and fresh meats," she said. "We also offer Continental breakfasts or the American-type breakfast with things like scrambled eggs and bacon."

Betty mentioned another service for their guests that I think is quite thoughtful: it's possible to use Egan's as a forwarding address to hold mail.

The whole atmosphere is very informal and homey, but I noticed that there were many experienced travelers who found the place much to their liking.

Overseas guests arriving at Shannon Airport can phone Egan's when they get to the outskirts of Dublin and good directions will be provided. Guests arriving at the Dublin Airport can take either a cab or bus—those directions will also be provided by telephone.

Betty Egan, knowing that I was leaving very early in the morning, gave me a tray with a big bowl of cornflakes and some milk and a flask of coffee to sustain me for the long flight back to New York. She has a little store with all kinds of small items people might have lost or run out of, such as shaving cream, toothpaste, shampoo, and a few souvenirs of Ireland.

Egan's hotel is small and unassuming, and a great way to get acquainted with the informal friendliness of Ireland.

EGAN'S HOUSE, 7 Iona Park, Glasnevin, Dublin, Ireland 9. Tel: (01) Dublin 303611 or 305283. A 26-room in-town guest house in the middle of Dublin, 15 mi. from the airport. Meals served to residents only. Arrangements can be made for the evening meal. Breakfasts included in room rates. Convenient to all of the Dublin shops, museums, and other attractions. Mr. & Mrs. John Egan, Proprietors.

Directions: If arriving at Dublin airport, I'd suggest a taxi to Egan's hotel. From there, arrangements can be made to pick up a rental car in Dublin city. If arriving by car, have Dublin city center map available to note directions, and telephone the hotel for specific directions from outside of Dublin.

HUNTER'S HOTEL
Rathnew, County Wicklow

"This hotel has been in my family for four generations; it's a way of life for us." Mrs. Maureen Gelletlie, the owner of Hunter's Hotel, and I were having a mid-morning cup of tea in the gardens. It was a dewy morning and the weather promised to be beautiful for the remainder of the day.

The garden, dear to the hearts of Irish people, has sloping lawns, pebbled walks, rustic seats, and flowering shrubs alongside a small river, the Vartry, which flows through one end. A strange phenomenon was the presence of tropical palm trees here and there.

"The hotel has been here for over 200 years. It used to be what is called a coaching inn, the first stop after a good run from Dublin, and horses were changed and coach riders stayed overnight. Today, by car, it is less than an hour.

"I guess we have always been known for our good food," Mrs. Gelletlie continued. "Many people come just for our salmon and sea trout. We have vegetables and fruits from our own gardens. Many people come for afternoon tea for which we make our own cakes and scones; we really are famous for our strawberry jam. The garden always has quite a few people in the late afternoon."

Earlier at breakfast, I had talked to a man from northern Ireland and his wife, from Yorkshire, about their holiday in Wicklow and they told me that this hotel is especially nice for people with children. There were, so they told me, many things for people with families to enjoy in the vicinity. Their plans included touring and walking in the Wicklow Mountains and a visit to the beaches which are located a short distance away.

Rooms at Hunter's Hotel are quite similar to those of many country inns that I have visited in the United States. Two that come to mind are Colby Hill Inn in Henniker, New Hampshire, and the Barrows House in Dorset, Vermont. I found comfortable vintage furniture with gay touches in each of the rooms. Five rooms have their own WCs; others share one on the corridor.

A visitor to Hunter's Hotel in 1815 wrote in the visitor's book, "This superior family hotel has long been celebrated for the beauty of its situation and the excellence of its internal arrangement." Another more recent visitor wrote, "Pleasantly furnished with

plenty of bathrooms, hot water, and smiling Irish faces that provide good service."

It looks as if Hunter's Hotel has successfully spanned the centuries.

HUNTER'S HOTEL, Rathnew, Co. Wicklow, Ireland. Tel: (0404) Wicklow 4106. A 17-room (5 rooms with private bath/shower) country inn situated 1 hr. south of Dublin. Open all year. Breakfast, lunch, afternoon tea, and dinner served to non-residents. Touring, hiking, golf, tennis, fishing, horse riding, beaches nearby. Mrs. Maureen Gelletlie, Resident Owner.

Directions: From Dublin, take the Wexford road, and at Ashford Village there's a sign on the left that says Hunter's Hotel.

KNOCKROBIN HOUSE
Wicklow, County Wicklow

In 1976 when I first visited Knockrobin House,it was by chance. I was driving on the Dublin-Wexford road and saw a sign indicating that this was a "residential farmhouse."

What I found instead was a rather elegant country house in a secluded parkland with the main entrance through some graceful arches. It was here that I met Anne Marie Bittel, who was kind enough to show me through most of the house, which at that time had a number of guests from France. She told me that she and her husband were able to communicate in many European languages. There were four very attractive rooms with fine views of the countryside.

With the memory of that visit in my mind, on this trip I decided to fly to Dublin from Manchester and spend my first night in Ireland with the Bittels.

Both Anne Marie and Herbert were warm and friendly in their greeting, and we picked up the conversation almost where we left off three years earlier. They assigned me to a very pleasant corner room with a homelike atmosphere.

Other guests included two Britons from Surrey doing a leisurely tour of Ireland, and Mr. and Mrs. John Syke from Roanoke, Virginia, who were enjoying a plan-as-you-go excursion, which can be done in the low season. They commented that they were able to make bookings on a night-to-night basis most of the time.

Dinner was served family-style, and I was delighted to learn that the main course would be Weiner schnitzel which was served with a pineapple sauce. There was a very good green salad, homemade bread, and a Bavarian torte. Mr. and Mrs. Bittel are German, so there is usually something German on the menu.

Groaning with the pleasure that comes from eating well, if not wisely, we all took a short stroll through the gardens and grounds and returned to the main living room where a pleasant fire invited even more conversation.

A final reunion at a hearty breakfast the next morning found us exchanging names and addresses, and agreeing that some of the most genuine warmth and concern for guests in Ireland was to be found at Knockrobin House.

A letter from Anne Marie Bittel last spring carried the sad news that her husband, Herbert, has passed on. She is continuing, however, to offer her special hospitality to her guests.

KNOCKROBIN HOUSE, Wicklow, Co. Wicklow, Ireland. Tel: (0404) 2344. A 4-room guest house on Ireland's east coast, 30 mi. from Dublin. Rooms not available from Nov. 1 to Mar. 1. Dinners available year-round except Sunday and Monday night. Sunday lunch served (1 p.m. to 2 p.m.). Fishing, walking, sea bathing, and boating nearby. Many excellent backroads. Mrs. Anne Marie Bittel, Resident Owner.

Directions: From Dublin: follow Wicklow-Wexford Road sometimes marked M11. At Rathnew the road separates, the right fork going to Wexford which is to be ignored. Stay on road marked Wicklow; 500 yds. past Rathnew is the sign for Knockrobin House on the left.

For room rates and times for last dinner orders see Addendum-Index.

LORUM OLD RECTORY
Bagenalstown, County Carlow

I liked Lorum Old Rectory and Mrs. Young immediately. She was a most accommodating and entertaining person and, like many of my new Irish friends, a great conversationalist. She explained that her husband was a bank manager and that they both enjoyed running this 130-year-old cut-stone farmhouse in the country. I met her strapping young son who had just come off the fields.

All of the rooms in the Old Rectory are pleasant and homey—they are not luxurious, but clean and comfortable. One of the first things that attracted me was all of the books that are to be found on shelves throughout the house.

Guests all gather around the table in the evening and enjoy a real Irish farm meal which includes many homemade preserves, breads, patés, and the like. Salmon and trout have been freshly caught from nearby streams.

"We've had quite a few visitors from your European book," she wrote in one of her recent letters. "Americans who are looking for the 'real Ireland' come for a night and decide to spend two or three, because we are located quite conveniently for many of the attractions of the south of Ireland. In the evening after dinner we spend a lot of time sitting and visiting. That's one of the nicest things about keeping a guest house, sooner or later all of the world comes to us."

LORUM OLD RECTORY, Bagenalstown, Co. Carlow, Ireland. Tel: (0503) 75282. A 5-room rural guest house in the southeast of Ireland, 64 mi. from Dublin. Breakfast and dinner served to houseguests only. Open year-round except Christmas. Tennis, golf, river fishing, riding nearby. Within convenient distance of the sea. Beautiful mountain scenery nearby. Betty Young, Owner.

Directions: Bagenalstown is south of Carlow just off the road to Kilkenny. From Carlow, go to Leighlinbridge and then turn sharp left for Muine Bheag. At Muine Bheag take the Borris Rd. Lorum Old Rectory is 4 mi. out on the left-hand side. (All of these are on map.)

MARLFIELD HOUSE HOTEL
Gorey, County Wexford

Mrs. Mary Bowe and I were in the sumptuous, but comfortable, main lounge of the Marlfield House discussing the problems of keeping a country house hotel in Ireland in general, and the dinner menu for the previous evening, Friday, the 12th of October, in particular.

"I usually have twelve or fourteen starters and nine or ten main courses," she said. "It's a bit limited tonight."

I glanced down the list of offerings and it seemed more than sufficient to me. The starters included Kilmore crab salad, butter-fried sea trout, and soused herring. There was a choice of three soups, and among the main dishes were roast ribs of beef in a Bernaise sauce, grilled turbot, seafood pancakes, scallops in cream, and pork chops Normandy. The vegetables were from the garden. Mrs. Bowe told me that they make their own ice cream and butterscotch sauce.

While we were discussing the dinner menu, houseguests and other people from the nearby area had begun dropping in for the Saturday bar lunch. Mrs. Bowe excused herself several times to greet her guests, and this gave me an opportunity to observe the scene.

The lounge takes up one end of this beautiful old country house which is set on 35 acres of woodland about one mile from the town of Gorey on the Courtown Road. Marlfield House was the former residence of the Earls of Courtown. My attention was caught by the beautiful flower arrangements on the tables and on the baby grand piano in one corner and also by the several tastefully chosen country prints. The room had very high ceilings with decorated moldings and there was a handsome marble fireplace.

Mary Bowe rejoined me and suggested that we had better take a tour of the bedrooms before guests began to check in. I followed her up the very impressive winding staircase which curves around a sparkling crystal chandelier hanging from the two-and-a-half-story ceiling. There were eleven double bedrooms, all with baths, and all furnished most appropriately. Those on the top floor have a panoramic view of the fields and the low hills of county Wexford.

We took just a moment or two to look at some of the beautiful and frequently rare trees on the grounds, including a flowering ash tree, many oaks and evergreens, beeches, and pink and white flowering chestnut trees. She called my attention to a very sturdy California redwood. "We have quite a lot of birds here and about 30 wild ducks. Our two peacocks always amuse our guests."

Marlfield House, situated midway between Dublin and Wexford, is within a short drive of beaches, rugged mountains and richly timbered valleys, and is in what is known as the "Garden of Ireland."

MARLFIELD HOUSE, Gorey, Co. Wexford, Ireland. Tel: (055) 21124. An 11-room country house hotel on Ireland's southeast coast, 57 mi. from Dublin. Closed Dec. 10 to Feb. 14. Lunch, tea, dinner served to non-residents. County Wicklow with beautiful beaches and mountains nearby, Mount Usher Gardens, Russborough House, and other celebrated beauty spots within easy driving distance. Grass tennis court, croquet on grounds. Golfing, sea bathing, hunting, and fishing nearby. Children allowed under strict supervision. Mrs. Mary Bowe, Proprietress.

Directions: Gorey is on the Dublin-Wexford Road; just before Gorey, turn left before the road goes under the railroad bridge and proceed on the Courtown Rd. Hotel entrance is on right.

BALLYMALOE HOUSE
Shanagarry, County Cork

The Ballymaloe House is one of Ireland's manor house accommodations. The house is part of an old Geraldine Castle which has been rebuilt and modernized through the centuries, one portion dating back to the 14th century. It is in the middle of a 400-acre farm on the Cork-Ballycotton road about 2 miles from the coast of southern Ireland.

The dining room is open to the public from Tuesday through Saturday and is reserved for houseguests only at the other times.

Fifteen of the twenty-five bedrooms are in the main house and there are other lodging facilities in a 16th-century gate house and other farm outbuildings.

My room was located on the front overlooking a very pleasant terrace and some beautiful fields and meadows which stretched out to some low hills a few miles away. I understand that this

particular part of Ireland is not developed as a tourist area as yet. The coastal area is just a few minutes away.

After leaving Mrs. Young's in Bagenalstown, I followed the main road south through Thomastown and into Waterford, which is the home of the famous Irish Waterford crystal. From there, the main road heads south-westward with frequent glimpses of the Irish coast passing through Dungarvan and Youghal. At Ladysbridge, I began another "cat and mouse" game of directions to try and find Shanagarry, which is the town closest to Ballymaloe. It is quite beyond my limited description to explain how I arrived, but it took at least four stops.

I arrived in the late afternoon and had time enough for a good long soak in the tub and a few moments' rest before coming down for dinner.

Shortly before dinner I met some other houseguests in one of the living rooms who were on holiday from Dublin. I realized then that there were a great many children in residence and discovered that it was a long weekend. My new acquaintances had two children and explained that they had been in Ballymaloe several times because there is horseback riding which, along with the golf, tennis and swimming is free. "We Irish are great lovers of horses," one of them explained. "Our children get a chance to ride here as much as they wish."

Dinner was very informal, served by waitresses in attractive costumes who were efficient and answered questions in a very pleasant manner. The menu offerings were basically English and Irish, rather than Continental.

After dinner I took a short walk in the gathering darkness, strolling on the country lanes between the fields of ripening wheat. The lights of Ballymaloe gleamed softly and occasionally I could hear the delighted cries of some young people who were being allowed to stay up a little longer because it was a special occasion.

After many centuries of existence, I felt that Ballymaloe had really come into its own.

BALLYMALOE HOUSE, Shanagarry, Co. Cork, Ireland. Tel: (021) 652531. A 25-room country house hotel 3 mi. from the sea on Ireland's southern coast. Lunch and dinner served to non-residents. Closed Dec. 23 to 27. Tennis, golf, swimming pool, fishing, riding on grounds. Mrs. Myrtle Allen, Manager.

Directions: From Cork Road: At Midleton, take Cloyne-Ballycotton road towards Shanagarry. Ballymaloe House is on L-27, 2 mi. outside Cloyne.

LONGUEVILLE HOUSE
Mallow, County Cork

It was at Longueville House that I had my most intriguing contact with Irish history. Michael O'Callaghan, the resident owner of this handsome Georgian manor house, and his wife, Jane, entertained me royally with a high tea that included some simply fabulous homemade ginger cookies. (I unashamedly pocketed two of them as I was leaving.) Jane, as a Cordon Bleu-trained chef, has won several awards for her cuisine and supervises all the cooking.

The house overlooks one of the most beautiful river valleys in Ireland, the Blackwater Valley. The central portion was built about 1720 on a 500-acre wooded estate which was then the property of an ancestor of Michael O'Callaghan. As Michael said, "Since then, Longueville has had a checkered history." Now it has been considerably enlarged and is an excellent country house surrounded by an area particularly rich in scenery.

The size of the building took my breath away. The entrance is through a stately arch, and the first thing I noticed approaching the front entrance was a tremendous brass lock on the door. The center hallway and reception area are most elegant, as are the library, living room, smaller parlors, and dining rooms. The impressive main staircase rises to the full height of the house on both sides and repeats from the second to the third floor. One of the most unusual areas is a glass conservatory which is left over from Victorian days and contains many tropical plants, trees, and flowers. All the lodging rooms that I saw were comfortable, large, and very tastefully furnished.

Over tea I asked Michael about the outdoor sports and

recreation in the area. He replied, "Well, athletic salmon abound, as do trout also, in the river which runs across the southern boundary of our estate. We are just a few miles from the south coast where there is good sea fishing and shore angling. There are 18 golf courses in the county including one at Mallow which is free to our guests. We have horses and ponies available for trekking nearby.

"Many of our guests spend a great deal of time on the back roads here in County Cork, and driving out to the coast to some of the places of great natural beauty such as Glengarriff, Blarney, and Limerick. Killarney is also not far away.

"There are many castles in this section of Ireland that are open to the public, and quite a lot of history was made in this vicinity. For example, the oak trees that you see out the window were planted in the formation of the English and the French battle lines at Waterloo," he said.

"What about the history that took place nearby?" I asked.

"Well, this part of Ireland was known as Rebel Country," Michael said. "The O'Callaghans had owned this land for 1000 years including the remains of a castle which you can see from our front windows. It is one of my fondest wishes to completely restore this monument and make it available once again. When Cromwell's army invaded Ireland this was one of the few places that was not burned. Cromwell's son-in-law, who was in charge of the army, stayed nearby."

I could see that Michael was beginning to warm to his subject, and I settled back comfortably in the luxurious chair to get a good lesson in Irish history.

LONGUEVILLE HOUSE, Mallow, Co. Cork, Ireland. Tel: (022) 27156. A 20-room country house hotel situated west of Mallow on the Killarney Rd., 64 mi. from Shannon Airport. Open from Easter to October 13. Dinner served to non-residents by telephone booking. Fishing on grounds; horse riding, complimentary golf nearby. No credit cards. Michael and Jane O'Callaghan, Resident Owners.

Directions: From Shannon: take the road to Limerick, then the Cork road into Mallow. Take the Killarney road for 2 mi. west. From Dublin: take the Cork Road to Mitchell's Town and then on to Mallow. Continue on following above directions on the Killarney Road.

KNOCK-SAINT-LOUR HOUSE
Cashel, County Tipperary

I was sitting in Mrs. O'Brien's kitchen enjoying a cup of tea and watching her prepare the evening meal. "Tonight it is ham and chicken," she said, "and we'll have roast pork tomorrow night."

Mrs. O'Brien loves flowers. The house is surrounded on three sides by a truly intricate rock garden of myriad colors. "My mother tends the flowers outside," she said, "and I do the arranging on the inside. It keeps both of us very busy, but we love it."

Color is found throughout the house. Each bedroom is pastel-hued with harmonizing sheets and pillowcases and curtains.

Knock-Saint-Lour House is a farmhouse and almost everything served is homegrown. "I do a lot of freezing in the summer and early fall," she explained, "so that we have our own produce through most of the year."

I noticed a donkey grazing in a nearby field. "Oh, that's for the children. They love it."

She pointed out that there was a good view of the famous Rock of Cashel through one of the kitchen windows. "Everyone wants to visit there."

KNOCK-SAINT-LOUR HOUSE, Cashel, Co. Tipperary, Ireland. Tel: Cashel 275. A 6-bedroom farmhouse serving dinner and breakfast. Just 1½ mi. from the town of Cashel, where the famous Rock of Cashel is located. Golfing, tennis, horse riding and pony trekking available nearby. Open all year except Christmas. Mrs. E. O'Brien, Proprietress.

Directions: Knock-Saint-Lour is on the Dublin-Cork Road (T9), just south of Cashel.

BEECHMOUNT FARM
Mallow, County Cork

I followed Mrs. Myra Fitzpatrick up the stairs of the 17th-century stone farmhouse to the second floor where I found five bedrooms all furnished in bright colors and all very neat and clean. The second floor view included the fields and the meadows, and I was happy to see a reading lamp with each bed and many books. The countryside also offers a splendid view of the Boggerogh mountains.

This was a working farm with several dairy cows. Mrs. Fitzpatrick is most conscientious and obviously makes an effort to make her guests feel as comfortable as possible.

I asked her about the meals, and she said that the menu offered things such as homemade soup, roast stuffed turkey, mashed potatoes with cream, white turnips and cauliflower. "For dinner tonight I am making a banana surprise." Other things served on the evening menus included ham and cabbage, roast beef, Irish stew, roast pork and applesauce. "Most everything comes from the farm here," she said.

I wrote the above paragraphs for *Country Inns and Back Roads, Europe* in 1976, and according to several letters from Mrs. Fitzpatrick nothing has changed, except that she has had many of our American readers visit her in the last four years.

Myra's letters are lively, to say the least, and I hope anyone who visits will thank her again for the invitation she sent me to spend New Year's Eve with the family.

BEECHMOUNT FARM, Mallow, Co. Cork, Ireland. Tel: (022) 21764. A 17th-century 5-bedroom farmhouse on 187 acres. Fishing, golfing, horse riding, all within 2 mi. Ideal touring center for Cork and Kerry. Open May to Sept. Mrs. Myra Fitzpatrick, Proprietress.

Directions: Beechmount Farm is located just west of the centre of Mallow on the road to Killarney. Leaving Mallow, watch for Beechmount sign on right-hand side, pointing uphill.

AGHADOE HEIGHTS HOTEL
Killarney, County Kerry

Ah, the lakes and mountains of Killarney! It was one of those magic moments when there wasn't a more beautiful place in all the world.

Sandra Williamson, the manageress of the Aghadoe Heights Hotel joined me for a few minutes on the terrace and we stood quietly looking out over the green fields to the island-dotted blue lake and the gentle contours of the tree-clad mountains beyond. "That is Carrantuohill," she said. "It is 3,414 feet high, the highest mountain in Ireland."

The morning mist was burning off, although we counted three different rainbows that seemed to disappear into the azure waters of the lake.

"There are 23 lakes in all," she said. This is called the Lower Lake and mountains to the west are known as the McGillycuddy Reeks. We are centrally located for guests to visit Dingle Bay and the Ring of Kerry. There is good salmon and trout fishing on our own river bank and pony trekking and sunbathing on the beaches. We are surrounded by two 18-hole championship golf courses."

The Aghadoe Heights Hotel is a somewhat conventional hotel-type modern building with panoramic views from every bedroom. Dining room facilities include a rooftop restaurant and almost nightly entertainment of Irish music and dancing.

As Sandra pointed out, "Business visitors to Killarney from North America enjoy it here because it provides many of the amenities to which they have become accustomed in American hotels and motels, plus the advantage of our beautiful scenery, the opportunity for sports and relaxation."

AGHADOE HEIGHTS HOTEL, Killarney, Co. Kerry, Ireland. Tel: (064) 31766. Telex: 6942. (U.S.A. Reservations: 800-223-6764.) A 46-room conventional hotel with a beautiful view of the Killarney lakes and mountains. Closed the last three weeks in Dec. Breakfast, lunch, tea, dinner served to non-residents. Lake and mountain scenery, championship golf courses, fishing, sun bathing, swimming, pony trekking nearby.

Directions: The best way to find it from the town of Killarney is to ask for directions for the Hotel Europe. Just before Hotel Europe, there's a road to the right that goes up the hill, signposted Aghadoe. Coming south from the Tarbert Ferry: look for signpost on right, just before Killarney.

THE BURREN

Ireland is certainly a land of surprises, and one of the most paradoxical and contradictory surprises is the Burren, a 100-square-mile region in county Clare that provides endless browsing and opportunities for discovery.

Eerie and yet fascinating, the landscape of the Burren appears bleak, yet is far from barren. There are very few trees or shrubs and apart from one small stream there is no trace of a river. Yet the Burren supports a selection of flowers and plants that are found elsewhere as far north as the Arctic regions and in climes far south of Ireland.

Rock and stone predominate, and in their own way support the luxurious growth of rare flowers. Because the area has been inhabited for 4000 years, the region is dotted with monuments representing almost every century of man's habitation.

There are forts, ruined castles, caves, tombs, limestone pavements, cairns, abandoned churches, turloughs (dry lakes) and most of all, rare Burren plants which are a delight of the botanist.

Just outside the Burren at the village of Kilfenora there is an interpretive center which gives visual and sound explanations of the geology, botany, and history of the area.

Be prepared to be amazed by the Burren. Information is available on the area at Gregans Castle Hotel.

GREGANS CASTLE HOTEL
Ballyvaughan, County Clare

So entranced was I watching the sunset from the cliffs of Moher that before I realized it a full darkness had fallen. I started driving across county Clare and entered the desolate-appearing section known as the Burren. The lights of the occasional farm-

houses along the road reassured me that even if I didn't see any of the inhabitants, I knew there must be someone nearby.

I inquired of a passing motorcyclist as to the road to Ballyvaughan and he assured me that it was "straight ahead." I came upon a reassuring signpost for Gregans Hotel, pointing in the same direction for Corkscrew Hill. Reaching the brow of the hill, I looked down into the deep valley and saw a cluster of lights; I knew that this must be Gregans and following the road (quite aptly named "Corkscrew"), I dropped into the valley and turned into the driveway which was flanked by beautiful fir trees.

While I was fascinated by the Burren and its strange lunarlike landscape, I must say I was completely surprised and unprepared for the casual luxury at Gregans Castle. It stands at the head of the valley with dramatic views of the countryside. The owners are Peter and Moira Haden who arrived here just a few years ago and have created a most comfortable, tasteful, and stylish country hotel. It's an old family house from the mid-17th century and has now been restored and converted with every modern comfort including private bathroom facilities for most bedrooms. Previous to their venture into county Clare, Peter and Moira had been professional hoteliers. All the cooking is done under Peter's supervision, and Moira is in charge of the dining room service.

The menu on the night of my stay had six starters, including Galway Bay oysters and a seafood quiche. Following the soup, there were stuffed and baked mussels from Ballyvaughan harbor, estouffade of beef in the style of Provence, grilled lobster from the nearby Atlantic, and a cold baked Burren lamb salad.

On the evening of my stay, all of the hotel guests plus many local patrons enjoyed a recital of Irish songs by Deirdre O'Brien-Vaughn, a titian-haired songstress who accompanied herself on the Irish harp. Deirdre's explanations of the meanings of the words and stories of the songs, most of which were sung in Gaelic, heightened everyone's pleasure.

Moira and I talked about the Burren. "I believe that it's the flora, rather than the history, for which the Burren is famous," she said. "In the late spring and early summer, the orchids, mountain avens, rock roses, maidenhair fern, and blue gentian are in bloom, and the magnificent colors of the flowers turn the grey landscape into a natural rock garden. You don't really have to know much about botany to appreciate its beauty."

Gregans Castle is fortunately located on the coastal road around the western side of Ireland. It is only fifteen miles from the cliffs of Moher, and the Hadens can arrange one-day outings to the Aran Isles.

GREGANS CASTLE HOTEL, Ballyvaughan, Co. Clare, Ireland. Tel: 065-77005. Telex: 70130. A 16-room country hotel located in the Burren area on Ireland's west side, 37 mi. from Shannon Airport. Closed Nov. 1 to Mar. 13. Breakfast, lunch, afternoon tea, dinner served to non-residents. Besides walking and touring the Burren, there are beaches, fishing, caves, castles, and monuments nearby. The cliffs of Moher are 15 mi. distant. Moira and Peter Haden, Resident Owners.

Directions: From Dublin take one of the several roads to Loughrea which is on the main road to Galway. At Loughrea, take signs left to Gort, Kinvara, and Ballyvaughan (these are all on map).

CASHEL HOUSE HOTEL
Cashel, Connemara, County Galway

Here's a bit of Relais de Campagne luxury in one of Ireland's beauty spots.

The setting is typical of Connemara. Surrounded on three sides by rugged mountains, Cashel House Hotel stands at the head of Cashel Bay in a fifty-acre award-winning garden of flowering shrubs and woodland walks. During my late October visit, there were literally thousands of yellow flowers in bloom whose gay colors were shown to great advantage against the rather austere white lines of a Georgian-style house. I could hear songbirds who evidently found the exotic flowering shrubs, including rhododendrons, azaleas, camellias, and magnolias, much to their liking.

In contrast to the exterior, the interior furnishings and

decorations have many bright colors interspersed with gentle pastels. There were a number of paintings of Cashel Bay throughout all of the public rooms and dining rooms.

I arrived during the Sunday lunch, and among the local well-dressed Galway patrons was a table of beaming clergymen who were also enjoying the noontide comestibles.

The resident owners are Dermot and Kay McEvilly. They passed me back and forth between the two of them because Sunday lunchtime is one of the busiest of the week.

From Kay I learned that Dermot is in charge of the kitchen and the menus. "He places a great deal of emphasis on seafood because we're so close to the water," she said. "We have fresh turbot, sea trout and salmon, as well as scallops from Cashel Bay. Lamb and beef are plentiful. We serve them in many varieties of sauces. The vegetables come from our own garden whenever possible.

"I think the main emphasis here is on a restful holiday," she said. "Our guests can use our hard tennis court, or swim from our little private beach, golf at Ballyconneely, or fish in any of the lakes and rivers. A lot of them go in for mountain climbing, bird watching, horse riding, or just driving around on a picnic. We have two good day-trips from Cashel House which are shaped like a figure 8. I believe that guests using these excursions can see most of Connemara."

The beauties of Connemara provide a splendid backdrop for the understated elegance of the Cashel House Hotel.

CASHEL HOUSE HOTEL, Cashel,Connemara, Co. Galway, Ireland. Tel: Cashel, County Galway 9 or Clifden 252 [operator assisted].

Telex: 28812. A 23-room country house hotel located in the Connemara area of County Galway, 174 mi., from Dublin. Open from March to Nov. 1. A member of the Relais de Campagne. Lunch, tea, dinner served to non-residents. Golf, fishing, boating nearby. McEvilly Family, Proprietors.

Directions: From Galway, Cashel can be reached via the Oughterard-Clifden Road, or by the coast road which is the longer way around. Plainly marked on the map. (Note: There is another Cashel in County Tippperary.)

ROSLEAGUE MANOR HOTEL
Letterfrack, Connemara, County Galway

The visit to this country house hotel began with a sinking sensation. It all happened this way:

Driving on the Connemara coastal road between Clifden and Leenane I saw the sign for the Rosleague Manor Hotel, rembered Peter and Moira Haden's recommendation, and turned into a pleasant, woodland road which afforded many glimpses of a splendid bay. Just as I pulled into the car park of a Georgian house, I felt the left front corner of my automobile descending and experienced the said sinking sensation. I had a flat tire.

From that point on, it was all uphill. Anne Foyle, one of the resident owners of the hotel was good enough to ask a young man to help me change the "tyre," and also conducted me on a tour of the house which wound up with tea in the library.

"We are essentially a friendly family-run hotel with much emphasis on what I think is superb home cooking," she said. "My brother Patrick is the principal chef, and Nigel, the assistant chef, who was your temporary tyre-changer, is an old friend of the family. He was trained in London."

Her eyes sparkled when I remarked on the unusual number of oil paintings. "Yes, Patrick and I, as well as our mother, are art lovers and we've had a great deal of enjoyment in supplementing the period furniture with bright spots of color."

Characteristic of Georgian houses, the public rooms in the main part of the house have high ceilings and very comfortable, conversation-inviting furniture. A very pleasing collection of English bone china was displayed on one wall of the dining room; I believe Anne said it was English Darby, which is basically white with a wide blue border.

The bedrooms in the older portion of the house are large and decorated with harmonious draperies, bedspreads, and wallpaper. All of them have a view of Ballinakill Bay.

Back in the main sitting room, Nigel and Patrick, resplendent in their chef's whites joined us for just a few moments. They were making their preparations for the evening's repast.

"The one thing that we insist on is fresh food," said Patrick. "Everything comes locally—the vegetables are either from our own garden or are grown nearby; the meat all comes from Galway; and the fish comes from the bay out there. At the beginning of the season, we have salmon—that's the main attraction, especially for the tourists. We also serve lamb, pork, and beef. Most of our dishes are served with sauces which gives some of them a very nice French touch."

Anne was able to fill me in a little bit more on this beautiful section of Ireland. "Mountains dominate the Connemara landscape," she said. "There are many picturesque, hidden villages, and the coastline, as you've already seen, has dozens of little bays interspersed with very wide beaches. Ireland's language, customs, and crafts are kept alive in Connemara.

"Our guests can fish for salmon or sea trout, enjoy pony trekking, golf, or hill climbing. I think one of our principal virtues is the traffic-free roads."

And so my visit at Roseleague Manor, which began with a sinking sensation, ended with a real lift as I drove out of the driveway, taking one last look at Ballinakill Bay which is encircled by the Twelve Bens Mountains. The water looked warm and there were lazy ripples tempting me to stay even longer.

ROSLEAGUE MANOR HOTEL, Letterfrack, Connemara, Co. Galway, Ireland. Tel: MOYARD 7. A 16-room country house hotel in the west of Ireland, 100 mi. from Shannon Airport. Open from Easter to the end of Oct. Lunch, tea, and dinner served to non-residents. Salmon and sea trout fishing, pony trekking, golf, and hill climbing nearby. No credit cards. Anne Foyle, Resident Proprietor.

Directions: Letterfrack is located on the coastal road in the Connemara section of Co. Galway between Clifden and Leenane.

MOUNT FALCON CASTLE
Ballina, County Mayo

Almost every country house hotelier that I met in Britain and Ireland considered his hotel his home, and his patrons as houseguests, and the Mount Falcon Castle was no exception to this.

Owner Mrs. Constance Aldridge moved here with her husband from England in the 1930s and has maintained it as a country house hotel ever since. "I think I'm probably one of the earliest country house hoteliers in Ireland," she said. "It's become quite fashionable now to run a country house hotel."

The country house feeling is quite pervasive just before dinner when all of the guests meet in the main drawing room and are introduced by Mrs. Aldridge. She has the knack of making everybody feel most comfortable and very much at home. The room itself contributes to this feeling of well-being with walls that are lined from floor to high ceiling with all kinds of books, and with all the family possessions that have been accumulating for more than forty-five years. Guests are naturally drawn together not only by her skillful conversation, but also by a cheery log fire.

On that particular evening, Constance Aldridge had invited a neighboring friend to join the guests at dinner, and the three of us plus four other Americans were a lively group discussing such diverse subjects as salmon and trout fishing, and the poetry and drama of William Butler Yeats.

Dinner was announced and we all filed across the imposing entrance hall to an equally imposing and graceful candlelit dining room where the table was impressively laid with splendid china and silverware. Consulting her seating chart, Mrs. Aldridge assigned all of us to our places, and after a brief grace we continued as before.

As it is every evening, dinner was a set meal, and the main dish was a splendid roast beef accompanied by vegetables from the garden, and served on a handsome silver tray. It was presented by two pleasant Irish Colleens who also performed a number of other services at Mount Falcon.

During the lull in the badinage we all learned that the building, which resembles a small castle and has many acres of grounds and woodlands, was built in 1876. "When we purchased it in 1922, it was known as a fashionable country house," Constance noted. "We brought most of our home furnishings with us from England, but spent many years adding to them. In the early days one could find beautiful things. My husband and I were always collectors, and this has been our home for such a long time."

Because it was originally built as a palatial country home, ten of the eleven bedrooms are double rooms and some are quite large with views on two sides. Even the smaller rooms have their own private bathrooms today.

The "country house" feeling can also be found in strolling about the one hundred acres surrounding the house where there are many varieties of trees and flowers including cypress, beech, and chestnut, as well as delphiniums, dahlias, and gladiolas. I saw a flock of gold finches chattering about in the branches. A clay tennis court is playable during dry weather, and many of the guests enjoy fishing in the stream on the grounds, or nearby. A fishing guide can be provided.

There's a very pleasant rumpled informality about Mount Falcon Castle, and even if Mrs. Aldridge weren't there, it would be an enjoyable place to visit. However, it is the presence of this gracious lady that makes any stay memorable.

When I asked her about her innkeeping philosophy, she replied, "I don't have any in mind—I just love giving happiness—it's just a part of me." She reached down and patted the two very lovable dogs which all the guests take for walks in the woods. "I know that we're a little different, and sometimes guests who are more used to big formal hotels and obsequious servants find it a bit hard to adjust, but, after all, this is really my home, and I just love having houseguests. I wish that some of your countrymen would arrange for longer stays. I love Americans."

Mrs. Aldridge, I'm sure that Americans would love you.

MOUNT FALCON CASTLE, Ballina, Co. Mayo, Ireland. Tel: (096) 21172. An 11-room country house hotel in a castle, 140 mi. from Dublin. Open year-round. Salmon and trout fishing, tennis on grounds. Winter shooting for snipe and woodcock. Estuary and sea fishing, pony riding, golf nearby. No credit cards. Constance Aldridge, Resident Proprietress.

Directions: Ballina is on the coastal road on Ireland's west side. Mount Falcon Castle is on the Foxford Rd. between Castlebar and Ballina. From Ballina, take the Castlebar Rd. south about 1½ mi. to a "Y." Bear left at the Y and drive another 2½ mi. The hotel gate is on the right.

GLENCOLUMBKILLE

Since I've returned from Glencolumbkille I have been amazed at how many people also have either been there or have heard about it. It is located in the southwest corner of county Donegal on a peninsula of land thrust out into the Atlantic about 170 miles northwest of Dublin.

Glencolumbkille comprises five parallel glens, each opening out to beautiful expansive beaches and the sea. Within a radius of five miles there are twenty-three lakes, three rivers, and countless streams. The mountains end in precipitous cliffs which hurl defiance at the changing moods of an unpolluted ocean. One of these cliffs is reputed to be the highest in Europe at 1,972 feet.

The lore, legends, antiquities, scenic views, tranquillity and peace of Glencolumbkille are such that the area is extremely

popular among the Irish themselves. I caution against arriving in high season without advance reservations.

Besides all these things I have enumerated, Glencolumbkille is very well-known in Ireland because of the efforts of Father McDyer who has become the guiding spirit of a cooperative which is known as the Glencolumbkille Association.

Briefly, and with apologies to Father McDyer whose small booklet I am paraphrasing; the isolation, poor land resources, and the tyranny of landlordism all conspired in their own way to subject Glencolumbkille to massive emigration over the past 150 years.

Father McDyer saw the need for providing a way for the people of the area to help themselves and, among other things, a Holiday Village was built and new industries were fostered. There is an excellent folk museum and a craft shop.

I have a suggestion: whether you're going to Glencolumbkille or not, send $2 in American currency to the manager of the Glenbay Hotel, request an inn brochure and a copy of The Riches of Glencolumbkille *by J. McDyer. The booklet contains not only the history of the area, but also several walks in the countryside and* *some excellent four-color photographs. I promise the reader an unusual literary journey.*

I shall quote briefly from this booklet: "I hope you are not a careless driver, for, although the road to the car park overlooking the cliff (2,000 feet) is quite safe, the driver must proceed very slowly and keep his eyes riveted on the road until he parks his car. On the right side of the road driving upwards there can be seen many outcrops of large flagstones from which the mountain "Sliabh a Liag" takes its name. I hope, too, that the day is fine and that you brought your luncheon basket and your camera for here you can remain for a long time, absorbed by the riot of colours, the majesty and the peace, and entranced by the distant prospect of the mountains of Connaught far across the bay. It is also an engaging thought as you look westwards that there is no land between you and the American continent. Looking downwards you will see the seagulls gliding lazily on the air currents or occasionally plummeting toward the fish beneath."

The booklet is the next best thing to being there, and being there is to catch a brief glimpse of the magic of Ireland.

GLENCOLUMBKILLE HOTEL
Malinmore, Glencolumbkille, County Donegal

This hotel is the only hotel in the Glencolumbkille area. The accommodations are warm and comfortable and the menu is adequate. The hotel also has frequent Irish gatherings and songfests.

Oddly enough, for an accommodation that seems rather remote, there is also a telex service available and arrangements can probably be made by a North American travel agent.

GLENCOLUMBKILLE HOTEL, Malinmore, Glencolumbkille, Co. Donegal, Ireland. Tel: Glencolumbkille 3 (Necessary to go through operator). Telex: 33517 DWPEI. A 20-room conventional hotel (private baths) on Ireland's west coast, 142 mi. from Dublin. Open all year. Breakfast, lunch, dinner served to non-residents. (This particular section of Donegal is extremely popular and reservations must be made considerably in advance in the high season.) Bicycles (free to hotel guests), deep-sea fishing, boat trips, archaeology, folk museum, evenings of Irish music and dancing, tennis, and sandy beaches all available. No credit cards.

Directions: There are several different choices of roads from Dublin or Shannon to Donegal town. From there follow the road west through Killybegs to the farthest end of the peninsula.

FROM DONEGAL TO DUBLIN VIA NORTHERN IRELAND

The shortest distance between Donegal town and Dublin is to travel across the Black Gap following the signs to Pettigo, Kesh, Irvinestown and Enniskillen. This road leads through two border-crossing points which, I must confess, I was through before I had even realized it. It introduced me to the Erne Lakes which afford some of the most beautiful scenes in Ireland.

MANOR HOUSE HOTEL
Killadeas, Enniskillen, Northern Ireland

On the aforementioned journey from Donegal to Dublin across a corner of Northern Ireland, just outside of Enniskillen, I saw a signpost for the Manor House Hotel and the stone columns at the gates so impressed me that I decided to follow the road and see what was at the other end.

It proved to be an imposing and stately manor house-villa with Mediterranean overtones, filled with "Olde World" atmosphere, on the shores of Lough Erne.

Besides the 24 large bedrooms, many with private bathrooms or showers, there is also a group of chalets on the shore of the lake which offers holidays of a different dimension. A marina supplies boats for hire in which to explore the 300 square miles of waterways.

Almost everything at the Manor House is done in a grand manner. The high ceilings, the dimensions of the dining room, the many large oil paintings, and the length of the hallways and breadth of the terraces all bespeak bygone days of grandeur. It has lovely views of the lakes and countryside and there are a couple of corner bedrooms where I would have loved to settle down for a week's stay.

Among the many scenic forest walks and drives, is the Lough Navar Forest Drive which incorporates a wide variety of scenery, picnic areas, and a magnificent panoramic view of Lough Erne. The Manor House Hotel is only 12 miles from Eire and has easy access to Donegal and the Atlantic Coast.

Although this hotel appears to be privately owned, it is a touch on the commercial side. The size of the dining room and bar indicates that it must be very popular with the local people as well as travelers.

MANOR HOUSE HOTEL, Killadeas, Inniskillen, Northern Ireland. Tel: (036562) 545/561. Telex: 747912. A manor house hotel in the Irish Lake District, 100 mi. from Dublin. Closed on Christmas day only. Breakfast, lunch, tea, dinner served to non-residents. Situated on the shores of Lough Erne, where cruisers and day boats are available for hire. Many scenic walks and drives nearby. Self-catering chalet cottages also available. Hugo McVey, General Manager.

Directions: Inniskillen is 12 mi. from Eire and 86 mi. from Belfast. Make inquiries in village for correct road.

KILLYHEVLIN HOTEL
Enniskillen, Northern Ireland

I stopped at the Killyhevlin Hotel on the recommendation of the manager of the Manor House Hotel, which was just a few miles away. The two places make an interesting contrast, because the Killyhevlin is a bit more "Americanized" and is a conference center as well as a travelers' accommodation.

One of the principal attractions is the fact that it's located right on the Lough Erne shore and is very popular with fishermen.

Bedrooms are available with private bathrooms, television, channel radio, telephones, and a private balcony overlooking the countryside and the lake.

Amenities also include a ladies' hairdressing salon, a recreation room, a kiddies' paddling pool, paddle boats, and a dinner dance every Saturday night.

As in the case of the Manor House Hotel, the Killyhevlin also has some self-catering chalets on the lake shore.

KILLYHEVLIN HOTEL, Enniskillen, Northern Ireland. Tel: (0365) 3481. A 25-room hotel with 13 self-contained chalets. Open year-round. Breakfast, lunch, dinner served to non-residents. Salmon fishing, golf, boating on grounds. Located in the Lake District of northern Ireland. This hotel is more luxurious than the average accommodation described in this book.

Directions: Enniskillen is on one of the main roads from Dublin to Donegal. It's tucked into the southwest corner of northern Ireland. On my visit I found no problems at the border crossing points.

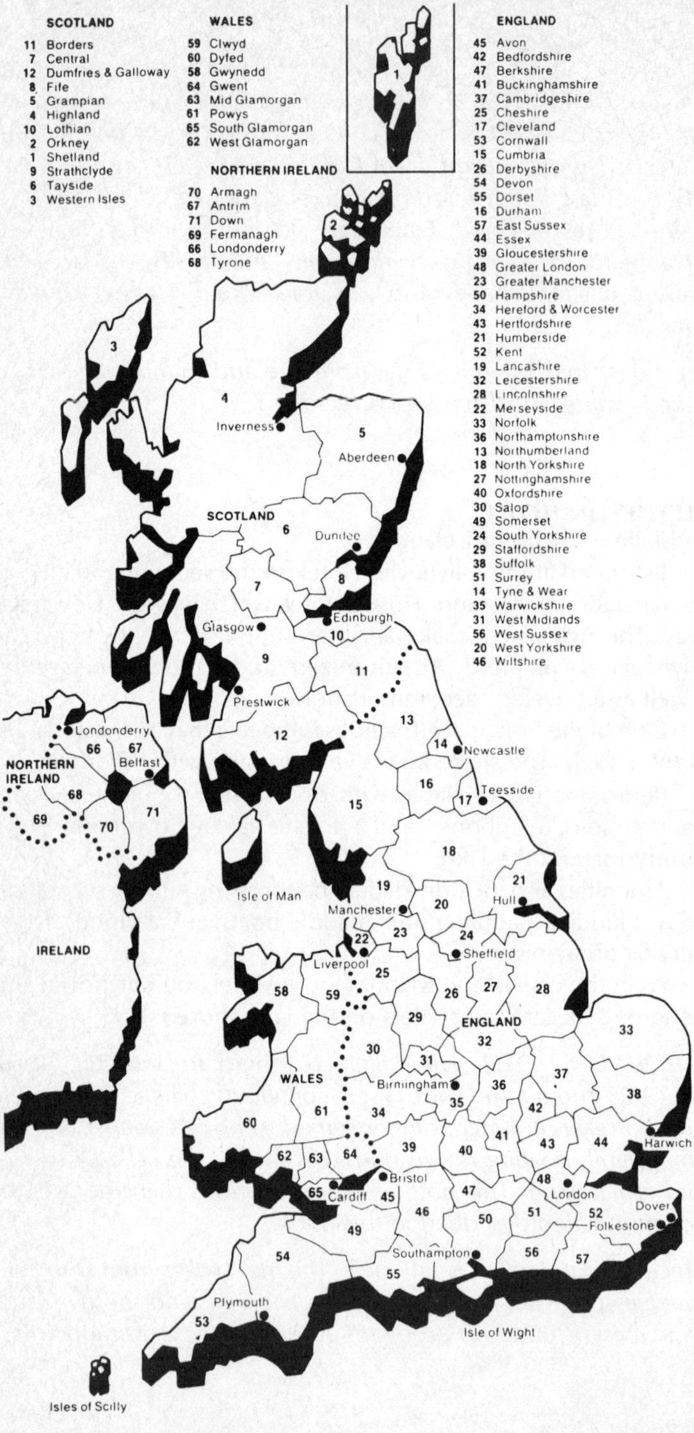
SCOTLAND
11 Borders
7 Central
12 Dumfries & Galloway
8 Fife
5 Grampian
4 Highland
10 Lothian
2 Orkney
1 Shetland
9 Strathclyde
6 Tayside
3 Western Isles
WALES
59 Clwyd
60 Dyfed
58 Gwynedd
64 Gwent
63 Mid Glamorgan
61 Powys
65 South Glamorgan
62 West Glamorgan
NORTHERN IRELAND
70 Armagh
67 Antrim
71 Down
69 Fermanagh
66 Londonderry
68 Tyrone
ENGLAND
45 Avon
42 Bedfordshire
47 Berkshire
41 Buckinghamshire
37 Cambridgeshire
25 Cheshire
17 Cleveland
53 Cornwall
15 Cumbria
26 Derbyshire
54 Devon
55 Dorset
16 Durham
57 East Sussex
44 Essex
39 Gloucestershire
48 Greater London
23 Greater Manchester
50 Hampshire
34 Hereford & Worcester
43 Hertfordshire
21 Humberside
52 Kent
19 Lancashire
32 Leicestershire
28 Lincolnshire
22 Merseyside
33 Norfolk
36 Northamptonshire
13 Northumberland
18 North Yorkshire
27 Nottinghamshire
40 Oxfordshire
30 Salop
49 Somerset
24 South Yorkshire
29 Staffordshire
38 Suffolk
51 Surrey
14 Tyne & Wear
35 Warwickshire
31 West Midlands
56 West Sussex
20 West Yorkshire
46 Wiltshire
Inverness
Aberdeen
SCOTLAND
Dundee
Edinburgh
Glasgow
Prestwick
Londonderry
Belfast
NORTHERN IRELAND
Newcastle
Teesside
Isle of Man
Manchester
Hull
Liverpool
Sheffield
IRELAND
ENGLAND
WALES
Birmingham
Harwich
Bristol
Cardiff
London
Dover
Folkestone
Southampton
Plymouth
Isle of Wight
Isles of Scilly

POSTSCRIPT

It was raining in London, but it was a Sunday and the bus from Euston station to Heathrow Airport was making fairly good progress right through the heart of the city. We careened down the Strand and Haymarket, continued on around Marble Arch, Hyde Park Corner, and Harrods. This was the London where I had spent so many happy visits with Stewart and Françoise in their little mews flat.

This trip to the British Isles was now almost behind me and I was looking forward to a good PanAm flight to Kennedy and Hartford. Back in the Berkshires I would put all the notes from four trips together and complete yet another revision of this book.

I must say my final night in Britain was spent in an unusual, for me, bit of travel. I can recommend it to anyone who finds himself in the north of England or Scotland, with a morning flight from London back to the States. About 10:30 p.m., I boarded a sleeping car, where I had my own compartment. Everything was very neat and all tied up with bows. There were two bunk beds and a wash basin, the W.C. being down the corridor. There was plenty of room to put my bags and generally to spread out.

I read for awhile on the top bunk, turned off the light, and the next thing I knew the train was speeding south for London. It arrived on time at 7:30 a.m. I must congratulate Britrail for maintaining this service.

All four of my trips for further research had been most successful. I visited with old friends and made many new ones, all of which are reflected in the pages of this revision. I had added to my knowledge of how to travel in Britain, where to stay, and more places to visit.

Once again I was leaving Britain and, except perhaps for a brief visit, I would not be returning for some time, hence I was making a mental list of the things I would miss: cheery "good mornings" from everybody, the built-in courtesy of all Britons, friendly pubs, extremely comfortable country house hotels, English blue sky (none bluer) and green lawns (none greener). I'd also miss the capricious English weather at certain times of the year, when quick showers are followed by wonderful bright sunshine. I'd cherish wonderful village names, the sweet little farms, and the glorious countryside.

My list grew longer: the journey over Kirkstone Pass, the single passage roads on the Lancashire fells and the Yorkshire moors, Rye at dawn, the ferry from Oban to Mull and Colonsay, Cornish creamed teas, the gentle Constable country, the seaside villages of Northumbria, tea every afternoon everywhere, London theatre, the beige hues of the Cotwolds, Bosham Harbor, ad infinitum.

The nice part of all these things is that they will still be here the next time I return.

ADDENDUM/INDEX

The following alphabetical listings under each country provide approximate rates in British pounds sterling (£) for two people for one night, including breakfast. In most cases, these rates include the Value Added Tax (VAT) of 15%. However, it is always wise to check the rates and what they cover when you make your reservation. There are a few places where breakfast is not offered with the room tariff, as well as others where *both breakfast and dinner* ARE included in the room rate. This latter situation is identified in the listing as "MAP" (Modified American Plan). (American Plan includes 3 meals.) These rates are estimated through 1985.

Why "Last Orders"?

It's not that the distances are very long in the British Isles, it's the many diversions along the way that sometimes make it impossible to estimate traveling and arrival times. Last order times for dinner are included in these listings so that you can see what time you must arrive in order not to find the kitchen door locked. If you are going to arrive later, call ahead—there isn't a hotel/inn listed here that will not make some provision to feed you if they know you can't make it before the kitchen closes.

ADDENDUM-INDEX

ENGLAND

Rates shown are for lodgings and breakfast for two people for one night; in most cases, inclusive of VAT (Value Added Tax, 15%). Prices are in British money: pounds sterling (£). Check exchange rate. Rates estimated through 1985.

*Breakfast add'l.
**MAP

	LAST ORDERS	RATES	PAGE
HUNSTRETE HOUSE Pensford, Avon	9:15 p.m.	From £70	143
INN AT WHITEWELL, THE Clitheroe, Lancashire	9:00 p.m.	£31.50	183
KENNEL HOLT COUNTRY HOUSE HOTEL Cranbrook, Kent	8:00 p.m.	£60-70**	34
KING'S HEAD INN Orford, Suffolk	9:00 p.m.	£30.00	76
LAMB, THE Hindon, Wiltshire	9:00 p.m.	£40.00**	140
LESCEAVE CLIFF HOTEL Praa Sands, Cornwall	8:30 p.m.	£32-44	169
LINDEN HALL HOTEL Longhorsley, Northumberland	9:30 p.m.	From £45	224
LOBSTER POT, THE Mousehole, Cornwall	9:45 p.m.	£20-44	176
LOW HOUSE Patterdale, Cumbria	7:30 p.m.	£24.00**	197
LUCCOMBE CHINE HOUSE Shaklin, Isle of Wight	9:00 p.m.	£30.00	51
LYGON ARMS Broadway, Worcestershire	9:15 p.m.	£70-80	99
MAISON TALBOOTH Dedham, Essex	9:00 p.m.	£55-75	68
MALLYAN SPOUT HOTEL Goathland, North Yorkshire	8:30 p.m.	£17-25	211
MANOR FARM, THE Broadway, Worcestershire	———	£17-22	101
MANOR HOUSE HOTEL Moreton-in-Marsh, Gloucestershire	9:00 p.m.	From £35	102
MANOR HOUSE HOTEL Castle Combe, Wiltshire	9:15 p.m.	£35-50	141
MARINE HOUSE PRIVATE HOTEL Alnmouth, Northumberland	6:00 p.m.	£24.00	223

**MAP

**MAP

	LAST ORDERS	RATES	PAGE
RAISE VIEW BED & BREAKFAST Grasmere, Cumbria	———	£20.00	190
RECTORY FARM Church Stretton, Shropshire	———	£14.00	106
RIBER HALL Matlock, Derbyshire	9:30 p.m.	£50.00	132
RISING SUN HOTEL, THE Lynmouth, Devon	9:00 p.m.	£28.00	167
RIVER HOUSE, THE Skippool Creek, Lancashire	9:00 p.m.	£30.00	184
RIVERSIDE Helford, Cornwall	9:30 p.m.	£51-55	170
ROTHAY MANOR HOTEL Ambleside, Cumbria	9:00 p.m.	From £55	188
ROWAN HOUSE Gt. Hucklow, Derbyshire	———	£15.00	136
ROYAL HOTEL, THE Deal, Kent	9:15 p.m.	From £35	35
ROYAL OAK HOTEL, THE Yattendon, Berkshire	9:30 p.m.	£50.00	56
SCALE HILL HOTEL Loweswater, Cumbria	7:45 p.m.	£58.00	204
SHARROW BAY HOTEL Penrith, Cumbria	8:30 p.m.	£88-150**	198
SLEPE HALL HOTEL St. Ives, Cambridgeshire	9:45 p.m.	£38-45	85
SOUTH SANDS HOTEL Salcombe, South Devon	9:30 p.m.	£35.00	162
SPREAD EAGLE HOTEL Midhurst, Sussex	9:15 p.m.	From £40	39
STAFFORD HOTEL St. James's Place, London	9:30 p.m.	£108.00*	24
STONE HOUSE HOTEL Sedbusk, North Yorkshire	8:00 p.m.	£24.00	214
STUDLEY PRIORY Horton-cum-Studley, Oxford	9:30 p.m.	£40-90	57

Rates shown are for lodgings and breakfast for two people for one night; in most cases, inclusive of VAT (Value Added Tax, 15%). Prices are in British money: pounds sterling (£). Check exchange rate. Rates estimated through 1985.

*Breakfast add'l.
**MAP

LONDON

*Breakfast add'l.
**MAP

	LAST ORDERS	RATES	PAGE
DURRANTS HOTEL George St., W1H	10:00 p.m.	£38-53	25
GORING HOTEL Beeston Place, SW1	10:30 p.m.	£72.00*	25
NUMBER SIXTEEN 16 Sumner Place, SW7	———	£49-65	26
STAFFORD HOTEL St. James's Place, SW1A	9:30 p.m.	£108.00*	24

Rates shown are for lodgings and breakfast for two people for one night; in most cases, inclusive of VAT (Value Added Tax, 15%). Prices are in British money: pounds sterling (£). Check exchange rate. Rates estimated through 1985.

WALES

BONTDDU HALL Bontddu, Gwynedd	9:15 p.m.	£35.00	121
BWLCH-Y-FEDWEN Penmorfa, Gwynedd	7:30 p.m.	£21-23	124
CROWN AT WHITEBROOK Whitebrook, Gwent	10:00 p.m.	£38.00	110
FFRIDD UCHAF (Mrs. Wynne-Robert's B&B) Rhyd Ddu, Gwynedd	———	£14.00	126
GOLDEN LION ROYAL HOTEL Dolgellau, Gwynedd	9:00 p.m.	£32.00	119
KING'S HEAD HOTEL Monmouth, Gwent	9:30 p.m.	£39.00	111
MRS. ROWLAND'S B&B Taliesin, Gwynedd	———	£16.00	117
PLAS MYNACH CASTLE Barmouth, Gwynedd	7:45 p.m.	£24.00	122
RHIWIAU RIDING CENTRE Llanfairfechan, Gwynedd	Call ahead	£15.00	128
SYGUN FAWR HOTEL Beddgelert, Gwynedd	7:45 p.m.	£25-30	127
TY MAWR Brechfa, Dyfed	9:00 p.m.	£32.00	112
TYN-Y-CORNEL HOTEL Talyllyn, Gwynedd	8:45 p.m.	£45.00	118
Y NEUADD (Mrs. Morgan's B&B) Pentre-Ty-Gwyn, Dyfed	8:00 p.m.	£18.00	115

*Breakfast add'l.

SCOTLAND

Rates shown are for lodgings and breakfast for two people for one night; in most cases, inclusive of VAT (Value Added Tax, 15%). Prices are in British money: pounds sterling (£). Check exchange rate. Rates estimated through 1985.

	LAST ORDERS	RATES	PAGE
ARDSHEAL HOUSE Kentallen of Appin, Strathclyde	8:30 p.m.	From– £86**	261
AUCHEN CASTLE Beattock, Dumfriesshire	9:00 p.m.	£40.00	276
BALCARY BAY HOTEL Auchencairn, Dumfries & Galloway	9:15 p.m.	£70.00**	277
BALGEDDIE HOUSE HOTEL Glenrothes, Fife	9:00 p.m.	£38.00*	238
BALLATHIE HOUSE Kinclaven by Stanley, Perthshire	9:30 p.m.	£52.00	240
CLIFTON HOTEL Nairn, Invernesshire	9:30 p.m.	£44.00	255
COUNTY HOTEL BANFF Banff, Grampian	9:30 p.m.	£40-46	250
CREGGANS INN, THE Strachur, Strathclyde	8:30 p.m.	£22-26	274
DUNAIN PARK Inverness, Highland	9:00 p.m. Mon-Sat 8:00 p.m. Sun	£66.00	256
DUNKELD HOUSE Dunkeld, Tayside	9:00 p.m.	From £30	241
GLEDDOCH HOUSE Langbank, Strathclyde	9:30 p.m.	£60.00	281
GREYWALLS Gullane, Lothian	9:30 p.m.	£50-77	235
HOUSTOUN HOUSE Uphall, Lothian	9:00 p.m.	£39.00	233
HOWARD HOTEL Great King St., Edinburgh	9:30 p.m.	£46-48	232
INVERLOCHY CASTLE Fort William, Highland	8:30 p.m.	£140.00**	259
ISLE OF COLONSAY HOTEL Colonsay, Strathclyde	8:00 p.m.	£40.00	267

*Breakfast add'l.
**MAP

	LAST ORDERS	RATES	PAGE
ISLE OF ERISKA Ledaig, Strathclyde	8:30 p.m.	£104-124**	263
KENMORE HOTEL Kenmore, Tayside	9:00 p.m.	£40-45	243
KNOCKINAAM LODGE HOTEL Portpatrick, Wigtownshire	9:00 p.m.	£70-108**	278
MARINE HOTEL Troon, Ayrshire	10:15 p.m.	£50.00	280
OPEN ARMS Dirleton, Lothian	10:00 p.m.	£46.00	234
PHILIPBURN HOUSE HOTEL Selkirk	10:00 p.m.	£26.00	282
PITTODRIE Pitcaple, Grampian	9:00 p.m.	From £70	251
PORT-AN-EILEAN Strathtummel, Tayside	9:00 p.m.	£30.00	246
PRESTONFIELD HOUSE RESTAURANT Edinburgh	8:30 p.m.	——	237
ROSE VILLA Fortingall, Highlands, Perthshire	9:00 p.m.	£45.00**	245
ROTHES GLEN Rothes, Grampian	8:30 p.m.	£45-50	254
TAYCHREGGAN HOTEL Kilchrenan, Argyll	9:00 p.m.	£70.00**	272
THRUSHWOOD B&B Mouswald, Dumfriesshire	——	£13.00	277
TIGH-AN-EILEAN Shieldaig, Highland	8:00 p.m.	£40.00**	258
TULLICH LODGE Ballater, Grampian	8:30 p.m.	£75.00**	248
WESTERN ISLES HOTEL Tobermory, Isle of Mull, Strathclyde	8:45 p.m.	£36-40	269

*Breakfast add'l.
**MAP

IRELAND

Rates shown are for lodgings and breakfast for two people for one night; in most cases, inclusive of VAT (Value Added Tax, 15%). Prices are in British money: pounds sterling (£). Check exchange rate. Rates estimated through 1985.